CW00552231

PRIESTS OF JESUS CHRIST

VOL II

Pope Benedict XVI

PRIESTS OF JESUS CHRIST
REFLECTIONS ON THE PRIESTHOOD

VOL II

*Extracts from his writings and speeches
selected by Fr Gerard Skinner*

ST PAULS

Papal Texts © Libreria Editrice Vaticana
Cover Image © Stefano Spaziani 2008
All rights reserved

ST PAULS Publishing
187 Battersea Bridge Road, London SW11 3AS, UK
www.stpaulspublishing.com

Copyright © ST PAULS Publishing, 2010

ISBN 978-0-85439-806-5

A catalogue record is available for this book from the British Library.

Set by Tukan DTP, Stubbington, Fareham, UK
Printed by Intype Libra Ltd, Wimbledon, London, UK

ST PAULS is an activity of the priests and brothers of the Society of St Paul
who proclaim the Gospel through the media of social communication.

CONTENTS

Introduction   7

I.   Letters   9

II.   Homilies   39

III.   Addresses   105

IV.   Lectio Divina   207

V.   Messages   231

VI.   Meetings with the Clergy   249

INTRODUCTION

'Faithfulness of Christ, faithfulness of priests', was the theme chosen by Pope Benedict XVI for a Year for Priests that he declared to be held beginning with the Solemnity of the Sacred Heart of Jesus, 19 June 2009, and ending on the same Solemnity in 2010. The catalyst for the year of prayer was the 150th anniversary of the death of St John Mary Vianney, the Curé d'Ars, a simple yet radiantly holy parish priest who is invoked as the patron saint of all parish priests.

The majority of texts to be found in this book are taken from the various writings, speeches and homilies that Pope Benedict gave during the 'Year for Priests'. Some of the entries, however, are a little older than this, thus making the present volume a continuation of 'Priests of Jesus Christ', a book originally published by Family Publications. I am delighted that this second volume, as well as its predecessor, are now being published by ST PAULS Publishing.

Fr Gerard Skinner
London, 12 July 2010

I.
LETTERS

LETTER PROCLAIMING A YEAR FOR PRIESTS ON THE OCCASION OF THE 150th ANNIVERSARY OF THE DEATH OF THE CURÉ D'ARS

18 June 2009

Dear Brother Priests,

On the forthcoming Solemnity of the Most Sacred Heart of Jesus, Friday, 19 June 2009 – a day traditionally devoted to prayer for the sanctification of the clergy – I have decided to inaugurate a "Year for Priests" in celebration of the 150th anniversary of the *"dies natalis"* of John Mary Vianney, the patron saint of parish priests worldwide.[1] This Year, meant to deepen the commitment of all priests to interior renewal for the sake of a more forceful and incisive witness to the Gospel in today's world, will conclude on the same Solemnity in 2010. *The priesthood is the love of the heart of Jesus",* the saintly Curé of Ars would often say.[2] This touching expression makes us reflect, first of all, with heartfelt gratitude on the immense gift which priests represent, not only for the Church, but also for humanity itself. I think of all those priests who quietly present Christ's words and actions each day to the faithful and to the whole world, striving to be one with the Lord in their thoughts and their will, their sentiments and their style of life. How can I not pay tribute to their apostolic labours, their tireless and hidden service, their universal charity? And how can I not praise the courageous fidelity of so many priests who, even amid difficulties and incomprehension, remain faithful to their vocation as "friends of Christ", whom he has called by name, chosen and sent?

I still treasure the memory of the first parish priest at whose side I exercised my ministry as a young priest: he left me an example of unreserved devotion to his pastoral duties, even to meeting death in the act of bringing viaticum to a gravely ill person. I also recall the countless confreres whom I have met and continue to meet, not least in my pastoral visits to different countries: men generously dedicated to the daily exercise of their priestly ministry. Yet the expression of St John Mary also makes us think of Christ's pierced Heart and the crown of thorns which surrounds it. I am also led to think, therefore, of the countless situations of suffering endured by many priests, either because they themselves share in the manifold human experience of pain or because they encounter misunderstanding from the very persons to whom they minister. How can we not also think of all those priests who are offended in their dignity, obstructed in their mission and persecuted, even at times to offering the supreme testimony of their own blood?

There are also, sad to say, situations which can never be sufficiently deplored where the Church herself suffers as a consequence of infidelity on the part of some of her ministers. Then it is the world which finds grounds for scandal and rejection. What is most helpful to the Church in such cases is not only a frank and complete acknowledgment of the weaknesses of her ministers, but also a joyful and renewed realization of the greatness of God's gift, embodied in the splendid example of generous pastors, religious afire with love for God and for souls, and insightful, patient spiritual guides. Here the teaching and example of St John Mary Vianney can serve as a significant point of reference for us all. The Curé of Ars was quite humble, yet as a priest he was conscious of being an immense gift to his people: "A good shepherd, a pastor after God's heart, is the greatest treasure which the good Lord can grant to a parish, and one of the most precious gifts of divine mercy".[3] He spoke of the priesthood as if incapable of fathoming the grandeur of the *gift* and *task* entrusted to a human creature: "O, how great is the priest! ... If he realized what he is, he would die... God obeys him: he utters a few words and the Lord descends from heaven at his voice, to be contained within a small host..."[4] Explaining to his parishioners the importance of the sacraments, he would say: "Without the Sacrament of Holy Orders, we would not have the Lord. Who put him there in that tabernacle? The priest. Who welcomed your soul at the beginning of your life? The priest. Who feeds your soul and gives it strength for its journey? The priest. Who will prepare it to appear before God, bathing it one last time in the blood of Jesus Christ? The priest, always the priest. And if this soul should happen to die [as a result of sin], who will raise it up, who will restore its calm and peace? Again, the priest... After God, the priest is everything! ... Only in heaven will he fully realize what he is".[5] These words, welling up from the priestly heart of the holy pastor, might sound excessive. Yet they reveal the high esteem in which he held the sacrament of the priesthood. He seemed overwhelmed by a boundless sense of responsibility: "Were we to fully realize what a priest is on earth, we would die: not of fright, but of love... Without the priest, the passion and death of our Lord would be of no avail. It is the priest who continues the work of redemption on earth... What use would be a house filled with gold, were there no one to open its door? The priest holds the key to the treasures of heaven: it is he who opens the door: he is the steward of the good Lord; the administrator of his goods ... Leave a parish for twenty years without a priest, and they will end by worshiping the beasts there ... The priest is not a priest for himself, he is a priest for you".[6]

He arrived in Ars, a village of 230 souls, warned by his Bishop beforehand that there he would find religious practice in a sorry state: "There is little love of God in that parish; you will be the one to put it there". As a result, he was deeply aware that he needed to go there to embody Christ's presence and to bear witness to his saving mercy: "[Lord,] grant me the conversion of my parish; I am willing to suffer whatever you wish, for my entire life!": with this prayer he entered upon his mission.[7] The Curé devoted himself completely to his parish's conversion, setting before all else the Christian education of the people in his care.

Dear brother priests, let us ask the Lord Jesus for the grace to learn for ourselves something of the pastoral plan of St John Mary Vianney! The first thing we need to learn is the complete identification of the man with his ministry. In Jesus, person and mission tend to coincide: all Christ's saving activity was, and is, an expression of his "filial consciousness" which from all eternity stands before the Father in an attitude of loving submission to his will. In a humble yet genuine way, every priest must aim for a similar identification. Certainly this is not to forget that the efficacy of the ministry is independent of the holiness of the minister; but neither can we overlook the extraordinary fruitfulness of the encounter between the ministry's objective holiness and the subjective holiness of the minister. The Curé of Ars immediately set about this patient and humble task of harmonizing his life as a minister with the holiness of the ministry he had received, by deciding to *"live"*, physically, in his parish church: As his first biographer tells us: "Upon his arrival, he chose the church as his home. He entered the church before dawn and did not leave it until after the evening *Angelus*. There he was to be sought whenever needed".[8]

The pious excess of his devout biographer should not blind us to the fact that the Curé also knew how to "live" actively within the entire territory of his parish: he regularly visited the sick and families, organized popular missions and patronal feasts, collected and managed funds for his charitable and missionary works, embellished and furnished his parish church, cared for the orphans and teachers of the *"Providence"* (an institute he founded); provided for the education of children; founded confraternities and enlisted lay persons to work at his side.

His example naturally leads me to point out that there are sectors of cooperation which need to be opened ever more fully to the lay faithful. Priests and laity together make up the one priestly people[9] and in virtue of their ministry priests live in the midst of the lay faithful, "that they may lead everyone to the unity of charity, 'loving one another with mutual affection; and outdoing one another in sharing honour'" (Rom 12:10).[10] Here we ought to recall the Second Vatican Council's hearty encouragement to priests "to be sincere in their appreciation and promotion of the dignity of the laity and of the special role they have to play in the Church's mission. ... They should be willing to listen to lay people, give brotherly consideration to their wishes, and acknowledge their experience and competence in the different fields of human activity. In this way they will be able together with them to discern the signs of the times".[11]

St John Mary Vianney taught his parishioners primarily by the witness of his life. It was from his example that they learned to pray, halting frequently before the tabernacle for a visit to Jesus in the Blessed Sacrament.[12] "One need not say much to pray well" – the Curé explained to them – "We know that Jesus is there in the tabernacle: let us open our hearts to him, let us rejoice in his sacred presence. That is the best prayer".[13] And he would urge them: "Come to communion, my brothers and sisters, come to Jesus. Come to live from him in order to live with him…[14] "Of course you are not worthy of him, but *you need him!*"[15] This way of educating the faithful *to the Eucharistic presence and to communion* proved most effective when they saw him celebrate the Holy Sacrifice of the Mass. Those present said that "it was not possible to find a finer example of worship… He gazed upon the Host with immense love".[16] "All good works, taken together, do not equal the sacrifice of the Mass" – he would say – "since they are human works, while the Holy Mass is the work of God".[17] He was convinced that the fervour of a priest's life depended entirely upon the Mass: "The reason why a priest is lax is that he does not pay attention to the Mass! My God, how we ought to pity a priest who celebrates as if he were engaged in something routine!".[18] He was accustomed, when celebrating, also to offer his own life in sacrifice: "What a good thing it is for a priest each morning to offer himself to God in sacrifice!".[19]

This deep personal identification with the Sacrifice of the Cross led him – by a sole inward movement – from the altar to the confessional. Priests ought never to be resigned to empty confessionals or the apparent indifference of the faithful to this sacrament. In France, at the time of the Curé of Ars, confession was no more easy or frequent than in our own day, since the upheaval caused by the revolution had long inhibited the practice of religion. Yet he sought in every way, by his preaching and his powers of persuasion, to help his parishioners to rediscover the meaning and beauty of the sacrament of Penance, presenting it as an inherent demand of the Eucharistic presence. He thus created a *"virtuous" circle*. By spending long hours in church before the tabernacle, he inspired the faithful to imitate him by coming to visit Jesus with the knowledge that their parish priest would be there, ready to listen and offer forgiveness. Later, the growing numbers of penitents from all over France would keep him in the confessional for up to sixteen hours a day. It was said that Ars had become "a great hospital of souls".[20] His first biographer relates that "the grace he obtained [for the conversion of sinners] was so powerful that it would pursue them, not leaving them a moment of peace!".[21] The saintly Curé reflected something of the same idea when he said: "It is not the sinner who returns to God to beg his forgiveness, but God himself who runs after the sinner and makes him return to him".[22] "This good Saviour is so filled with love that he seeks us everywhere."[23]

We priests should feel that the following words, which he put on the lips of Christ, are meant for each of us personally: "I will charge my ministers to proclaim to sinners that I am ever ready to welcome them, that my mercy is infinite".[24] From St John Mary Vianney we can learn to put our unfailing trust in the sacrament of Penance, to set it once more at the centre of our pastoral concerns, and to take up the "dialogue of salvation" which it entails. The Curé of Ars dealt with different penitents in different ways. Those who came to his confessional drawn by a deep and humble longing for God's forgiveness found in him the encouragement to plunge into the "flood of divine mercy" which sweeps everything away by its vehemence. If someone was troubled by the thought of his own frailty and inconstancy, and fearful of sinning again, the Curé would unveil the mystery of God's love in these beautiful and touching words: "The good Lord knows everything. Even before you confess, he already knows that you will sin again, yet he still forgives you. How great is the love of our God: he *even forces himself to forget the future*, so that he can grant us his forgiveness!".[25] But to those who made a lukewarm and rather indifferent confession of sin, he clearly demonstrated by his own tears of pain how "abominable" this attitude was: "I weep because you don't weep",[26] he would say. "If only the Lord were not so good! *But he is so good!* One would have to be a brute to treat so good a Father this way!".[27] He awakened repentance in the hearts of the lukewarm by forcing them to see God's own pain at their sins reflected in the face of the priest who was their confessor. To those who, on the other hand, came to him already desirous of and suited to a deeper spiritual life, he flung open the abyss of God's love, explaining the untold beauty of living in union with him and dwelling in his presence: "Everything in God's sight, everything with God, everything to please God... How beautiful it is!".[28] And he taught them to pray: "My God, grant me the grace to love you as much as I possibly can".[29]

In his time the Curé of Ars was able to transform the hearts and the lives of so many people because he enabled them to experience the Lord's merciful love. Our own time urgently needs a similar proclamation and witness to the truth of Love: *Deus caritas est* (1 Jn 4:8). Thanks to the word and the sacraments of Jesus, John Mary Vianney built up his flock, although he often trembled from a conviction of his personal inadequacy, and desired more than once to withdraw from the responsibilities of the parish ministry out of a sense of his unworthiness. Nonetheless, with exemplary obedience he never abandoned his post, consumed as he was by apostolic zeal for the salvation of souls. He sought to remain completely faithful to his own vocation and mission through the practice of an austere asceticism: "The great misfortune for us parish priests – he lamented – is that our souls grow tepid"; meaning by this that a pastor can grow dangerously inured to the state of sin or of indifference in which so many of his flock are living.[30] He himself kept a tight rein on his body, with vigils and fasts, lest it rebel against his priestly soul. Nor did he avoid self-mortification for the good of the souls in his care and as a help to expiating the many sins he heard in confession. To a priestly confrere he explained: "I will tell you my recipe: I give sinners a small penance and the rest I do in their place".[31] Aside from the actual penances which the Curé of Ars practiced, the core of his teaching remains valid for each of us: souls have been won at the price of Jesus' own blood, and a priest cannot devote himself to their salvation if he refuses to share personally in the "precious cost" of redemption.

In today's world, as in the troubled times of the Curé of Ars, the lives and activity of priests need to be distinguished by *a forceful witness to the Gospel.* As Pope Paul VI rightly noted, "modern man listens more willingly to witnesses than to teachers, and if he does listen to teachers, it is because they are witnesses".[32] Lest we experience existential emptiness and the effectiveness of our ministry be compromised, we need to ask ourselves ever anew: "Are we truly pervaded by the word of God? Is that word truly the nourishment we live by, even more than bread and the things of this world? Do we really know that word? Do we love it? Are we deeply engaged with this word to the point that it really leaves a mark on our lives and shapes our thinking?".[33] Just as Jesus called the Twelve to be with him (cf. Mk 3:14), and only later sent them forth to preach, so too in our days priests are called to assimilate that "new style of life" which was inaugurated by the Lord Jesus and taken up by the Apostles.[34]

It was complete commitment to this "new style of life" which marked the priestly ministry of the Curé of Ars. Pope John XXIII, in his Encyclical Letter *Sacerdotii nostri primordia*, published in 1959 on the first centenary of the death of St John Mary Vianney, presented his asceticism with special reference to the "three evangelical counsels" which the Pope considered necessary also for priests: "even though priests are not bound to embrace these evangelical counsels by virtue of the clerical state, these counsels nonetheless offer them, as they do all the faithful, the surest road to the desired goal of Christian perfection".[35] The Curé of Ars lived the "evangelical counsels" in a way suited to his priestly state. His *poverty* was not the poverty of a religious or a monk, but that proper to a priest: while managing much money (since well-to-do pilgrims naturally took an interest in his charitable works), he realized that everything had been donated to his church, his poor, his orphans, the girls of his "*Providence*",[36] his families of modest means. Consequently, he "was rich in giving to others and very poor for himself".[37] As he would explain: "My secret is simple: give everything away; hold nothing back".[38] When he lacked money, he would say aimiably to the poor who knocked at his door: "Today I'm poor just like you, I'm one of you".[39] At the end of his life, he could say with absolute tranquillity: "I no longer have anything. The good Lord can call me whenever he wants!".[40] His *chastity*, too, was that demanded of a priest for his ministry. It could be said that it was a chastity suited to one who must daily touch the Eucharist, who contemplates it blissfully and with that same bliss offers it to his flock. It was said of him that "he radiated chastity"; the faithful would see this when he turned and gazed at the tabernacle with loving eyes".[41] Finally, St John Mary Vianney's *obedience* found full embodiment in his conscientious fidelity to the daily demands of his ministry. We know how he was tormented by the thought of his inadequacy for parish ministry and by a desire to flee "in order to bewail his poor life, in solitude".[42] Only obedience and a thirst for souls convinced him to remain at his post. As he explained to himself and his flock: "There are no two good ways of serving God. There is only one: serve him as he desires to be served".[43] He considered this the golden rule for a life of obedience: "Do only what can be offered to the good Lord".[44]

In this context of a spirituality nourished by the practice of the evangelical counsels, I would like to invite all priests, during this Year dedicated to them, to welcome the new springtime which the Spirit is now bringing about in the Church, not least through the ecclesial movements and the new communities. "In his gifts the Spirit is multifaceted... He breathes where he wills. He does so unexpectedly, in unexpected places, and in ways previously unheard of... but he also shows us that he works with a view to the one body and in the unity of the one body".[45] In this regard, the statement of the Decree *Presbyterorum Ordinis* continues to be timely: "While testing the spirits to discover if they be of God, priests must discover with faith, recognize with joy and foster diligently the many and varied charismatic gifts of the laity, whether these be of a humble or more exalted kind".[46] These gifts, which awaken in many people the desire for a deeper spiritual life, can benefit not only the lay faithful but the clergy as well. The communion between ordained and charismatic ministries can provide "a helpful impulse to a renewed commitment by the Church in proclaiming and bearing witness to the Gospel of hope and charity in every corner of the world".[47] I would also like to add, echoing the Apostolic Exhortation *Pastores Dabo Vobis* of Pope John Paul II, that the ordained ministry has a radical *"communitarian form"* and can be exercised only in the communion of priests with their Bishop.[48] This communion between priests and their Bishop, grounded in the sacrament of Holy Orders and made manifest in Eucharistic concelebration, needs to be translated into various concrete expressions of an effective and affective priestly fraternity.[49] Only thus will priests be able to live fully the gift of celibacy and build thriving

Christian communities in which the miracles which accompanied the first preaching of the Gospel can be repeated.

The Pauline Year now coming to its close invites us also to look to the Apostle of the Gentiles, who represents a splendid example of a priest entirely devoted to his ministry. "The love of Christ urges us on" – he wrote – "because we are convinced that one has died for all; therefore all have died" (2 Cor 5:14). And he adds: "He died for all, so that those who live might live no longer for themselves, but for him who died and was raised for them" (2 Cor 5:15). Could a finer programme could be proposed to any priest resolved to advance along the path of Christian perfection?

Dear brother priests, the celebration of the 150th anniversary of the death of St John Mary Vianney (1859) follows upon the celebration of the 150th anniversary of the apparitions of Lourdes (1858). In 1959 Blessed Pope John XXIII noted that "shortly before the Curé of Ars completed his long and admirable life, the Immaculate Virgin appeared in another part of France to an innocent and humble girl, and entrusted to her a message of prayer and penance which continues, even a century later, to yield immense spiritual fruits. The life of this holy priest whose centenary we are commemorating in a real way anticipated the great supernatural truths taught to the seer of Massabielle. He was greatly devoted to the Immaculate Conception of the Blessed Virgin; in 1836 he had dedicated his parish church to Our Lady Conceived without Sin and he greeted the dogmatic definition of this truth in 1854 with deep faith and great joy."[50] The Curé would always remind his faithful that "after giving us all he could, Jesus Christ wishes in addition to bequeath us his most precious possession, his Blessed Mother".[51]

To the Most Holy Virgin I entrust this Year for Priests. I ask her to awaken in the heart of every priest a generous and renewed commitment to the ideal of complete self-oblation to Christ and the Church which inspired the thoughts and actions of the saintly Curé of Ars. It was his fervent prayer life and his impassioned love of Christ Crucified that enabled John Mary Vianney to grow daily in his total self-oblation to God and the Church. May his example lead all priests to offer that witness of unity with their Bishop, with one another and with the lay faithful, which today, as ever, is so necessary. Despite all the evil present in our world, the words which Christ spoke to his Apostles in the Upper Room continue to inspire us: "In the world you have tribulation; but take courage, I have overcome the world" (Jn 16:33). Our faith in the Divine Master gives us the strength to look to the future with confidence. Dear priests, Christ is counting on you. In the footsteps of the Curé of Ars, let yourselves be enthralled by him. In this way you too will be, for the world in our time, heralds of hope, reconciliation and peace!

With my blessing.
From the Vatican, 16 June 2009.
BENEDICTUS PP. XVI

1. He was proclaimed as such by Pope Pius XI in 1929.
2. *"Le Sacerdoce, c'est l'amour du cœur de Jésus"* (in *Le curé d'Ars. Sa pensée – Son cœur.* Présentés par l'Abbé Bernard Nodet, éd. Xavier Mappus, Foi Vivante, 1966, p. 98). Hereafter: *NODET*. The expression is also quoted in the *Catechism of the Catholic Church*, No. 1589).
3. NODET, p. 101.
4. Ibid., p. 97.
5. Ibid., pp. 98-99.
6. Ibid., pp. 98-100.
7. Ibid., p. 183.
8. MONNIN, A., *Il Curato d'Ars. Vita di Gian. Battista-Maria Vianney*, vol. I, ed. Marietti, Turin, 1870, p. 122.
9. Cf. *Lumen Gentium*, 10.
10. *Presbyterorum Ordinis*, 9.
11. Ibid.

12. "Contemplation is a gaze of faith, fixed on Jesus. 'I look at him and he looks at me': this is what a certain peasant of Ars used to say to his holy Curé about his prayer before the tabernacle" (*Catechism of the Catholic Church*, No. 2715).
13. NODET, p. 85.
14. Ibid., p. 114.
15. Ibid., p. 119.
16. MONNIN, A., op. cit., II, pp. 430ff.
17. NODET, p. 105.
18. Ibid.
19. Ibid., p. 104.
20. MONNIN, A., op. cit., II, p. 293.
21. Ibid., II, p. 10.
22. NODET, p. 128.
23. Ibid., p. 50.
24. Ibid., p. 131.
25. Ibid., p. 130.
26. Ibid., p. 27.
27. Ibid., p. 139.
28. Ibid., p. 28.
29. Ibid., p. 77.
30. Ibid., p. 102.
31. Ibid., p. 189.
32. *Evangelii nuntiandi*, 41.
33. BENEDICT XVI, *Homily at the Chrism Mass*, 9 April 2009.
34. Cf. BENEDICT XVI, Address to the Plenary Assembly of the Congregation for the Clergy, 16 March 2009.
35. P. I.
36. The name given to the house where more than sixty abandoned girls were taken in and educated. To maintain this house he would do anything: *"J'ai fait tous les commerces imaginables"*, he would say with a smile (NODET, p. 214).
37. NODET, p. 216.
38. Ibid., p. 215.
39. Ibid., p. 216.
40. Ibid., p. 214.
41. Cf. ibid., p. 112.
42. Cf. ibid., pp. 82-84; 102-103.
43. Ibid., p. 75.
44. Ibid., p. 76.
45. BENEDICT XVI, *Homily for the Vigil of Pentecost*, 3 June 2006.

46. No. 9.
47. BENEDICT XVI, Address to Bishop-Friends of the Focolare Movement and the Sant'Egidio Community, 8 February 2007
48. Cf. No. 17.
49. Cf. JOHN PAUL II, Apostolic Exhortation *Pastores Dabo Vobis*, 74.
50. Encyclical Letter *Sacerdotii nostri primordia*, P. III.
51. NODET, p. 244.

PASTORAL LETTER
TO THE CATHOLICS OF IRELAND

20 March 2010

1. Dear Brothers and Sisters of the Church in Ireland, it is with great concern that I write to you as Pastor of the universal Church. Like yourselves, I have been deeply disturbed by the information which has come to light regarding the abuse of children and vulnerable young people by members of the Church in Ireland, particularly by priests and religious. I can only share in the dismay and the sense of betrayal that so many of you have experienced on learning of these sinful and criminal acts and the way Church authorities in Ireland dealt with them.

As you know, I recently invited the Irish bishops to a meeting here in Rome to give an account of their handling of these matters in the past and to outline the steps they have taken to respond to this grave situation. Together with senior officials of the Roman Curia, I listened to what they had to say, both individually and as a group, as they offered an analysis of mistakes made and lessons learned, and a description of the programmes and protocols now in place. Our discussions were frank and constructive. I am confident that, as a result, the bishops will now be in a stronger position to carry forward the work of repairing past injustices and confronting the broader issues associated with the abuse of minors in a way consonant with the demands of justice and the teachings of the Gospel.

2. For my part, considering the gravity of these offences, and the often inadequate response to them on the part of the ecclesiastical authorities in your country, I have decided to write this Pastoral Letter to express my closeness to you and to propose a path of healing, renewal and reparation.

It is true, as many in your country have pointed out, that the problem of child abuse is peculiar neither to Ireland nor to the Church. Nevertheless, the task you now face is to address the problem of abuse that has occurred within the Irish Catholic community, and to do so with courage and determination. No one imagines that this painful situation will be resolved swiftly. Real progress has been made, yet much more remains to be done. Perseverance and prayer are needed, with great trust in the healing power of God's grace.

At the same time, I must also express my conviction that, in order to recover from this grievous wound, the Church in Ireland must first acknowledge before the Lord and before others the serious sins committed against defenceless children. Such an acknowledgement, accompanied by sincere sorrow for the damage caused to these victims and their families, must lead to a concerted effort to ensure the protection of children from similar crimes in the future.

As you take up the challenges of this hour, I ask you to remember "the rock from which you were hewn" (Isa 51:1). Reflect upon the generous, often heroic, contributions made by past generations of Irish men and women to the Church and to humanity as a whole, and let this provide the impetus for honest self-examination and a committed programme of ecclesial and individual renewal. It is my prayer that, assisted by the intercession of her many saints and purified through penance, the Church in Ireland will overcome the present crisis and become once more a convincing witness to the truth and the goodness of Almighty God, made manifest in his Son Jesus Christ.

3. Historically, the Catholics of Ireland have proved an enormous force for good at home and abroad. Celtic monks like St Columbanus spread the Gospel in Western Europe and laid the foundations of medieval monastic culture. The ideals of holiness, charity and transcendent wisdom born of the Christian faith found expression in the building of churches and

monasteries and the establishment of schools, libraries and hospitals, all of which helped to consolidate the spiritual identity of Europe. Those Irish missionaries drew their strength and inspiration from the firm faith, strong leadership and upright morals of the Church in their native land.

From the sixteenth century on, Catholics in Ireland endured a long period of persecution, during which they struggled to keep the flame of faith alive in dangerous and difficult circumstances. St Oliver Plunkett, the martyred Archbishop of Armagh, is the most famous example of a host of courageous sons and daughters of Ireland who were willing to lay down their lives out of fidelity to the Gospel. After Catholic Emancipation, the Church was free to grow once more. Families and countless individuals who had preserved the faith in times of trial became the catalyst for the great resurgence of Irish Catholicism in the nineteenth century. The Church provided education, especially for the poor, and this was to make a major contribution to Irish society. Among the fruits of the new Catholic schools was a rise in vocations: generations of missionary priests, sisters and brothers left their homeland to serve in every continent, especially in the English-speaking world. They were remarkable not only for their great numbers, but for the strength of their faith and the steadfastness of their pastoral commitment. Many dioceses, especially in Africa, America and Australia, benefited from the presence of Irish clergy and religious who preached the Gospel and established parishes, schools and universities, clinics and hospitals that served both Catholics and the community at large, with particular attention to the needs of the poor.

In almost every family in Ireland, there has been someone – a son or a daughter, an aunt or an uncle – who has given his or her life to the Church. Irish families rightly esteem and cherish their loved ones who have dedicated their lives to Christ, sharing the gift of faith with others, and putting that faith into action in loving service of God and neighbour.

4. In recent decades, however, the Church in your country has had to confront new and serious challenges to the faith arising from the rapid transformation and secularization of Irish society. Fast-paced social change has occurred, often adversely affecting people's traditional adherence to Catholic teaching and values. All too often, the sacramental and devotional practices that sustain faith and enable it to grow, such as frequent confession, daily prayer and annual retreats, were neglected. Significant too was the tendency during this period, also on the part of priests and religious, to adopt ways of thinking and assessing secular realities without sufficient reference to the Gospel. The programme of renewal proposed by the Second Vatican Council was sometimes misinterpreted and indeed, in the light of the profound social changes that were taking place, it was far from easy to know how best to implement it. In particular, there was a well-intentioned but misguided tendency to avoid penal approaches to canonically irregular situations. It is in this overall context that we must try to understand the disturbing problem of child sexual abuse, which has contributed in no small measure to the weakening of faith and the loss of respect for the Church and her teachings.

Only by examining carefully the many elements that gave rise to the present crisis can a clear-sighted diagnosis of its causes be undertaken and effective remedies be found. Certainly, among the contributing factors we can include: inadequate procedures for determining the suitability of candidates for the priesthood and the religious life; insufficient human, moral, intellectual and spiritual formation in seminaries and novitiates; a tendency in society to favour the clergy and other authority figures; and a misplaced concern for the reputation of the Church and the avoidance of scandal, resulting in failure to apply existing canonical penalties and to safeguard the dignity of every person. Urgent action is needed to address these factors, which have had such tragic consequences in the lives of victims and their families, and have obscured the light of the Gospel to a degree that not even centuries of persecution succeeded in doing.

5. On several occasions since my election to the See of Peter, I have met with victims of sexual abuse, as indeed I am ready to do in the future. I have sat with them, I have listened to their stories, I have acknowledged their suffering, and I have prayed with them and for them. Earlier in my pontificate, in my concern to address this matter, I asked the bishops of Ireland, "to establish the truth of what happened in the past, to take whatever steps are necessary to prevent it from occurring again, to ensure that the principles of justice are fully respected, and above all, to bring healing to the victims and to all those affected by these egregious crimes" (*Address to the Bishops of Ireland*, 28 October 2006).

With this Letter, I wish to exhort *all of you*, as God's people in Ireland, to reflect on the wounds inflicted on Christ's body, the sometimes painful remedies needed to bind and heal them, and the need for unity, charity and mutual support in the long-term process of restoration and ecclesial renewal. I now turn to you with words that come from my heart, and I wish to speak to each of you individually and to all of you as brothers and sisters in the Lord.

6. *To the victims of abuse and their families*
You have suffered grievously and I am truly sorry. I know that nothing can undo the wrong you have endured. Your trust has been betrayed and your dignity has been violated. Many of you found that, when you were courageous enough to speak of what happened to you, no one would listen. Those of you who were abused in residential institutions must have felt that there was no escape from your sufferings. It is understandable that you find it hard to forgive or be reconciled with the Church. In her name, I openly express the shame and remorse that we all feel. At the same time, I ask you not to lose hope. It is in the communion of the Church that we encounter the person of Jesus Christ, who was himself a victim of injustice and sin. Like you, he still bears the wounds of his own unjust suffering. He understands the depths of your pain and its enduring effect

upon your lives and your relationships, including your relationship with the Church. I know some of you find it difficult even to enter the doors of a church after all that has occurred. Yet Christ's own wounds, transformed by his redemptive sufferings, are the very means by which the power of evil is broken and we are reborn to life and hope. I believe deeply in the healing power of his self-sacrificing love – even in the darkest and most hopeless situations – to bring liberation and the promise of a new beginning.

Speaking to you as a pastor concerned for the good of all God's children, I humbly ask you to consider what I have said. I pray that, by drawing nearer to Christ and by participating in the life of his Church – a Church purified by penance and renewed in pastoral charity – you will come to rediscover Christ's infinite love for each one of you. I am confident that in this way you will be able to find reconciliation, deep inner healing and peace.

7. *To priests and religious who have abused children*
You betrayed the trust that was placed in you by innocent young people and their parents, and you must answer for it before Almighty God and before properly constituted tribunals. You have forfeited the esteem of the people of Ireland and brought shame and dishonour upon your confreres. Those of you who are priests violated the sanctity of the sacrament of Holy Orders in which Christ makes himself present in us and in our actions. Together with the immense harm done to victims, great damage has been done to the Church and to the public perception of the priesthood and religious life.

I urge you to examine your conscience, take responsibility for the sins you have committed, and humbly express your sorrow. Sincere repentance opens the door to God's forgiveness and the grace of true amendment. By offering prayers and penances for those you have wronged, you should seek to atone personally for your actions. Christ's redeeming sacrifice has the power to forgive even the gravest of sins, and to bring forth good from even the most terrible evil. At the same time, God's justice summons us to give an account of our actions and to conceal nothing. Openly acknowledge your guilt, submit yourselves to the demands of justice, but do not despair of God's mercy.

8. *To parents*

You have been deeply shocked to learn of the terrible things that took place in what ought to be the safest and most secure environment of all. In today's world it is not easy to build a home and to bring up children. They deserve to grow up in security, loved and cherished, with a strong sense of their identity and worth. They have a right to be educated in authentic moral values rooted in the dignity of the human person, to be inspired by the truth of our Catholic faith and to learn ways of behaving and acting that lead to healthy self-esteem and lasting happiness. This noble but demanding task is entrusted in the first place to you, their parents. I urge you to play your part in ensuring the best possible care of children, both at home and in society as a whole, while the Church, for her part, continues to implement the measures adopted in recent years to protect young people in parish and school environments. As you carry out your vital responsibilities, be assured that I remain close to you and I offer you the support of my prayers.

9. *To the children and young people of Ireland*

I wish to offer you a particular word of encouragement. Your experience of the Church is very different from that of your parents and grandparents. The world has changed greatly since they were your age. Yet all people, in every generation, are called to travel the same path through life, whatever their circumstances may be. We are all scandalized by the sins and failures of some of the Church's members, particularly those who were chosen especially to guide and serve young people. But it is *in the Church* that you will find Jesus Christ, who is the same yesterday, today and for ever (cf. Heb 13:8). He loves you and he has offered himself on the cross for you. Seek a personal relationship with him within the communion of his Church, for he will never betray your trust! He alone can satisfy your deepest longings and give your lives their fullest meaning by directing them to the service of others. Keep your eyes fixed on Jesus and his goodness, and shelter the flame of faith in your heart. Together with your fellow Catholics in Ireland, I look to you to be faithful disciples of our Lord and to bring your much-needed enthusiasm and idealism to the rebuilding and renewal of our beloved Church.

10. *To the priests and religious of Ireland*
All of us are suffering as a result of the sins of our confreres who betrayed a sacred trust or failed to deal justly and responsibly with allegations of abuse. In view of the outrage and indignation which this has provoked, not only among the lay faithful but among yourselves and your religious communities, many of you feel personally discouraged, even abandoned. I am also aware that in some people's eyes you are tainted by association, and viewed as if you were somehow responsible for the misdeeds of others. At this painful time, I want to acknowledge the dedication of your priestly and religious lives and apostolates, and I invite you to reaffirm your faith in Christ, your love of his Church and your confidence in the Gospel's promise of redemption, forgiveness and interior renewal. In this way, you will demonstrate for all to see that where sin abounds, grace abounds all the more (cf. Rom 5:20).

I know that many of you are disappointed, bewildered and angered by the way these matters have been handled by some of your superiors. Yet, it is essential that you cooperate closely with those in authority and help to ensure that the measures adopted to respond to the crisis will be truly evangelical, just and effective. Above all, I urge you to become ever more clearly men and women of prayer, courageously following the path of conversion, purification and reconciliation. In this way, the

Church in Ireland will draw new life and vitality from your witness to the Lord's redeeming power made visible in your lives.

11. *To my brother bishops*

It cannot be denied that some of you and your predecessors failed, at times grievously, to apply the long-established norms of canon law to the crime of child abuse. Serious mistakes were made in responding to allegations. I recognize how difficult it was to grasp the extent and complexity of the problem, to obtain reliable information and to make the right decisions in the light of conflicting expert advice. Nevertheless, it must be admitted that grave errors of judgement were made and failures of leadership occurred. All this has seriously undermined your credibility and effectiveness. I appreciate the efforts you have made to remedy past mistakes and to guarantee that they do not happen again. Besides fully implementing the norms of canon law in addressing cases of child abuse, continue to cooperate with the civil authorities in their area of competence. Clearly, religious superiors should do likewise. They too have taken part in recent discussions here in Rome with a view to establishing a clear and consistent approach to these matters. It is imperative that the child safety norms of the Church in Ireland be continually revised and updated and that they be applied fully and impartially in conformity with canon law.

Only decisive action carried out with complete honesty and transparency will restore the respect and good will of the Irish people towards the Church to which we have consecrated our lives. This must arise, first and foremost, from your own self-examination, inner purification and spiritual renewal. The Irish people rightly expect you to be men of God, to be holy, to live simply, to pursue personal conversion daily. For them, in the words of St Augustine, you are a bishop; yet with them you are called to be a follower of Christ (cf. Sermon 340, 1). I therefore exhort you to renew your sense of accountability before God, to grow in solidarity with your people and to deepen your pastoral concern for all the members of your flock. In particular, I ask you to be attentive to the spiritual and moral lives of each one of your priests. Set them an example by your own lives, be close to them, listen to their concerns, offer them encouragement at this difficult time and stir up the flame of their love for Christ and their commitment to the service of their brothers and sisters.

The lay faithful, too, should be encouraged to play their proper part in the life of the Church. See that they are formed in such a way that they can offer an articulate and convincing account of the Gospel in the midst of modern society (cf. 1 Pet 3:15) and cooperate more fully in the Church's life and mission. This in turn will help you once again become credible leaders and witnesses to the redeeming truth of Christ.

12. *To all the faithful of Ireland*

A young person's experience of the Church should always bear fruit in a personal and life-giving encounter with Jesus Christ within a loving, nourishing community. In this environment, young people should be encouraged to grow to their full human and spiritual stature, to aspire to high ideals of holiness, charity and truth, and to draw inspiration from the riches of a great religious and cultural tradition. In our increasingly secularized society, where even we Christians often find it difficult to speak of the transcendent dimension of our existence, we need to find new ways to pass on to young people the beauty and richness of friendship with Jesus Christ in the communion of his Church. In confronting the present crisis, measures to deal justly with individual crimes are essential, yet on their own they are not enough: a new vision is needed, to inspire present and future generations to treasure the gift of our common faith. By treading the path marked out by the Gospel, by observing the commandments and by conforming your lives ever more closely to the figure of Jesus Christ, you will surely experience the profound renewal that is so urgently needed at this time. I invite you all to persevere along this path.

13. Dear brothers and sisters in Christ, it is out of deep concern for all of you at this painful time in which the fragility of the human condition has been so starkly revealed that I have wished to offer these words of encouragement and support. I hope that you will receive them as a sign of my spiritual closeness and my confidence in your ability to respond to the challenges of the present hour by drawing renewed inspiration and strength from Ireland's noble traditions of fidelity to the Gospel, perseverance in the faith and steadfastness in the pursuit of holiness. In solidarity with all of you, I am praying earnestly that, by God's grace, the wounds afflicting so many individuals and families may be healed and that the Church in Ireland may experience a season of rebirth and spiritual renewal.

14. I now wish to propose to you some concrete initiatives to address the situation.

At the conclusion of my meeting with the Irish bishops, I asked that Lent this year be set aside as a time to pray for an outpouring of God's mercy and the Holy Spirit's gifts of holiness and strength upon the Church in your country. I now invite all of you to devote your Friday penances, for a period of one year, between now and Easter 2011, to this intention. I ask you to offer up your fasting, your prayer, your reading of Scripture and your works of mercy in order to obtain the grace of healing and renewal for the Church in Ireland. I encourage you to discover anew the sacrament of Reconciliation and to avail yourselves more frequently of the transforming power of its grace.

Particular attention should also be given to Eucharistic adoration, and in every diocese there should be churches or chapels specifically devoted to this purpose. I ask parishes, seminaries, religious houses and monasteries to organize periods of Eucharistic adoration, so that all have an opportunity to take part. Through intense prayer before the real presence of the Lord, you can make reparation for the sins of abuse that have done so much harm, at the same time imploring the grace of renewed strength and a deeper sense of mission on the part of all bishops, priests, religious and lay faithful.

I am confident that this programme will lead to a rebirth of the Church in Ireland in the fullness of God's own truth, for it is the truth that sets us free (cf. Jn 8:32).

Furthermore, having consulted and prayed about the matter, I intend to hold an Apostolic Visitation of certain dioceses in Ireland, as well as seminaries and religious congregations. Arrangements for the Visitation, which is intended to assist the local Church on her path of renewal, will be made in cooperation with the competent offices of the Roman Curia and the Irish Episcopal Conference. The details will be announced in due course.

I also propose that a nationwide Mission be held for all bishops, priests and religious. It is my hope that, by drawing on the expertise of experienced preachers and retreat-givers from Ireland and from elsewhere, and by exploring anew the conciliar documents, the liturgical rites of ordination and profession, and recent pontifical teaching, you will come to a more profound appreciation of your respective vocations, so as to rediscover the roots of your faith in Jesus Christ and to drink deeply from the springs of living water that he offers you through his Church.

In this Year for Priests, I commend to you most particularly the figure of St John Mary Vianney, who had such a rich understanding of the mystery of the priesthood. "The priest", he wrote, "holds the key to the treasures of heaven: it is he who opens the door: he is the steward of the good Lord; the administrator of his goods." The Curé d'Ars understood well how greatly blessed a community is when served by a good and holy priest: "A good shepherd, a pastor after God's heart, is the greatest treasure which the good Lord can grant to a parish, and one of the most precious gifts of divine mercy." Through the intercession of St John Mary Vianney, may the priesthood in Ireland be revitalized, and may the whole Church in Ireland grow in appreciation for the great gift of the priestly ministry.

I take this opportunity to thank in anticipation all those who will be involved in the work of organizing the Apostolic Visitation and the Mission, as well as the many men and women throughout Ireland already working for the safety of children in church environments. Since the time when the gravity and extent of the problem of child sexual abuse in Catholic institutions first began to be fully grasped, the Church has done an immense amount of work in many parts of the world in order to address and remedy it. While no effort should be spared in improving and updating existing procedures, I am encouraged by the fact that the current safeguarding practices adopted by local Churches are being seen, in some parts of the world, as a model for other institutions to follow.

I wish to conclude this Letter with a special *Prayer for the Church in Ireland,* which I send to you with the care of a father for his children and with the affection of a fellow Christian, scandalized and hurt by what has occurred in our beloved Church. As you make use of this prayer in your families, parishes and communities, may the Blessed Virgin Mary protect and guide each of you to a closer union with her Son, crucified and risen. With great affection and unswerving confidence in God's promises, I cordially impart to all of you my Apostolic Blessing as a pledge of strength and peace in the Lord.

From the Vatican, 19 March 2010,
on the Solemnity of St Joseph
BENEDICTUS PP. XVI

PRAYER FOR
THE CHURCH IN IRELAND

God of our fathers,
renew us in the faith which is our life and salvation,
the hope which promises forgiveness and interior renewal,
the charity which purifies and opens our hearts
to love you, and in you, each of our brothers and sisters.

Lord Jesus Christ,
may the Church in Ireland renew her age-old commitment
to the education of our young people in the way of truth and
goodness, holiness and generous service to society.

Holy Spirit, comforter, advocate and guide,
inspire a new springtime of holiness and apostolic zeal
for the Church in Ireland.

May our sorrow and our tears,
our sincere effort to redress past wrongs,
and our firm purpose of amendment
bear an abundant harvest of grace
for the deepening of the faith
in our families, parishes, schools and communities,
for the spiritual progress of Irish society,
and the growth of charity, justice, joy and peace
within the whole human family.

To you, Triune God,
confident in the loving protection of Mary,
Queen of Ireland, our Mother,
and of Saint Patrick, Saint Brigid and all the saints,
do we entrust ourselves, our children,
and the needs of the Church in Ireland.

Amen.

II.
HOMILIES

Homily given during the

CHRISM MASS

Saint Peter's Basilica
Holy Thursday, 9 April 2009

"Sanctify them in the truth; your word is truth"

In the Upper Room, on the eve of his Passion, the Lord prayed
for his disciples gathered about him. At the same time he looked
ahead to the community of disciples of all centuries, "those who
believe in me through their word" (Jn 17:20). In his prayer for
the disciples of all time, he saw us too, and he prayed for us. Let
us listen to what he asks for the Twelve and for us gathered here:
"Sanctify them in the truth; your word is truth. As you sent
me into the world, so I have sent them into the world. And
for their sake I consecrate myself, so that they also may be
consecrated in truth" (17:17ff.). The Lord asks for our
sanctification, our consecration in truth. And he sends us forth
to carry on his own mission. But in this prayer there is one
word which draws our attention, and appears difficult to
understand. Jesus says: "For their sake I consecrate myself".
What does this mean? Is Jesus not himself "the Holy One of
God", as Peter acknowledged at that decisive moment in
Capharnaum (cf. Jn 6:69)? How can he now consecrate –
sanctify – himself?

To understand this, we need first to clarify what the Bible
means by the words "holy" and "sanctify – consecrate". "Holy"
– this word describes above all God's own nature, his completely
unique, divine, way of being, one which is his alone. He alone
is the true and authentic Holy One, in the original sense of the
word. All other holiness derives from him, is a participation in
his way of being. He is purest Light, Truth and untainted Good.
To consecrate something or someone means, therefore, to give

that thing or person to God as his property, to take it out of the context of what is ours and to insert it in his milieu, so that it no longer belongs to our affairs, but is totally of God. Consecration is thus a taking away from the world and a giving over to the living God. The thing or person no longer belongs to us, or even to itself, but is immersed in God. Such a giving up of something in order to give it over to God, we also call a sacrifice: this thing will no longer be my property, but his property. In the Old Testament, the giving over of a person to God, his "sanctification", is identified with priestly ordination, and this also defines the essence of the priesthood: it is a transfer of ownership, a being taken out of the world and given to God. We can now see the two directions which belong to the process of sanctification-consecration. It is a departure from the milieux of worldly life – a "being set apart" for God. But for this very reason it is not a segregation. Rather, being given over to God means being charged to represent others. The priest is removed from worldly bonds and given over to God, and precisely in this way, starting with God, he must be available for others, for everyone. When Jesus says: "I consecrate myself", he makes himself both priest and victim. Bultmann was right to translate the phrase: "I consecrate myself" by "I sacrifice myself". Do we now see what happens when Jesus says: "I consecrate myself for them"? This is the priestly act by which Jesus – the Man Jesus, who is one with the Son of God – gives himself over to the Father for us. It is the expression of the fact that he is both priest and victim. I consecrate myself – I sacrifice myself: this unfathomable word, which gives us a glimpse deep into the heart of Jesus Christ, should be the object of constantly renewed reflection. It contains the whole mystery of our redemption. It also contains the origins of the priesthood in the Church, of our priesthood.

Only now can we fully understand the prayer which the Lord offered the Father for his disciples – for us. "Sanctify them in the truth": this is the inclusion of the Apostles in the priesthood of Jesus Christ, the institution of his new priesthood for the community of the faithful of all times. "Sanctify them in truth": this is the true prayer of consecration for the Apostles. The Lord prays that God himself draw them towards him, into his holiness. He prays that God take them away from themselves to make them his own property, so that, starting from him, they can carry out the priestly ministry for the world. This prayer of Jesus appears twice in slightly different forms. Both times we need to listen very carefully, in order to understand, even dimly the sublime reality that is about to be accomplished. "Sanctify them in the truth". Jesus adds: "Your word is truth". The disciples are thus drawn deep within God by being immersed in the word of God. The word of God is, so to speak, the bath which purifies them, the creative power which transforms them into God's own being. So then, how do things stand in our own lives? Are we truly pervaded by the word of God? Is that word truly the nourishment we live by, even more than bread and the things of this world? Do we really know that word? Do we love it? Are we deeply engaged with this word to the point that it really leaves a mark on our lives and shapes our thinking? Or is it rather the case that our thinking is constantly being shaped by all the things that others say and do? Aren't prevailing opinions the criterion by which we all too often measure ourselves? Do we not perhaps remain, when all is said and done, mired in the superficiality in which people today are generally caught up? Do we allow ourselves truly to be deeply purified by the word of God? Nietzsche scoffed at humility and obedience as the virtues of slaves, a source of repression. He replaced them with pride and man's absolute freedom. Of course there exist caricatures of a misguided humility and a mistaken submissiveness, which we do not want to imitate. But there also exists a destructive pride and a presumption which tear every community apart and result in violence. Can we learn from Christ the correct humility which corresponds to the truth of our being, and the obedience which submits to truth, to the will of God? "Sanctify them in the truth; your word is truth": this word of inclusion in the priesthood lights up our lives and calls us to become ever anew disciples of that truth which is revealed in the word of God.

We can advance another step in the interpretation of these words. Did not Christ say of himself: "I am the truth" (cf. Jn 14:6)? Is he not himself the living Word of God, to which every other word refers? Sanctify them in the truth – this means, then, in the deepest sense: make them one with me, Christ. Bind them to me. Draw them into me. Indeed, when all is said and done, there is *only one* priest of the New Covenant, Jesus Christ himself. Consequently, the priesthood of the disciples can only be a participation in the priesthood of Jesus. Our being priests is simply a new and radical way of being united to Christ. In its substance, it has been bestowed on us for ever in the sacrament. But this new seal imprinted upon our being can become for us a condemnation, if our lives do not develop by entering into the truth of the Sacrament. The promises we renew today state in this regard that our will must be directed along this path: *"Domino Iesu arctius coniungi et conformari, vobismetipsis abrenuntiantes"* ("Those who renounce themselves are more closely [to be] joined and confirmed to the Lord Jesus"). Being united to Christ calls for renunciation. It means not wanting to impose our own way and our own will, not desiring to become someone else, but abandoning ourselves to him, however and wherever he wants to use us. As St Paul said: "It is no longer I who live, but Christ who lives in me" (Gal 2:20). In the words "I do", spoken at our priestly ordination, we made this fundamental renunciation of our desire to be independent, "self-made". But day by day this great "yes" has to be lived out in the many little "yeses" and small sacrifices. This "yes" made up of tiny steps which together make up the great "yes", can be lived out without bitterness and self-pity only if Christ is truly the center of our lives. If we enter into true closeness to him. Then indeed we experience, amid sacrifices which can at first be painful, the growing joy of friendship with him, and all the small and sometimes great signs of his love, which he is constantly showing us. "The one who loses himself, finds himself". When we dare to lose ourselves for the Lord, we come to experience the truth of these words.

To be immersed in the Truth, in Christ – part of this process is prayer, in which we exercise our friendship with him and also come to know him: his way of being, of thinking, of acting. Praying is a journey in personal communion with Christ, setting before him our daily life, our successes and failures, our struggles and our joys – in a word, it is to stand in front of him. But if this is not to become a form of self-contemplation, it is important that we constantly learn to pray by praying with the Church. Celebrating the Eucharist means praying. We celebrate the Eucharist rightly if with our thoughts and our being we enter into the words which the Church sets before us. There we find the prayer of all generations, which accompany us along the way towards the Lord. As priests, in the Eucharistic celebration we are those who by their prayer blaze a trail for the prayer of today's Christians. If we are inwardly united to the words of prayer, if we let ourselves be guided and transformed by them, then the faithful will also enter into those words. And then all of us will become truly "one body, one spirit" in Christ.

To be immersed in God's truth and thus in his holiness – for us this also means to acknowledge that the truth makes demands, to stand up, in matters great and small, to the lie which in so many different ways is present in the world; accepting the struggles associated with the truth, because its inmost joy is present within us. Nor, when we talk about being sanctified in the truth, should we forget that in Jesus Christ truth and love are one. Being immersed in him means being immersed in his goodness, in true love. True love does not come cheap, it can also prove quite costly. It resists evil in order to bring men true good. If we become one with Christ, we learn to recognize him precisely in the suffering, in the poor, in the little ones of this world; then we become people who serve, who recognize our brothers and sisters in him, and in them, we encounter him.

"Sanctify them in truth" – this is the first part of what Jesus says. But then he adds: "I consecrate myself, so that they also may be consecrated in truth" – that is, truly consecrated (Jn 17:19). I think that this second part has a special meaning of its own. In the world's religions there are many different ritual means of "sanctification", of the consecration of a human person. Yet all these rites can remain something merely formal. Christ asks for his disciples the true sanctification which transforms their being, their very selves; he asks that it not remain a ritual formality, but that it make them truly the "property" of God himself. We could even say that Christ prayed on behalf of us for that sacrament which touches us in the depths of our being. But he also prayed that this interior transformation might be translated day by day in our lives; that in our everyday routine and our concrete daily lives we might be truly pervaded by the light of God.

On the eve of my priestly ordination, fifty-eight years ago, I opened the Sacred Scripture, because I wanted to receive once more a word from the Lord for that day and for my future journey as a priest. My gaze fell on this passage: "Sanctify them in the truth; your word is truth". Then I realized: the Lord is speaking about me, and he is speaking to me. This very same thing will be accomplished tomorrow in me. When all is said and done, we are not consecrated by rites, even though rites are necessary. The bath in which the Lord immerses us is himself – the Truth in person. Priestly ordination means: being immersed in him, immersed in the Truth. I belong in a new way to him and thus to others, "that his Kingdom may come". Dear friends, in this hour of the renewal of promises, we want to pray to the Lord to make us men of truth, men of love, men of God. Let us implore him to draw us ever anew into himself, so that we may become truly priests of the New Covenant.
Amen.

HOLY MASS FOR THE ORDINATION TO THE PRIESTHOOD OF 19 DEACONS OF THE DIOCESE OF ROME

St Peter's Basilica
Fourth Sunday of Easter, 3 May 2009

'always be men of prayer and service'

According to a beautiful tradition, the Sunday of "the Good Shepherd" is when the Bishop of Rome meets with his clergy for the Ordination of new priests for the Diocese. This is a great gift from God every time; it is his grace! Therefore let a deep feeling of faith and gratitude in living today's celebration arise in us... The word of God that we have listened to offers many points for meditation: I will choose a few to shed an indelible light on the path of your life and your ministry.

"This [Jesus] is the stone... there is no other name... given among men by which we must be saved" (Acts 4:11-12). In the passage of the Acts of the Apostles the first reading the singular "homonymy" between Peter and Jesus strikes us and makes us reflect: Peter, who received his name from Jesus himself, here asserts that he, Jesus, is "the stone". In fact, the only true rock is Jesus. The only name that saves is his. The apostle, and therefore the priest, receives his "name", his very identity, from Christ. Everything he does is done in his name. His "I" becomes totally relative to the "I" of Jesus. In the name of Christ, and most certainly not in his own, the apostle may perform acts of healing for the brethren, may help the "crippled" to rise again and take their path (cf. Acts 4:9-10). In Peter's case, the miracle that had just occurred makes this especially evident. And even the reference to what was said in the Psalm is essential: "The stone which the builders rejected has become the corner stone" (Ps 118[117]:22). Jesus was "rejected", but the Father favoured him and put him as the foundation of the Temple of the New Covenant. Thus the apostle, like the priest, experiences in turn the Cross, and only through this can he become truly useful to the building of the Church. God loves to build his Church with people who, following Jesus, place their entire trust in God, as the Psalm itself mentions: "It is better to take refuge in the Lord than to put confidence in man. It is better to take refuge in the Lord than to put confidence in princes" (v. 8-9).

The disciple shares the same destiny as the Teacher, which ultimately is the destiny expressed in God the Father's own will! Jesus confessed at the end of his life, in the great prayer called "priestly": "O righteous Father, the world has not known you, but I have known you" (Jn 17:25). Even before he had asserted: "No one knows the Father except the Son" (Mt 11:27). Jesus himself experienced the rejection of God by the world, the misunderstanding, the indifference, the disfiguration of the Face of God. And Jesus passed the "witness" on to the disciples: "I made known to them your name", he further confides in the prayer to the Father, "and I will make it known, that the love with which you have loved me may be in them, and I in them" (Jn 17:26). Therefore the disciple and especially the apostle experiences the same joy that Jesus did, in knowing the name and the Face of the Father; and also shares his suffering, seeing that God is not recognized, that his love is not returned. On one hand we joyfully exclaim, like John did with joy in his first Letter: "See what love the Father has given us, that we should be called children of God; and so we are!"; and on the other with bitterness we observe: "The reason why the world does not know us is that it did not know him" (1 Jn 3:1). It is true, and we priests experience this: the "world" in an acceptance of the Johannine definition of the term does not understand the Christian, does not understand the ministers of the Gospel. Somewhat because it does not know God, and somewhat because it does not want to know him. The world does not want to know God so as not to be disturbed by his will, and therefore it does not want to listen to his ministers; this could cause a crisis.

Here we must pay attention to a de facto reality: that this "world", interpreted in the evangelical sense, also lures the Church, infecting her members and even ordained ministers. With the word "world", St John indicates and seeks to define a mentality, a way of thinking and living that can pollute even the Church, that in fact does pollute her, thereby requiring constant vigilance and purification. Until God is fully manifest, even his sons are not yet fully "like Him" (1 Jn 3:2). We are "in" the world, and we risk being also "of" the world, the world in the sense of this mentality. And in fact at times we are. Because of this, Jesus at the end did not pray for the world in this same sense but for his disciples, so that the Father may keep them from evil that they may be free and different from the world, while living in the world (cf. Jn 17:9,15). At that moment, at the end of the Last Supper, Jesus raised to the Father the prayer of consecration for the apostles and for all the priests of all times, when he said: "Sanctify them in the truth" (Jn 17:17). And he added: "And for their sake I consecrate myself, that they may also be consecrated in truth" (Jn 17:19). I emphasized these words of Jesus in the Homily of the Chrism Mass, last Holy Thursday. Today I take up this reflection referring to the Gospel of the Good Shepherd, when Jesus declared: "I give my life for the sheep" (cf. Jn 10:15,17,18).

To become priests in the Church means to enter into this self-donation of Christ through the Sacrament of Orders and to enter with all of one's being. Jesus gave his life for all, but in a special way he consecrated himself for those the Father had given to him, that they may be consecrated in truth, that is in him, and could speak and act in his name, represent him, continue his saving actions: breaking the Bread of life and remitting sins. Thus, the Good Shepherd offered his life for all the sheep, but he gave it and gave it in a special way for those that he himself, "with a feeling of favour", called and calls to follow him on the path of pastoral service. Then, in a singular way, Jesus prayed for Simon Peter, and sacrificed himself for him, because he would say to him one day, on the banks of the Sea of Tiberias: "Feed my sheep" (Jn 21:16-17). In the same way, every priest is the recipient of Christ's personal prayer, and only because of this he is able to collaborate with him in feeding the flock, which is completely and only the Lord's.

Here I would like to touch upon a point that is particularly dear to me: the prayer and its ties with service. We have seen that to be ordained priests means to enter in a sacramental and existential way into Christ's prayer for "his own". From this we priests derive a particular vocation to pray in a strongly Christocentric sense: we are called, that is, to "remain" in Christ as the evangelist John likes to repeat (cf. Jn 1:35-39; 15:4-10) and this abiding in Christ is achieved especially through prayer. Our ministry is totally tied to this "abiding" which is equivalent to prayer, and draws from this its efficacy. In this perspective, we must think of the different forms of prayer of a priest, first of all daily Holy Mass. The Eucharistic Celebration is the greatest and highest act of prayer, and constitutes the centre and the source from which even the other forms receive "nourishment": the Liturgy of the Hours, Eucharistic adoration, *Lectio divina*, the Holy Rosary, meditation. All these expressions of prayer, which have their centre in the Eucharist, fulfil the words of Jesus in the priest's day and in all his life: "I am the good shepherd; I know my own and my own know me, as the Father knows me and I know the Father; and I lay down my life for the sheep" (Jn 10:14-15). In fact, this "knowing" and "being known" in Christ and, through him, in the Most Holy Trinity, is none other than the most true and deep reality of prayer. The priest who prays a lot, and who prays well, is progressively drawn out of himself and evermore united to Jesus the Good Shepherd and the Servant of the Brethren. In conforming to him, even the priest "gives his life" for the sheep entrusted to him. No one takes it from him: he offers it himself, in unity with Christ the Lord, who has the power to give his life and the power to take it back not only for himself, but also for his friends, bound to him in the Sacrament of Orders. Thus the life of Christ, Lamb and Shepherd, is communicated to the whole flock, through the consecrated ministers.

Dear Deacons, may the Holy Spirit impress this divine word which I have briefly commented upon in your hearts, so that it may bear abundant and lasting fruit. We ask this through the intercession of the Holy Apostles Peter and Paul and St John Mary Vianney, the Curé d'Ars, to whose protection I have dedicated the next Presbyteral Year. And through the Mother of the Good Shepherd, Mary Most Holy. In every circumstance of your life, look to her, the star of your priesthood. As she said to the servants at the wedding in Cana, Mary repeats to you too: "Do whatever he tells you" (Jn 2:5). At the school of the Virgin, always be men of prayer and service, to become, in the faithful practice of your ministry, holy priests after God's heart.

HOLY MASS AND EUCHARISTIC PROCESSION TO THE BASILICA OF SAINT MARY MAJOR ON THE SOLEMNITY OF CORPUS CHRISTI

Square outside the Basilica of Saint John Lateran
Thursday, 11 June 2009

To become the Eucharist!

I address you in particular, dear priests, whom Christ has chosen so that with him you may be able to live your life as a sacrifice of praise for the salvation of the world. Only from union with Jesus can you draw that spiritual fruitfulness which generates hope in your pastoral ministry. St Leo the Great recalls that "our participation in the Body and Blood of Christ aspires to nothing other than to become what we receive" (*Sermo* 12, *De Passione* 3, 7, *PL* 54). If this is true for every Christian it is especially true for us priests. To become the Eucharist! May precisely this be our constant desire and commitment, so that the offering of the Body and Blood of the Lord which we make on the altar may be accompanied by the sacrifice of our existence. Every day, we draw from the Body and Blood of the Lord that free, pure love which makes us worthy ministers of Christ and witnesses to his joy. This is what the faithful expect of the priest: that is, the example of an authentic devotion to the Eucharist; they like to see him spend long periods of silence and adoration before Jesus as was the practice of the Holy Curé d'Ars, whom we shall remember in a special way during the upcoming Year for Priests.

SOLEMNITY OF
THE SACRED HEART OF JESUS

From the homily given at the

OPENING OF
THE YEAR FOR PRIESTS
ON THE 150th ANNIVERSARY OF
THE DEATH OF
SAINT JOHN MARY VIANNEY

Saint Peter's Basilica
Friday, 19 June 2009

"the priesthood is the love of the heart of Jesus"

In a little while we shall sing in the antiphon to the *Magnificat*: "The Lord has drawn us to his heart – *Suscepit nos Dominus in sinum et cor suum*". God's heart, as the expression of his will, is spoken of twenty-six times in the Old Testament. Before God's heart men and women stand judged. His heartfelt pain at the sins of mankind makes God decide on the flood, but then he is touched by the sight of human weakness and offers his forgiveness. Yet another passage of the Old Testament speaks of God's heart with absolute clarity: it is in the eleventh chapter of the book of the Prophet Hosea, whose opening lines portray the Lord's love for Israel at the dawn of its history: "When Israel was a child, I loved him, and out of Egypt I called my son" (Hos 11:1). Israel, however, responds to God's constant offer of love with indifference and even outright ingratitude. "The more I called them", the Lord is forced to admit, "the more they went from me" (v. 2). Even so, he never abandons Israel to the power of its enemies, because "my heart" – the the Creator of the

52

universe observes – "recoils within me, my compassion grows warm and tender" (v. 8).

The heart of God burns with compassion! On today's solemnity of the Sacred Heart of Jesus the Church presents us this mystery for our contemplation: the mystery of the heart of a God who feels compassion and who bestows all his love upon humanity. A mysterious love, which in the texts of the New Testament is revealed to us as God's boundless and passionate love for mankind. God does not lose heart in the face of ingratitude or rejection by the people he has chosen; rather, with infinite mercy he sends his only-begotten Son into the world to take upon himself the fate of a shattered love, so that by defeating the power of evil and death he could restore to human beings enslaved by sin their dignity as sons and daughters. But this took place at great cost – the only-begotten Son of the Father was sacrificed on the Cross: "Having loved his own who were in the world, he loved them to the end" (cf. Jn 13:1). The symbol of this love which transcends death is his side, pierced by a spear. The Apostle John, an eyewitness, tells us: "one of the soldiers pierced his side with a spear, and at once there came out blood and water" (cf. Jn 19:34)…

Together let us pause to contemplate the pierced heart of the Crucified One. Just now we heard once again, in the brief reading from St Paul's Letter to the Ephesians, that "God, who is rich in mercy, out of the great love with which he loved us, even when we were dead through our trespasses, made us alive together with Christ… raised us up with him, and made us sit with him in the heavenly places in Christ Jesus" (Eph 2:4-6). To be "in" Jesus Christ is already to be seated in heaven. The very core of Christianity is expressed in the heart of Jesus; in Christ the revolutionary "newness" of the Gospel is completely revealed and given to us: the Love that saves us and even now makes us live in the eternity of God. As the Evangelist John writes: "God so loved the world that he gave his only Son, that whoever believes in him should not perish but have eternal life" (3:16). God's heart calls to our hearts, inviting us to come out of ourselves, to forsake our human certainties, to trust in him and, by following his example, to make ourselves a gift of unbounded love.

While it is true that Jesus' invitation to "abide in my love" (cf. Jn 15:9) is addressed to all the baptized, on this feast of the Sacred Heart of Jesus, the day of prayer for the sanctification of priests, this invitation resounds all the more powerfully for us priests. It does so in a special way this evening, at the solemn inauguration of the Year for Priests which I have proclaimed to mark the 150th anniversary of the death of the saintly Curé of Ars. A lovely and touching saying of his, quoted in the *Catechism of the Catholic Church*, comes immediately to mind: "the priesthood is the love of the heart of Jesus" (n. 1589). How can we fail to be moved when we recall that the gift of our priestly ministry flows directly from this heart? How can we forget that we priests were consecrated to serve, humbly yet authoritatively, the common priesthood of the faithful? Ours is a mission which is indispensable for the Church and for the world, a mission which calls for complete fidelity to Christ and constant union with him. To abide in his love entails constantly striving for holiness, as did St John Mary Vianney.

In the Letter which I wrote to you for this special Jubilee Year, dear brother priests, I wished to highlight some essential aspects of our ministry by making reference to the example and teaching of the Curé of Ars, the model and protector of all priests, especially parish priests. I hope that my Letter will prove a help and encouragement to you in making this Year a graced opportunity to grow ever closer to Jesus, who counts on us, his ministers, to spread and build up his Kingdom, and to radiate his love and his truth. As I invited you at the conclusion of my Letter: "in the footsteps of the Curé of Ars, let yourselves be enthralled by Christ. In this way you too will be, for the world in our time, heralds of hope, reconciliation and peace!".

To be completely enthralled by Christ! This was the goal of the entire life of St Paul, to whom we looked throughout the Pauline Year now ending; this was the goal of the entire ministry of the Curé of Ars, whom we shall invoke in particular during this Year for Priests; may it also be the primary goal for each and every one of us. Certainly, to be ministers at the service of the Gospel, study and careful, ongoing pastoral and theological formation are useful and necessary, but even more necessary is that "knowledge of love" which can only be learned in a "heart to heart" encounter with Christ. For it is he who calls us to break the bread of his love, to forgive sins and to guide the flock in his name. And for that reason we must never step back from the source of love which is his heart, pierced on the Cross.

Only in this way can we cooperate effectively in the mysterious "plan of the Father" which consists in "making Christ the heart of the world"! This plan is accomplished in history as Jesus gradually becomes the Heart of human hearts, beginning with those called to be closest to him: namely his priests. We are reminded of this constant commitment by the "priestly promises" that we made on the day of our ordination and which we renew yearly on Holy Thursday during the Chrism Mass. Even our shortcomings, our limitations and our weaknesses ought to bring us back to the heart of Jesus. If it is true that by contemplating Christ sinners learn from him the "sorrow for sins" needed to bring them back to the Father, this is even more the case for sacred ministers. How can we forget, in this regard, that nothing causes more suffering for the Church, the Body of Christ, than the sins of her pastors, especially the sins of those who become "thieves and robbers" of the sheep (cf. Jn 10:1 ff.), lead them astray by their own private teachings, or ensnare them in the toils of sin and death? Dear priests, the summons to conversion and to trust in God's mercy also applies to us; we too must humbly, sincerely and unceasingly implore the heart of Jesus to preserve us from the terrifying risk of endangering the very people we are obliged to save.

A few moments ago, in the Choir Chapel, I was able to venerate the relic of the saintly Curé of Ars: his heart. A heart that blazed with divine love, experienced amazement at the thought of the dignity of the priest, and spoke to the faithful in touching and sublime tones, telling them that "after God, the priest is everything! ... Only in heaven will he fully realize what he is" (cf. *Letter for the Year for Priests*, p. 3). Dear brothers, let us cultivate this same amazement, in order to carry out our ministry with generosity and dedication, and to maintain the true "fear of God" in our hearts: the fear, that is, that we can deprive of so much good, by our negligence or fault, the souls entrusted to our care, or that – God forbid – we can do them harm. The Church needs holy priests; ministers capable of helping the faithful to experience the Lord's merciful love, and convinced witnesses of that love. In the Eucharistic Adoration which is to follow our celebration of Vespers, let us ask the Lord to set the heart of every priest afire with that "pastoral charity" which can make him one in heart and mind with Jesus the High Priest, and thus to imitate Jesus in complete self-giving. May the Virgin Mary, whose Immaculate Heart we shall contemplate with lively faith tomorrow, obtain this grace for us. The Curé of Ars had a filial devotion to Mary, a devotion so profound that in 1836, in anticipation of the proclamation of the dogma of the Immaculate Conception, he dedicated his parish to Mary "conceived without sin". He frequently renewed this offering of the parish to the Blessed Virgin, teaching his parishioners that "to be heard it is enough to speak to her", for the simple reason that she "desires above all else to see us happy". May the Blessed Virgin, our Mother, accompany us during the Year for Priests which we begin today, so that we can be wise and steady guides of the flock which the Lord has entrusted to our pastoral care. Amen!

PASTORAL VISIT TO
SAN GIOVANNI ROTONDO

From the homily given at the

EUCHARISTIC CONCELEBRATION

*Square outside the Church of Saint Pio of Pietrelcina
Sunday, 21 June 2009*

The Example of Padre Pio

At the heart of my pilgrimage to this place where everything speaks of the life and holiness of Padre Pio of Pietrelcina, I have the joy of celebrating for you and with you the Eucharist, a mystery that was the centre of his whole life, the origin of his vocation, the power of his witness, the consecration of his sacrifice...

We have just heard the Gospel reading of the calming of the storm, which was presented with a brief but incisive passage from the Book of Job, in which God reveals himself as the Lord of the sea. Jesus rebukes the wind and orders the sea to be calm, he speaks to it as if it were identified with the power of the devil. In fact, according to what the First Reading and Psalm 107[106] tell us, in the Bible the sea is considered a threatening, chaotic and potentially destructive element which God the Creator alone can dominate, govern and calm.

Yet, there is another force a positive force that moves the world, capable of transforming and renewing creatures: the power of "Christ's love" (2 Cor 5:14) as St Paul calls it in his Second Letter to the Corinthians not, therefore essentially a cosmic force, but rather divine, transcendent. It also acts on the cosmos but, in itself, Christ's love is "another" power and the Lord manifested this transcendent otherness in his Pasch, in the "holiness" of the "way" he chose to free us from the dominion of evil, as happened for the Exodus when he brought the Jews out of Egypt through the waters of the Red Sea. "Your way, O God, is holy", the Psalmist exclaims, "Your way was through the sea/ your path through the great waters" (Ps 77[76]:13, 19). In the Paschal Mystery, Jesus passed through the abyss of death, because in this way God wanted to renew the universe through the death and Resurrection of his Son, who "died for all", that all might live "for him who for their sake died and was raised" (2 Cor 5:15), and not live for their own sake alone.

The solemn gesture of calming the stormy sea was a clear sign of Christ's lordship over negative powers and induces one to think of his divinity: "Who then is this", his own Disciples asked fearfully, "that even wind and sea obey him?" (Mk 4:41). Their faith is not yet firm, it is being formed; it is a mingling of fear and trust; on the other hand, Jesus' confidant abandonment to the Father is total and pure. This is why he could sleep during the storm, completely safe in God's arms. The time would come, however, when Jesus too would feel fear and anguish, when his hour came he was to feel the full burden of humanity's sins upon him, like a wave at high tide about to break over him. That was indeed to be a terrible tempest, not cosmic but spiritual. It was to be the final, extreme assault of evil against the Son of God.

Yet, in that hour Jesus did not doubt in the power of God the Father or in his closeness, even though he had to experience to the full the distance of hatred from love, of falsehood from the truth, of sin from grace. He experienced this drama in himself with excruciating pain, especially in Gethsemane, before his arrest, and then throughout his Passion until his death on the Cross. In that hour, Jesus on the one hand was one with the Father, fully abandoned *to* him; on the other, since he showed solidarity to sinners, he was as it were separated and felt abandoned *by* him.

Some Saints have lived Jesus' experience intensely and personally. Padre Pio of Pietrelcina is one such. A simple man, of humble origin, whom "Christ made... his own" (Phil 3:12) as the Apostle Paul wrote of himself to make him a chosen instrument of the eternal power of his Cross: a power of love for souls, of forgiveness and of reconciliation, of spiritual fatherhood, of effective solidarity with the suffering. The stigmata that marked his Body closely united him with the Crucified and Risen One. A genuine follower of St Francis of Assisi, like the *Poverello* he made St Paul's experience his own, as he described it in his Letters: "I have been crucified with Christ; it is no longer I who live, but Christ who lives in me" (Gal 2:20); or: "death is at work in us, but life in you" (2 Cor 4:12). This does not mean alienation, the loss of one's personality: God never annihilates human beings but transforms them with his Spirit and orientates them to serving his plan of salvation. Padre Pio retained his own natural gifts and his own temperament, but he offered all things to God, who was able to make free use of them to extend Christ's work: to proclaim the Gospel, to forgive sins and to heal the sick in body and in mind.

Like Jesus, Padre Pio did not have to battle with earthly enemies, in radical combat, but rather with the spirit of evil (cf Eph 6:12). The greatest "storms" that threatened him were the assaults of the devil, from which he defended himself with "the armour of God", with "the shield of faith" and with the "sword of the Spirit, which is the word of God" (Eph 6:11, 16, 17). By staying united with Jesus, he always focussed on the depth of the human drama, and for this reason offered himself up as well as his many sufferings and could expend himself for the healing and relief of the sick, a privileged sign of God's mercy, of his Kingdom which comes, indeed, which is already in the world, of the victory of love and life over sin and death. To guide souls and to alleviate suffering; we may thus sum up St Pio of Pietrelcina in the words of the Servant of God Pope Paul VI: "he was a man of prayer and suffering" (*Address to the Capuchin Chapter Fathers,* 20 February 1971).

Dear friends, Friars Minor Capuchin, the members of prayer groups and all the faithful of San Giovanni Rotondo, you are the heirs of Padre Pio and the legacy he has bequeathed to you is his holiness. In one of his letters he wrote: "It seems that Jesus had no work for his hands other than to sanctify your soul" (Epist. II, p. 155). This was always his first concern, his priestly and paternal caring: so that people might return to God, might be able to experience his mercy and, inwardly renewed, rediscover the beauty and joy of being Christians, of living in communion with Jesus, of belonging to his Church and of putting the Gospel into practice. Padre Pio attracted people to the way of holiness with his own witness, pointing out by his example the "track" that leads to it: prayer and charity.

First of all *prayer*. Like all great men of God, Padre Pio himself had become prayer, body and soul. His days were a Rosary lived, that is, a continuous meditation and assimilation of Christ's mysteries in spiritual union with the Virgin Mary. This explains the unique coexistence within him of supernatural gifts and human reality.

And it all culminated in the celebration of holy Mass in which he was fully united with the dead and Risen Lord. From prayer, as an ever living source, flowed *charity*. The love that he carried in his heart and passed on to others was full of tenderness, always attentive to the real situations of people and families. Especially in the sick and the suffering, he encouraged special love for the Heart of Christ and it was precisely from this that the project of a great work dedicated to "the relief of suffering" took its origin and form. It is not possible to understand or interpret this institution adequately if it is separated from the source that inspired it, which is evangelical charity, enlivened, in its turn, by prayer.

Today, dear friends, Padre Pio presents all this to our attention anew. The risks of activism and secularization are ever present; thus my visit is also intended to strengthen your fidelity to the mission you have inherited from your most beloved Father. Many of you, men and women religious and lay people, are so taken up by the thousands of tasks demanded of you by the service to pilgrims or to the sick in hospital that you run the risk of neglecting the one truly necessary thing: listening to Christ in order to do God's will. When you realize that you are close to running this risk, look to Padre Pio: at his example, at his suffering, and invoke his intercession so that he may obtain for you from the Lord the light and strength that you need to continue your own mission, steeped in love for God and in fraternal charity. And may he continue from Heaven to exercise that exquisite spiritual fatherhood that distinguished him during his earthly existence; may he continue to accompany his confreres, his spiritual children and the entire work that he began. Together with St Francis and with Our Lady whom he so deeply loved and made loved in this world, may he always watch over all of you and protect you. And then, also in the storms that may suddenly break, you will be able to feel the breath of the Holy Spirit that is stronger than any contrary wind and impels the Barque of the Church and each one of us onward. This is why we must always live in serenity and cultivate in our hearts joy, giving thanks to the Lord. "His love is for ever" (Responsorial psalm).

Amen!

MASS FOR THE EPISCOPAL ORDINATION OF FIVE NEW BISHOPS

Vatican Basilica
Saturday, 12 September 2009

Fidelity, Prudence and Goodness

No man can make another man a priest or a Bishop. It is the Lord himself, through the words of prayer and the act of the imposition of hands, who takes that man totally into his service, draws him into his own Priesthood. It is he himself who consecrates those chosen. He himself the one High Priest who offered the one sacrifice for us all confers on him participation in his own Priesthood so that his word and his work may be present in all the ages...

The Gospel must penetrate him, the living word of God must, so to speak, permeate him. The Gospel is, at its core, not only a word: Christ himself is the Gospel. With the word, the very life of Christ must enter into that man so that he may become entirely one with him and so that Christ may live in him and give shape and content to his life. In this way what appears as the essence of the priestly ministry of Christ in the Readings of today's Liturgy must be brought about in him. The man consecrated must be filled with and live on the Spirit of God. He must bring to the poor the Good News the true freedom and hope that gives life to human beings and heal them. He must establish the Priesthood of Christ among men and women, the Priesthood after the order of Melchizedek, that is, the kingdom of justice and peace. Like the 72 disciples sent out by the Lord, he must be one who brings healing, who helps to heal man's inner wound, a person's distance from God. The first and essential good which man needs is closeness to God himself. The Kingdom of God of which the Gospel passage speaks today is not something "next to" God, not some worldly condition: it is simply the presence of God himself, which is the truly healing force.

Jesus summed up all these multiple aspects of his Priesthood in a single sentence: "The Son of Man also came not to be served but to serve, and to give his life as a ransom for many" (Mk 10:45). Serving, and in so doing giving oneself; existing not for oneself but for others, on behalf of God and in view of God: this is the innermost core of Jesus Christ's mission and at the same time the true essence of his Priesthood. Thus he made the term "servant" his highest title of honour. He brought about with it an overturning of values, he gave us a new image of God and of man. Jesus does not come in the guise of a master of this world but the One who is the true Master comes as a servant. His Priesthood is not dominion but service: this is the new Priesthood of Jesus Christ, in keeping with Melchizedek.

St Paul formulates very clearly the essence of the apostolic and priestly ministry. Confronting the disputes that existed in the Church of Corinth between the different factions that adhered to different Apostles, he asks: What then is an Apostle? What then is Apollos? What is Paul? They are servants, each according to what the Lord has assigned them (cf. 1 Cor 3:5). "This is how one should regard us, as servants of Christ and stewards of the mysteries of God. Moreover it is required of stewards that they be found trustworthy" (1 Cor 4:1-2). In Jerusalem, in the last week of his life, Jesus himself spoke in two parables of those servants to whom the Lord entrusts his goods in the time of the world. Through them he has pointed out to you three characteristics of correct service, in which the image of the priestly ministry is also actualized...

The first characteristic which the Lord requires of his servant is fidelity. He has been entrusted with a great good that does not belong to him. The Church is not our Church but his

Church, the Church of God. The servant must account for how he has managed the good that has been entrusted to him. We do not bind people to us; we do not seek power, prestige or esteem for ourselves. We lead men and women toward Jesus Christ, hence toward the living God. In so doing, we introduce them into truth and into freedom, which derives from truth. Fidelity is altruism and, in this very way, liberating for the minister himself and for all who are entrusted to him. We know how in civil society and often also in the Church things suffer because many people on whom responsibility has been conferred work for themselves rather than for the community, for the common good. With a few strokes the Lord sketches an image of the wicked servant, who begins by grovelling and beating the workers, thereby betraying the essence of his responsibility. In Greek, the word for "fidelity" coincides with the word for "faith". The fidelity of the servant of Jesus Christ also consists precisely in the fact that he does not attempt to adapt faith to the fashions of the times. Christ alone has the words of eternal life and we must bring these words to the people. They are the most precious good that has been entrusted to us. There is nothing sterile or static about such fidelity; it is creative. The master rebuked the servant who, attempting to avoid all risk, had buried the money given to him in the ground. With this apparent fidelity, the servant had in reality set aside the good of his master to dedicate himself exclusively to his own affairs. Fidelity is not fear but rather is inspired by love and by its dynamism. The master praises the servant who has invested his goods profitably. Faith demands to be passed on: it was not given to us merely for ourselves, for the personal salvation of our own souls, but for others, for this world and for our time. We must bring faith into this world so that it may become in it a living force; in order to increase God's presence in the world.

The second characteristic that Jesus asks of the servant is prudence. Here it is necessary first to eliminate a misunderstanding. Prudence is something other than shrewdness. Prudence, according to the Greek philosophical tradition, is the first of the cardinal virtues. It indicates the primacy of the truth which, through "prudence", becomes a criterion for our action. Prudence demands humble, disciplined and watchful reason that does not let itself be blinded by prejudices; it does not judge according to desires and passions but rather seeks the truth, even though it may prove uncomfortable. Prudence means searching for the truth and acting in conformity with it. The prudent servant is first and foremost a man of truth and a man of sincere reason. God, through Jesus Christ, has opened wide for us the window of the truth which, before our own mere forces, often remains narrow and only partially transparent. In Sacred Scripture and in faith in the Church, God shows us the essential truth about man, which impresses the right orientation upon our action. Thus, the first cardinal virtue of the priest as minister of Jesus Christ consists in letting himself be moulded by the truth that Christ shows us. In this way we become truly reasonable people, who judge on the basis of the whole and not on chance details. Let us not allow ourselves to be guided by what we see through the small window of our personal astuteness, but, rather, let us look at the world and at human beings through the large window that Christ has opened to us on the whole truth and thus recognize what truly counts in life.

The third characteristic of which Jesus speaks in the parables of the servant is goodness: "Good and faithful servant... enter into the joy of your master" (Mt 25:21, 23). What is meant by the characteristic of "goodness" can become clear to us if we think of Jesus' encounter with the rich young man. This man had addressed Jesus calling him "Good Teacher" and was given the surprising answer: "Why do you call me good? No one is good but God alone" (Mk 10:17 f.). Only God is good in the full sense. He is the Good, the Good par excellence, Goodness personified. In a creature, in man, being good is therefore necessarily based on a profound interior orientation towards God. Goodness increases in inner union with the living God. Goodness presupposes in particular a living communion with

God who is Good, a growing inner union with him. And in fact, from who else could one learn true goodness if not from the One who loved us to the end, to the very end (cf. Jn 13:1). We become good servants through our living relationship with Jesus Christ. Only if our life is lived in dialogue with him; only if his being, his characteristics enter into us and shape us can we become truly good servants.

In the Church's calendar the Holy Name of Mary is commemorated today. In Mary who was and is totally united with her Son, Christ, those amidst the darkness and sufferings of this world have found the face of the Mother who gives us the courage to go on. In the Western tradition, the name "Mary" was translated with "Star of the Sea". The title expresses exactly this experience: how often does the story which we are living appear like a dark sea whose waves pound threateningly against the small vessel of our life. At times, the night seems impenetrable. Often we can be under the impression that evil alone has power and that God is infinitely remote.

We often glimpse only from afar the great Light, Jesus Christ who has overcome death and evil. Yet then we see very near that light which is kindled when Mary says: "Behold, I am the handmaid of the Lord". We see the bright light of goodness that emanates from her. In the goodness with which she met and continually meets the needs of the great and small aspirations of numerous men and women, we recognize the goodness of God himself in a very human way. With his goodness he brings to the world ever anew Jesus Christ, hence the great Light of God. He gave us his Mother as our own Mother that we might learn from her to say the "yes" that makes us become good.

Dear friends, at this moment let us pray the Mother of the Lord for you, that she may always lead you towards her Son, the source of all goodness. And let us pray that you may become faithful servants, prudent and good, and thus that you may one day be able to hear the Lord of history speak these words: "Good and faithful servant, enter into the joy of your Master". Amen.

PASTORAL VISIT
TO BRESCIA AND CONCESIO

From the Homily given during the

EUCHARISTIC CONCELEBRATION

Paul VI Square – Brescia, Italy
Sunday, 8 November 2009

Pope Paul VI

Dear friends what an invaluable gift for the Church the lesson of the Servant of God Paul VI is! And how exciting it is, every time, to learn from him! It is a lesson that concerns all and involves all in accordance with the various gifts and ministries with which the action of the Holy Spirit has enriched the People of God. In this Year for Priests I would like to stress how this lesson concerns and involves priests in particular, for whom Pope Montini always reserved special affection and concern. In his Encyclical on priestly celibacy he wrote: "Laid hold of by Christ" unto the complete abandonment of one's entire self to him, the priest takes on a closer likeness to Christ, even in the love with which the eternal Priest has loved the Church his Body and offered himself entirely for her sake... In fact "the consecrated celibacy of the sacred ministers manifests the virginal love of Christ for the Church and above all the virginal and supernatural fecundity of this marriage" (*Sacerdotalis caelibatus*, n. 26). I dedicate the great Pope's words to the many priests of the Diocese of Brescia, well represented here, as well as to the young men in formation at the Seminary. And I would also like to recall the words that Paul VI addressed to the students at the Lombard Seminary on 7 December 1968, when the difficulties of the post-conciliar period had to contend with

67

the ferment in the world of youth: "So many", he said, "expect of the Pope sensational work, energetic and decisive interventions. The Pope does not consider he should follow any other line than that of trust in Jesus Christ, whose concern for his Church is greater than for anyone else. It will be he who rides out the storm.... This expectation is neither sterile nor inert; rather, it is attentive watching in prayer. This is the condition Jesus chose for us so that he might fully carry out his work. The Pope too needs the help of prayer" (*Insegnamenti* VI, [1968], 1189). Dear Brothers and Sisters, may the priestly example of the Servant of God Giovanni Battista Montini always guide you, and may St Arcangelo Tadini whom I have just venerated during my brief stop at Botticino intercede for you.

From the Homily given on the

MEMORIAL OF
OUR LADY OF LOURDES
18th WORLD DAY OF THE SICK

Vatican Basilica
Thursday, 11 February 2010

Priests and the Sick

At the same time this text, which contains the foundation and the praxis of the Sacrament of the Anointing of the Sick, also inspired a vision of the role of the sick in the Church an active role in "provoking", so to speak, faithful prayer. "Is any among you sick? Let him call for the elders". In this Year for Priests, I am pleased to emphasize the bond between the sick and priests, a sort of covenant of evangelical "complicity". Both have a task: the sick must "call" priests and priests must respond, to draw the presence and action of the Risen One and of his Spirit into the experience of illness. And here we can see the full importance of the pastoral care of the sick. Its value is truly incalculable because of the immense good it does, first of all to the sick person and to the priest himself and then also to relatives, acquaintances, the community and, in unknown and mysterious ways, to the whole of the Church and of the world. In fact, when the word of God speaks of the healing, salvation and health of the sick person, it means these concepts in an integral sense, never separating soul and body. A sick person healed by Christ's prayer through the Church is a joy on earth and in Heaven, a foretaste of eternal life.

Dear friends, as I wrote in my Encyclical *Spe Salvi,* "The true measure of humanity is essentially determined in relationship to suffering and to the sufferer" (n. 38). In setting up a Dicastery dedicated to the pastoral health care, the Holy See also wished to make its own contribution to promoting a world that is better able to accept and heal the sick as people. It wanted, in fact, to help them live the experience of sickness in a human way, not by denying it but by offering it meaning. I would like to end these reflections with a thought from Venerable Pope John Paul II, to which he witnessed with his own life. In his Apostolic Letter *Salvifici Doloris,* he wrote: "At one and the same time Christ has taught man *to do good by his suffering* and *to do good to those who suffer.* In this double aspect he has completely revealed the meaning of suffering" (n. 30). May the Virgin Mary help us live this mission to the full.

CHRISM MASS

Saint Peter's Basilica
Holy Thursday, 1st April 2010

The Holy Oils

At the centre of the Church's worship is the notion of "sacrament". This means that it is not primarily we who act, but God comes first to meet us through his action, he looks upon us and he leads us to himself. Another striking feature is this: God touches us through material things, through gifts of creation that he takes up into his service, making them instruments of the encounter between us and himself. There are four elements in creation on which the world of sacraments is built: water, bread, wine and olive oil. Water, as the basic element and fundamental condition of all life, is the essential sign of the act in which, through baptism, we become Christians and are born to new life. While water is the vital element everywhere, and thus represents the shared access of all people to rebirth as Christians, the other three elements belong to the culture of the Mediterranean region. In other words, they point towards the concrete historical environment in which Christianity emerged. God acted in a clearly defined place on the earth, he truly made history with men. On the one hand, these three elements are gifts of creation, and on the other, they also indicate the locality of the history of God with us. They are a synthesis between creation and history: gifts of God that always connect us to those parts of the world where God chose to act with us in historical time, where he chose to become one of us.

Within these three elements there is a further gradation. Bread has to do with everyday life. It is the fundamental gift of life day by day. Wine has to do with feasting, with the fine things of creation, in which, at the same time, the joy of the redeemed finds particular expression. Olive oil has a wide range of meaning. It is nourishment, it is medicine, it gives beauty, it prepares us for battle and it gives strength. Kings and priests are anointed with oil, which is thus a sign of dignity and responsibility, and likewise of the strength that comes from God. Even the name that we bear as "Christians" contains the mystery of the oil. The word "Christians", in fact, by which Christ's disciples were known in the earliest days of Gentile Christianity, is derived from the word "Christ" (Acts 11:20-21) – the Greek translation of the word "Messiah", which means "anointed one". To be a Christian is to come from Christ, to belong to Christ, to the Anointed One of God, to whom God granted kingship and priesthood. It means belonging to him whom God himself anointed – not with material oil, but with the One whom the oil represents: with his Holy Spirit. Olive oil is thus in a very particular way a symbol of the total compenetration of the Man Jesus by the Holy Spirit.

In the Chrism Mass on Holy Thursday, the holy oils are at the centre of the liturgical action. They are consecrated in the bishop's cathedral for the whole year. They thus serve also as an expression of the Church's unity, guaranteed by the episcopate, and they point to Christ, the true "shepherd and guardian" of our souls, as St Peter calls him (1 Pet 2:25). At the same time, they hold together the entire liturgical year, anchored in the mystery of Holy Thursday. Finally, they point to the Garden of Olives, the scene of Jesus' inner acceptance of his Passion. Yet the Garden of Olives is also the place from which he ascended to the Father, and is therefore the place of redemption: God did not leave Jesus in death. Jesus lives for ever with the Father, and is therefore omnipresent, with us always. This double mystery of the Mount of Olives is also always "at work" within the Church's sacramental oil. In four sacraments, oil is the sign of God's goodness reaching out to touch us: in baptism, in confirmation as the sacrament of the Holy Spirit, in the different grades of the sacrament of holy orders and finally in the anointing of the sick, in which oil is offered to us, so to speak, as God's medicine – as the medicine which now assures us of his goodness, offering us strength and consolation, yet at the same time points beyond the moment of the illness towards the definitive healing, the resurrection (cf. Jas 5:14). Thus oil, in its different forms, accompanies us throughout our lives: beginning with the catechumenate and baptism, and continuing right up to the moment when we prepare to meet God, our Judge and Saviour. Moreover, the Chrism Mass, in which the sacramental sign of oil is presented to us as part of the language of God's creation, speaks in particular to us who are priests: it speaks of Christ, whom God anointed King and Priest – of him who makes us sharers in his priesthood, in his "anointing", through our own priestly ordination.

I should like, then, to attempt a brief interpretation of the mystery of this holy sign in its essential reference to the priestly vocation. In popular etymologies a connection was made, even in ancient times, between the Greek word "*elaion*" – oil – and the word "*eleos*" – mercy. In fact, in the various sacraments, consecrated oil is always a sign of God's mercy. So the meaning of priestly anointing always includes the mission to bring God's mercy to those we serve. In the lamp of our lives, the oil of mercy should never run dry. Let us always obtain it from the Lord in good time – in our encounter with his word, in our reception of the sacraments, in the time we spend with him in prayer.

As a consequence of the story of the dove bearing an olive branch to signal the end of the flood – and thus God's new peace with the world of men – not only the dove but also the olive branch and oil itself have become symbols of peace. The Christians of antiquity loved to decorate the tombs of their dead with the crown of victory and the olive branch, symbol of peace. They knew that Christ conquered death and that their dead were resting in the peace of Christ. They knew that they themselves were awaited by Christ, that he had promised them the peace which the world cannot give. They remembered that the first words of the Risen Lord to his disciples were: "Peace be with you!" (Jn 20:19). He himself, so to speak, bears the olive branch, he introduces his peace into the world. He announces God's saving goodness. He is our peace. Christians should therefore be people of peace, people who recognize and live the mystery of the Cross as a mystery of reconciliation. Christ does not conquer through the sword, but through the Cross. He wins by conquering hatred. He wins through the force of his greater love. The Cross of Christ expresses his "no" to violence. And in this way, it is God's victory sign, which announces Jesus' new way. The one who suffered was stronger than the ones who exercised power. In his self-giving on the Cross, Christ conquered violence. As priests we are called, in fellowship with Jesus Christ, to be men of peace, we are called to oppose violence and to trust in the greater power of love.

A further aspect of the symbolism of oil is that it strengthens for battle. This does not contradict the theme of peace, but forms part of it. The battle of Christians consisted – and still consists – not in the use of violence, but in the fact that they were – and are – ready to suffer for the good, for God. It consists in the fact that Christians, as good citizens, keep the law and do what is just and good. It consists in the fact that they do not do whatever within the legal system in force is not just but unjust. The battle of the martyrs consists in their concrete "no" to injustice: by taking no part in idolatry, in Emperor worship, they refused to bow down before falsehood, before the adoration of human persons and their power. With their "no" to falsehood and all its consequences, they upheld the power of right and truth. Thus they served true peace. Today too it is important for Christians to follow what is right, which is the foundation of peace. Today too it is important for Christians not to accept a wrong that is enshrined in law – for example the killing of innocent unborn children. In this way we serve peace, in this way we find ourselves following in the footsteps of Jesus Christ, of whom St Peter says: "When he was reviled he did not revile in return; when he suffered, he did not threaten; but he trusted to him who judges justly. He himself bore our sins in his body on the tree, that we might die to sin and live to righteousness" (1 Pet 2:23f.).

The Fathers of the Church were fascinated by a phrase from Psalm 45 (44) – traditionally held to be Solomon's wedding psalm – which was reinterpreted by Christians as the psalm for the marriage of the new Solomon, Jesus Christ, to his Church. To the King, Christ, it is said: "Your love is for justice; your hatred for evil. Therefore God, your God, has anointed you with the oil of gladness above other kings" (v. 8). What is this oil of gladness with which the true king, Christ, was anointed? The Fathers had no doubt in this regard: the oil of gladness is the Holy Spirit himself, who was poured out upon Jesus Christ. The Holy Spirit is the gladness that comes from God. From Jesus this gladness sweeps over us in his Gospel, in the joyful message that God knows us, that he is good and that his goodness is the power above all powers; that we are wanted and loved by him. Gladness is the fruit of love. The oil of gladness, which was poured out over Christ and comes to us from him, is the Holy Spirit, the gift of Love who makes us glad to be alive. Since we know Christ, and since in him we know the true God, we know that it is good to be a human being. It is good to be alive, because we are loved, because truth itself is good.

In the early Church, the consecrated oil was considered a special sign of the presence of the Holy Spirit, who communicates himself to us as a gift from Christ. He is the oil of gladness. This gladness is different from entertainment and from the outward happiness that modern society seeks for itself. Entertainment, in its proper place, is certainly good and enjoyable. It is good to be able to laugh. But entertainment is not everything. It is only a small part of our lives, and when it tries to be the whole, it becomes a mask behind which despair lurks, or at least doubt over whether life is really good, or whether non-existence might perhaps be better than existence. The gladness that comes to us from Christ is different. It does indeed make us happy, but it can also perfectly well coexist with suffering. It gives us the capacity to suffer and, in suffering, to remain nevertheless profoundly glad. It gives us the capacity to share the suffering of others and thus by placing ourselves at one another's disposal, to express tangibly the light and the goodness of God. I am always struck by the passage in the *Acts of the Apostles* which recounts that after the Apostles had been whipped by order of the Sanhedrin, they "rejoiced that they were counted worthy to suffer dishonour for the name of Jesus" (Acts 5:41). Anyone who loves is ready to suffer for the beloved and for the sake of his love, and in this way he experiences a deeper joy. The joy of the martyrs was stronger than the torments inflicted on them. This joy was ultimately victorious and opened the gates of history for Christ. As priests, we are – in St Paul's words – "co-workers with you for your joy" (2 Cor 1:24). In the fruit of the olive-tree, in the consecrated oil, we are touched by the goodness of the Creator, the love of the Redeemer. Let us pray that his gladness may pervade us ever more deeply and that we may be capable of bringing it anew to a world in such urgent need of the joy that has its source in truth. Amen.

APOSTOLIC JOURNEY TO MALTA
ON THE OCCASION OF THE
1950th ANNIVERSARY OF SAINT PAUL'S
SHIPWRECK ON THE ISLAND
(17–18 APRIL 2010)

From the Homily given at the

EUCHARISTIC CELEBRATION

Floriana Granaries – Floriana
Third Sunday of Easter, 18 April 2010

St Dun Ġorġ Preca

As Moses taught the people of Israel, the words of the Lord "shall be upon your heart, and you shall teach them diligently to your children, and shall talk of them when you sit in your house, and when you walk by the way, and when you lie down and when you rise" (Deut 6:6-7). This was well understood by Malta's first canonized Saint, Dun Ġorġ Preca. His tireless work of catechesis, inspiring young and old with a love for Christian doctrine and a deep devotion to the Incarnate Word of God, set an example that I urge you to maintain. Remember that the exchange of goods between these islands and the world outside is a two-way process. What you receive, evaluate with care, and what you have that is of value, be sure to share with others.

I would like to address a particular word to the priests present here, in this year devoted to a celebration of the great gift of the priesthood. Dun Ġorġ was a priest of remarkable humility, goodness, meekness and generosity, deeply devoted to prayer and with a passion for communicating the truths of the Gospel. Let him serve as a model and an inspiration for you, as you strive to fulfil the mission you have received to feed the Lord's flock. Remember, too, the question that the Risen Lord put three times to Peter: "Do you love me?" That is the question he asks each of you. Do you love him? Do you wish to serve him through the gift of your whole lives? Do you long to bring others to know and love him? With Peter, have the courage to answer, "Yes, Lord, you know I love you," and accept with grateful hearts the beautiful task that he has assigned you. The mission entrusted to priests is truly a service to joy, to God's joy which longs to break into the world (cf. *Homily,* 24 April 2005).

PASTORAL VISIT TO TURIN

From the Homily given during the

EUCHARISTIC CONCELEBRATION

St Charles Square
Fifth Sunday of Easter, 2 May 2010

'love one another; even as I have loved you'

We are in the Easter Season which is the time of Jesus' glorification. The Gospel we have just heard reminds us that this glorification is brought about in the Passion. In the Paschal Mystery, passion and glorification are closely bound together and form an indissoluble unity. When Judas leaves the Upper Room to carry out his scheme of betrayal that will lead to the Master's death, Jesus says: "now is the Son of man glorified, and in him God is glorified" (Jn 13:31): the glorification of Jesus begins at that very moment. The Evangelist John makes it quite clear: he does not in fact say that Jesus was glorified only after his Passion, through his Resurrection; rather he shows that precisely with the Passion his glorification began. In it Jesus manifests his glory, which is the glory of love, which gives itself totally. He loved the Father, doing his will to the very end, with a perfect gift of self; he loved humanity, giving his life for us. Thus he was already glorified in his Passion and God was glorified in him. But the Passion as a very real and profound expression of his love is only a beginning. This is why Jesus says that his glorification is also to come (cf. *ibid.,* 13:32). Then, when he announces his departure from this world (cf. *ibid.,* 13:33), the Lord gives his disciples a new commandment, as it were a testament, so that they might continue his presence among them in a new way: "A new commandment I give to

79

you, that you love one another; even as I have loved you, that you also love one another" (Jn 13:34). If we love each other, Jesus will continue to be present in our midst, to be glorified in this world.

Jesus speaks of a "new commandment". But what is new about it? In the Old Testament, God had already given the commandment of love; but this commandment has become new now because Jesus makes a very important addition to it: "*As I have loved you*, that you also love one another". What is new is precisely this "loving as Jesus loved". All our loving is preceded by his love and refers to this love, it fits into this love and is achieved precisely through this love. The Old Testament did not present any model of love; it only formulated the precept of love. Instead, Jesus gave himself to us as a model and source of love a boundless, universal love that could transform all negative circumstances and all obstacles into opportunities to progress in love. And in this City's Saints we see the fulfilment of this love, always from the source of Jesus' love.

In past centuries, the Church in Turin had a rich tradition of holiness and generous service to the brethren ... thanks to the work of zealous priests and men and women religious of both active and contemplative life and faithful laypeople. Jesus' words thus acquire a special resonance for this Church of Turin, a generous and active Church, beginning with her priests. In giving us the new commandment, Jesus asks us to live his own love and on his own love, which is the truly credible, eloquent and effective sign for proclaiming the coming of the Kingdom of God to the world. Clearly, with our own strength alone we are weak and limited. In us there is always a resistance to love and in our existence there are very many difficulties that cause division, resentment and ill will. However, the Lord promised us that he would be present in our lives, making us capable of this generous, total love that can overcome all obstacles, even those in our own hearts. If we are united to Christ, we can truly love in this way. Loving others as Jesus loved us is only possible with that power which is communicated to us in the relationship with him, especially in the Eucharist, in which his Sacrifice of love that generates love becomes really present: this is the true newness in the world and the power of a permanent glorification of God who is glorified in the continuity of the love of Jesus in our love.

APOSTOLIC JOURNEY OF POPE BENEDICT XVI TO PORTUGAL ON THE OCCASION OF THE TENTH ANNIVERSARY OF THE BEATIFICATION OF JACINTA AND FRANCISCO, YOUNG SHEPHERDS OF FÁTIMA

Address given during the

CELEBRATION OF VESPERS WITH PRIESTS, RELIGIOUS, SEMINARIANS AND DEACONS

Church of the Most Holy Trinity, Fátima
Wednesday, 12 May 2010

Fidelity

"When the time had fully come, God sent forth his Son born of woman, [...] so that we might receive adoption as sons" (Gal 4:4,5). The fullness of time came when the Eternal broke into time; by the grace of the Holy Spirit the Son of the Most High was conceived and became man in the womb of a woman, the Virgin Mary, type and lofty model of the believing Church. The Church does not cease to beget new sons in the Son, whom the Father willed to be the first-born of many brothers. Each one of us is called to be with Mary and like Mary, a humble and simple sign of the Church who offers herself constantly as a spouse into the hands of her Lord.

To all of you who have given your life to Christ I wish to express this evening the Church's appreciation and recognition. Thank you for your witness, often silent and certainly not easy; thank you for your fidelity to the Gospel and to the Church. In

Jesus, present in the Eucharist, I embrace my brothers in the priesthood and the deacons, the consecrated women and men, the seminarians and the members of the movements and new ecclesial communities present. May the Lord reward, as he alone can and does, all those who have made it possible for us to gather together before the presence of Jesus in the Eucharist. I mention especially the Episcopal Commission for Vocations and Ministries, with its President, Bishop António Santos, whom I thank for his greeting, full of collegial and fraternal affection, at the beginning of Vespers. In this "upper room" of faith which is Fatima, the Virgin Mother shows us the way to place our pure and holy offering into the hands of the Father.

Let me open my heart and tell you that the greatest concern of every Christian, especially of every consecrated person or minister of the altar, must be fidelity, loyalty to one's own vocation, as a disciple who wishes to follow the Lord. Faithfulness over time is the name of love, of a consistent, true and profound love for Christ the Priest. "Since Baptism is a true entry into the holiness of God through incorporation into Christ and the indwelling of his Spirit, it would be a contradiction to settle for a life of mediocrity, marked by a minimalistic ethic and a shallow religiosity" (John Paul II, Apostolic Letter *Novo Millennio Ineunte*, 31). In this Year for Priests which is drawing to its close, may grace in abundance come down upon you that you may live joyfully your consecration and bear witness to your priestly fidelity grounded in the fidelity of Christ. This evidently supposes true intimacy with Christ in prayer, since it is the powerful and intense experience of the Lord's love that brings priests and consecrated persons to respond to his love in way that is exclusive and spousal.

This life of special consecration was born to keep the Gospel always before the People of God, as a reminder which manifests, certifies and proclaims to the whole Church the radical nature of the Gospel and the coming of the Kingdom. Dear consecrated men and women, by your dedication to prayer, asceticism and growth in the spiritual life, to apostolic action and mission, you are progressing towards the heavenly Jerusalem, you are a foretaste of the eschatological Church, solid in her possession and loving contemplation of God who is love. How much we need this witness today! Many of our brothers and sisters live as if there were nothing beyond this life, and without concern for their eternal salvation. Men and women are called to know and love God, and the Church has the mission to assist them in this calling. We know well that God is the master of his gifts and that conversion is a grace. But we are responsible for proclaiming the faith, the whole faith, with all its demands. Dear friends, let us imitate the Curé of Ars who prayed to the Lord in the following words: "Grant me the conversion of my parish, and I accept to suffer all that you wish for the rest of my life". And he did everything to pull people away from their own lukewarm attitude in order to lead them back to love.

There exists a deep solidarity among all the members of the Body of Christ. It is not possible to love Christ without loving his brothers and sisters. For their salvation John Mary Vianney decided to become a priest: "to win souls for the good God", as he said when, at eighteen years of age, he announced his vocation, just as Paul had said: "to win as many as I could" (1 Cor 9:19). The Vicar General had told him: "there is not much love of God in the parish; you will bring it there". In his priestly passion, this holy parish priest was merciful like Jesus in meeting each sinner. He preferred to insist on the attractive aspect of virtue, on God's mercy, in comparison to which our sins are like "grains of sand". He pointed to the merciful love of God which had been offended. He feared that priests would become "insensitive" and accustomed to the indifference of their faithful: "Woe to the Pastor – he would warn – who remains silent while God is offended and souls are lost".

Dear brother priests, in this place, which Mary has made special, keep before your eyes her vocation as a faithful disciple of her Son Jesus from the moment of his conception to the Cross, and then beyond, along the path of the nascent Church, and consider the unheard-of grace of your priesthood. Fidelity to one's vocation requires courage and trust, but the Lord also wishes that you join forces: that you be concerned for one another and support one another fraternally. Moments of common prayer and study, and sharing in the demands of the priestly life and work, are a necessary part of your life. It is a fine thing when you welcome one another into your homes with the peace of Christ in your hearts! It is important to assist one another with prayer, helpful advice and discernment! Be especially attentive to those situations where there is a certain weakening of priestly ideals or dedication to activities not fully consonant with what is proper for a minister of Jesus Christ. Then is the time to take a firm stand, with an attitude of warm fraternal love, as brother assisting his brother to "remain on his feet".

The priesthood of Christ is eternal (cf. Heb 5:6), but the life of priests is limited. Christ has willed that others continue in time the priestly ministry that he instituted. Keep alive in your hearts, and in others around you, the desire to raise up – in cooperation with the grace of the Holy Spirit – new priestly vocations among the faithful. Trustful and persevering prayer, joyful love of one's own vocation and commitment to the work of spiritual direction will allow you to discern the charism of vocation in those whom God calls.

Dear seminarians, who have taken the first step towards the priesthood and are preparing in the major seminary or in houses of formation, the Pope encourages you to be conscious of the great responsibility which you will have to assume. Carefully examine your intentions and your motivations. Devote yourselves with a steadfast heart and a generous spirit to your training. The Eucharist, which is the centre of Christian life and the school of humility and service, should be your first love. Adoration, piety and care for the Most Holy Sacrament during these years of preparation will lead you one day to celebrate the Sacrifice of the Altar in an edifying and devout manner.

Along this path of fidelity, beloved priests and deacons, consecrated men and women, seminarians and committed lay persons, may the Blessed Virgin Mary guide us. With her and like her, we are free so as to be saints; free so as to be poor, chaste and obedient; free for all because detached from all, free from self so that others may grow in Christ, the true Holy One of the Father and the Shepherd to whom priests, as his presence, lend their voice and their gestures; free to bring to today's world Jesus who died and rose again, Jesus who remains with us until the end of time and who gives himself to all in the Most Holy Eucharist.

HOLY MASS AND EUCHARISTIC PROCESSION TO THE BASILICA OF SAINT MARY MAJOR ON THE SOLEMNITY OF CORPUS CHRISTI

HOMILY

Square outside the Basilica of Saint John Lateran
Thursday, 3 June 2010

Christ the High Priest

The priesthood of the New Testament is closely linked to the Eucharist. For this reason today, on the Solemnity of *Corpus Christi* and almost at the end of the Year for Priests, we are invited to meditate on the relationship between the Eucharist and the priesthood of Christ. We are also oriented to this direction by the First Reading and the Responsorial Psalm that present Melchizedek. The brief passage from the Book of Genesis (cf. 14:18-20) says that Melchizedek, King of Salem, was "priest of God Most High" and therefore "brought out bread and wine" and "blessed him [Abram]", who had just returned after winning a battle. Abram himself gave Melchizedek a tenth of everything. In the last verse, the Psalm in turn contains solemn words, sworn by God himself who declares to the Messiah-King: "You are a priest for ever after the order of Melchizedek" (Ps 110[109]:4); thus the Messiah is not only proclaimed King but also Priest. It is from this passage that the author of the Letter to the Hebrews drew for his broad and articulate explanation. And we have re-echoed it in the refrain: "You are a priest for ever" Christ the Lord: almost a profession of faith that acquires special significance on today's Feast. It is the joy of the community, the joy of the whole Church which, in contemplating and adoring the Most Holy Sacrament, recognizes in it the real and permanent presence of Jesus, the Eternal High Priest.

The Second Reading and the Gospel focus attention on the Eucharistic mystery instead. From the First Reading of the Letter to the Corinthians (cf. 11:23-26) is taken the fundamental passage in which St Paul reminds this community of the meaning and value of the "Lord's Supper", which the Apostle had transmitted and taught and which risked being lost. Whereas the Gospel is St Luke's version of the account of the miracle of the loaves and fishes: a sign attested to by all the Evangelists and that foretells the gift that Christ was to make of himself in order to give to all humanity eternal life. Both these texts highlight the prayer of Christ, in the act of breaking bread. There is of course a clear difference between the two moments: when he breaks the loaves and fishes for the crowds, Jesus thanks the heavenly Father for his providence, trusting that he will not let the people go hungry. In the Last Supper, instead, Jesus transforms the bread and wine into his own Body and Blood so that the disciples may be nourished by him and live in close and real communion with him.

The first thing always to remember is that Jesus was not a priest in accordance with the Jewish tradition. He did not come from a family of priests. He did not belong to the lineage of Aaron but rather that of Judah and was therefore legally barred from taking the path of the priesthood. Jesus of Nazareth himself and his activities do not follow in the wake of the ancient priests but rather in that of the prophets. And in this line Jesus took his distance from the ritual conception of religion, criticizing the structure that gave value to human precepts linked to ritual purity rather than to the observance of God's commandments: namely, love of God and of one's neighbour *which, as the Lord says,* "is much more than all whole burnt offerings and sacrifices" (Mk 12:33). Even in the Temple of Jerusalem, a sacred place par excellence, Jesus makes an exquisitely prophetic gesture when he drives out the money changers and livestock vendors, all things that served for offering the traditional sacrifices. Thus Jesus was not recognized as a priestly but rather as a prophetic and royal Messiah. Even his death, which we Christians rightly call a "sacrifice", had nothing to do with the ancient sacrifices; indeed, it was quite the opposite; it was the execution of a death sentence by crucifixion, the most ignominious punishment, which took place outside the walls of Jerusalem.

In what sense, therefore, was Jesus a priest? The Eucharist itself tells us. We can start with the simple words that describe Melichizedek: He "brought out bread and wine" (Gen 14:18). This is what Jesus did at the Last Supper: he offered bread and wine and in that action recapitulated the whole of himself and his whole mission. That gesture, the prayer that preceded it and the words with which he accompanied it contain the full meaning of the mystery of Christ, as the Letter to the Hebrews expresses it in a crucial passage that we should quote: "In the days of his flesh", the author writes of Our Lord, "Jesus offered up prayers and supplications, with loud cries and tears, to him who was able to save him from death, and he was heard for his godly fear. Although he was a Son, he learned obedience through what he suffered; and being made perfect he became the source of eternal salvation to all who obey him, being designated by God a high priest after the order of Melchizedek" (5:8-10). In this text, which clearly alludes to the spiritual agony of Gethsemane, Christ's Passion is presented as a prayer and an offering. Jesus faces his "hour" which leads him to death on the Cross, immersed in a profound prayer that consists of the union of his own will with that of the Father. This dual yet single will is a will of love. Lived in this prayer, the tragic trial that Jesus faces is transformed into an offering, into a living sacrifice.

The Letter to the Hebrews says that Jesus "was heard". In what sense? In the sense that God the Father liberated him from death and restored him to life. He was heard precisely because of his total abandonment of himself to the Father's will: God's plan of love could be perfectly fulfilled in Jesus who, having obeyed to the end, to his death on the Cross, became a "cause of salvation" for all who obey him. In other words, he became the High Priest for having taken upon himself all the sin of the world, as the "Lamb of God". It is the Father who confers this priesthood upon him at the very moment in which Jesus passes over from his death to his Resurrection. He is not a priest according to the Mosaic law (cf. Lev 8-9), but "after the order of Melchizedek", according to a prophetic order, dependent only on his special relationship with God.

Let us return to the words of the Letter to the Hebrews which say: "Although he was a Son he learned obedience through what he suffered". Christ's priesthood entailed suffering. Jesus truly suffered and did so for our sake. He was the Son and did not need to learn obedience but we do, we did need to and we always will. Therefore the Son took upon himself our humanity and for our sake he let himself be "taught" obedience in the crucible of suffering, he let himself be transformed by it like the grain of wheat that has to die in the earth in order to bear fruit. By means of this process Jesus was "made perfect" in Greek, *teleiotheis*. We must pause to reflect on this term because it is very important. It indicates the fulfilment of a journey, that is, the very journey and transformation of the Son of God through suffering, through his painful Passion. It is through this transformation that Jesus Christ became the "high priest" and can save all who entrust themselves to him. The term *teleiotheis*, correctly translated by the words "made perfect", belongs to a verbal root which, in the Greek version of the Pentateuch, that is, the first five Books of the Bible, is always used to mean the consecration of the ancient priests. This discovery is very valuable because it tells us that for Jesus the Passion was like a priestly consecration. He was not a priest according to the Law but became one existentially in his Pasch of Passion, death and Resurrection: he gave himself in expiation and the Father, exalting him above every creature, made him the universal Mediator of salvation.

Let us return in our meditation, to the Eucharist that will shortly be the focus of our liturgical assembly. In it, Jesus anticipated his Sacrifice, a non-ritual but a personal sacrifice. At the Last Supper his actions were prompted by that "eternal spirit" with which he was later to offer himself on the Cross (cf. Heb 9:14). Giving thanks and blessing, Jesus transforms the bread and the wine. It is divine love that transforms them: the love with which Jesus accepts, in anticipation, to give the whole of himself for us. This love is nothing other than the Holy Spirit, the Spirit of the Father and of the Son, who consecrates the bread and the wine and changes their substance into the Body and Blood of the Lord, making present in the Sacrament the same sacrifice that is fulfilled in a bloody way on the Cross. We may therefore conclude that Christ is a true and effective priest because he was filled with the power of the Holy Spirit, he was filled with the whole fullness of God's love and precisely "in the night on which he was betrayed", precisely, "in the hour... of darkness" (cf. Lk 22:53). It is this divine power, the same power that brought about the Incarnation of the Word, that transformed the extreme violence and extreme injustice into a supreme act of love and justice. This is the work of the priesthood of Christ which the Church inherited and extended in history, in the dual form of the common priesthood of the baptized and the ordained priesthood of ministers, in order to transform the world with God's love. Let us all, priests and faithful, nourish ourselves with the same Eucharist, let us all prostrate ourselves to adore it, because in it our Master and Lord is present, the true Body of the Jesus is present in it, the Victim and the Priest, the salvation of the world. Come let us exult with joyful songs! Come, let us adore him! Amen.

APOSTOLIC JOURNEY TO CYPRUS
(4-6 JUNE 2010)

HOLY MASS ATTENDED BY PRIESTS, RELIGIOUS, DEACONS, CATECHISTS AND REPRESENTATIVES OF CYPRIAN ECCLESIAL MOVEMENTS

From the

HOMILY

Latin parish church of the Holy Cross – Nicosia
Saturday, 5 June 2010

"conform your life to the mystery of the Lord's Cross"

The Son of Man must be lifted up, so that whoever believes in him may have eternal life (cf. Jn 3:14-15). In this Votive Mass we adore and praise our Lord Jesus Christ, because by his Holy Cross he has redeemed the world. Through his death and resurrection he has thrown open the gates of heaven and he has prepared a place for us, so that we, his followers, may be granted a share in his glory…

The focus of our celebration today is the Cross of Christ. Many might be tempted to ask why we Christians celebrate an instrument of torture, a sign of suffering, defeat and failure. It is true that the Cross expresses all these things. And yet, because of him who was lifted up on the Cross for our salvation, it also represents the definitive triumph of God's love over all the evil in the world.

There is an ancient tradition that the wood of the Cross was taken from a tree planted by Adam's son Seth over the place where Adam was buried. On that very spot, known as Golgotha, the place of the skull, Seth planted a seed from the tree of the knowledge of good and evil, the tree in the midst of the Garden of Eden. Through God's providence, the work of the Evil One would be undone by turning his own weapons against him.

Beguiled by the serpent, Adam had foresaken his filial trust in God and sinned by biting into the fruit of the one tree in the garden that was forbidden to him. In consequence of that sin, suffering and death came into the world. The tragic effects of sin, suffering and death were all too evident in the history of Adam's descendants. We see this in our first reading today, with its echoes of the Fall and its prefiguring of Christ's redemption.

As a punishment for their sin, the people of Israel, languishing in the desert, were bitten by serpents and could only be saved from death by looking upon the emblem that Moses raised up, foreshadowing the Cross that would put an end to sin and death once and for all. We see clearly that man cannot save himself from the consequences of his sin. He cannot save himself from death. Only God can release him from his moral and physical enslavement. And because he loved the world so much, he sent his only-begotten Son, not to condemn the world – as justice seemed to demand – but so that through him the world might be saved. God's only-begotten Son had to be lifted up just as Moses lifted up the serpent in the desert, so that all who looked upon him with faith might have life.

The wood of the Cross became the vehicle for our redemption, just as the tree from which it was fashioned had occasioned the Fall of our first parents. Suffering and death, which had been a consequence of sin, were to become the very means by which sin was vanquished. The innocent Lamb was slain on the altar of the Cross, and yet from the immolation of the victim new life burst forth: the power of evil was destroyed by the power of self-sacrificing love.

The Cross, then, is something far greater and more mysterious than it at first appears. It is indeed an instrument of torture, suffering and defeat, but at the same time it expresses the complete transformation, the definitive reversal of these evils: that is what makes it the most eloquent symbol of hope that the world has ever seen. It speaks to all who suffer – the oppressed, the sick, the poor, the outcast, the victims of violence – and it offers them hope that God can transform their suffering into joy, their isolation into communion, their death into life. It offers unlimited hope to our fallen world.

That is why the world needs the Cross. The Cross is not just a private symbol of devotion, it is not just a badge of membership of a certain group within society, and in its deepest meaning it has nothing to do with the imposition of a creed or a philosophy by force. It speaks of hope, it speaks of love, it speaks of the victory of non-violence over oppression, it speaks of God raising up the lowly, empowering the weak, conquering division, and overcoming hatred with love. A world without the Cross would be a world without hope, a world in which torture and brutality would go unchecked, the weak would be exploited and greed would have the final word. Man's inhumanity to man would be manifested in ever more horrific ways, and there would be no end to the vicious cycle of violence. Only the Cross puts an end to it. While no earthly power can save us from the consequences of our sins, and no earthly power can defeat injustice at its source, nevertheless the saving intervention of our loving God has transformed the reality of sin and death into its opposite. That is what we celebrate when we glory in the Cross of our Redeemer. Rightly does St Andrew of Crete describe the Cross as "more noble, more precious than anything on earth [...] for in it and through it and for it all the riches of our salvation were stored away and restored to us" (*Oratio* X; *PG* 97, 1018-1019).

Dear brother priests, dear religious, dear catechists, the message of the Cross has been entrusted to us, so that we can offer hope to the world. When we proclaim Christ crucified we are proclaiming not ourselves, but him. We are not offering our own wisdom to the world, nor are we claiming any merit of our own, but we are acting as channels for his wisdom, his love, his saving merits. We know that we are merely earthenware vessels, and yet, astonishingly, we have been chosen to be heralds of the saving truth that the world needs to hear. Let us never cease to marvel at the extraordinary grace that has been given to us, let us never cease to acknowledge our unworthiness, but at the same time let us always strive to become less unworthy of our noble calling, lest through our faults and failings we weaken the credibility of our witness.

In this Year for Priests, let me address a special word to the priests present today, and to those who are preparing for ordination. Reflect on the words spoken to a newly ordained priest as the Bishop presents him with the chalice and paten: "Understand what you do, imitate what you celebrate, and conform your life to the mystery of the Lord's Cross". As we proclaim the Cross of Christ, let us always strive to imitate the selfless love of the one who offered himself for us on the altar of the Cross, the one who is both priest and victim, the one in whose person we speak and act when we exercise the ministry that we have received. As we reflect on our shortcomings, individually and collectively, let us humbly acknowledge that we have merited the punishment that he, the innocent Lamb, suffered on our behalf. And if, in accordance with what we have deserved, we should have some share in Christ's sufferings, let us rejoice because we will enjoy a much greater gladness when his glory is revealed.

In my thoughts and prayers I am especially mindful of the many priests and religious in the Middle East who are currently experiencing a particular call to conform their lives to the mystery of the Lord's Cross. Through the difficulties facing their communities as a result of the conflicts and tensions of the region, many families are taking the decision to move away, and it can be tempting for their pastors to do likewise. In situations of this kind, though, a priest, a religious community, a parish that remains steadfast and continues to bear witness to Christ is an extraordinary sign of hope, not only for the Christians but for all who live in the region. Their presence alone is an eloquent expression of the Gospel of peace, the determination of the Good Shepherd to care for all the sheep, the Church's unyielding commitment to dialogue, reconciliation and loving acceptance of the other. By embracing the Cross that is held out to them, the priests and religious of the Middle East can truly radiate the hope that lies at the heart of the mystery we are celebrating in our liturgy today.

Let us all take heart from the words of our second reading today, which speak so beautifully of the triumph that was in store for Christ after his death on the Cross, a triumph in which we are invited to share. "For God raised him high and bestowed on him the name which is above every name, that at the name of Jesus every knee should bow in heaven and on earth and under the earth" (Phil 2:9-10).

Ναι, αγαπητές εν Χριστώ αδελφές και αγαπητοί αδελφοί, εμάς δε μή γένοιτο καυχάσθαι ει μή εν τώ σταυρώ του Κυρίου ημών Ιησού Χριστού (cf. Gal 6:14). Αυτος ειναι η σωτηρία, η ζωή και η ανάστασις. Δια μέσου αυτου εσωθήκαμε και ελευθερωθήκαμε.*

* Yes, beloved brothers and sisters in Christ, far be it from us to glory except in the cross of our Lord Jesus Christ (cf. Gal 6:14). He is our life, our salvation and our resurrection; through him we are saved and set free.

CONCLUSION OF THE YEAR FOR PRIESTS HOLY MASS

HOMILY

Solemnity of the Sacred Heart of Jesus
St Peter's Square
Friday, 11 June 2010

The Year for Priests which we have celebrated on the one hundred and fiftieth anniversary of the death of the holy Curè of Ars, the model of priestly ministry in our world, is now coming to an end. We have let the Curé of Ars guide us to a renewed appreciation of the grandeur and beauty of the priestly ministry. The priest is not a mere office-holder, like those which every society needs in order to carry out certain functions. Instead, he does something which no human being can do of his own power: in Christ's name he speaks the words which absolve us of our sins and in this way he changes, starting with God, our entire life. Over the offerings of bread and wine he speaks Christ's words of thanksgiving, which are words of transubstantiation – words which make Christ himself present, the Risen One, his Body and Blood – words which thus transform the elements of the world, which open the world to God and unite it to him. The priesthood, then, is not simply "office" but sacrament: God makes use of us poor men in order to be, through us, present to all men and women, and to act on their behalf. This audacity of God who entrusts himself to human beings – who, conscious of our weaknesses, nonetheless considers men capable of acting and being present in his stead – this audacity of God is the true grandeur concealed in the word "priesthood". That God thinks that we are capable of this; that in this way he calls men to his service and thus from within binds himself to them: this is what we wanted to reflect upon and appreciate anew over the course of the past year. We wanted to reawaken our joy at how close God is to us, and our gratitude for the fact that he entrusts himself to our infirmities; that he guides and sustains us daily. In this way we also wanted to demonstrate once again to young people that this vocation, this fellowship of service for God and with God, does exist – and that God is indeed waiting for us to say "yes". Together with the whole Church we wanted to make clear once again that we have to ask God for this vocation. We have to beg for workers for God's harvest, and this petition to God is, at the same time, his own way of knocking on the hearts of young people who consider themselves able to do what God considers them able to do. It was to be expected that this new radiance of the priesthood would not be pleasing to the "enemy"; he would have rather preferred to see it disappear, so that God would ultimately be driven out of the world. And so it happened that, in this very year of joy for the sacrament of the priesthood, the sins of priests came to light – particularly the abuse of the little ones, in which the priesthood, whose task is to manifest God's concern for our good, turns into its very opposite. We too insistently beg forgiveness from God and from the persons involved, while promising to do everything possible to ensure that such abuse will never occur again; and that in admitting men to priestly ministry and in their formation we will do everything we can to weigh the authenticity of their vocation and make every effort to accompany priests along their journey, so that the Lord will protect them and watch over them in troubled situations and amid life's dangers. Had the Year for Priests been a glorification of our individual human performance, it would have been ruined by these events. But for us what happened was precisely the opposite: we grew in gratitude for God's gift, a gift concealed in "earthen vessels" which ever anew, even amid human weakness, makes his love concretely present in this world. So let us look upon all that happened as a summons to purification, as a task which we bring to the future and which makes us acknowledge and love all the more the great gift we have received from God. In this way, his gift becomes a commitment to respond to God's courage and humility by our own courage and our own humility. The word of God, which we have sung in the Entrance Antiphon of the liturgy, can speak to us, at this hour, of what it means to become and to be priests: "Take my yoke upon you, and learn from me; for I am gentle and humble of heart" (Mt 11:29).

We are celebrating the feast of the Sacred Heart of Jesus, and in the liturgy we peer, as it were, into the heart of Jesus opened in death by the spear of the Roman soldier. Jesus' heart was indeed opened for us and before us – and thus God's own heart was opened. The liturgy interprets for us the language of Jesus' heart, which tells us above all that God is the shepherd of mankind, and so it reveals to us Jesus' priesthood, which is rooted deep within his heart; so too it shows us the perennial foundation and the effective criterion of all priestly ministry, which must always be anchored in the heart of Jesus and lived out from that starting-point. Today I would like to meditate especially on those texts with which the Church in prayer responds to the word of God presented in the readings. In those chants, word (*Wort*) and response (*Antwort*) interpenetrate. On the one hand, the chants are themselves drawn from the word of God, yet on the other, they are already our human response to that word, a response in which the word itself is communicated and enters into our lives. The most important of those texts in today's liturgy is Psalm 23(22) – "The Lord is my shepherd" – in which Israel at prayer received God's self-revelation as shepherd, and made this the guide of its own life. "The Lord is my shepherd, I shall not want": this first verse expresses joy and gratitude for the fact that God is present to and concerned for us. The reading from the Book of Ezechiel begins with the same theme: "I myself will look after and tend my sheep" (Ez 34:11). God personally looks after me, after us, after all mankind. I am not abandoned, adrift in the universe and in a society which leaves me ever more lost and bewildered. God looks after me. He is not a distant God, for whom my life is worthless. The world's religions, as far as we can see, have always known that in the end there is only one God. But this God was distant. Evidently he had abandoned the world to other powers and forces, to other divinities. It was with these that one had to deal. The one God was good, yet aloof. He was not dangerous, nor was he very helpful. Consequently one didn't need to worry about him. He did not lord it over us. Oddly, this kind of thinking re-emerged during the Enlightenment. There was still a recognition that the world presupposes a Creator. Yet this God, after making the world, had evidently withdrawn from it. The world itself had a certain set of laws by which it ran, and God did not, could not, intervene in them. God was only a remote cause. Many perhaps did not even want God to look after them. They did not want God to get in the way. But wherever God's loving concern is perceived as getting in the way, human beings go awry. It is fine and consoling to know that there is someone who loves me and looks after me. But it is far more important that there is a God who knows me, loves me and is concerned about me. "I know my own and my own know me" (Jn 10:14), the Church says before the Gospel with the Lord's words. God knows me, he is concerned about me. This thought should make us truly joyful. Let us allow it to penetrate the depths of our being. Then let us also realize what it means: God wants us, as priests, in one tiny moment of history, to share his concern about people. As priests, we want to be persons who share his concern for men and women, who take care of them and provide them with a concrete experience of God's concern. Whatever the field of activity entrusted to him, the priest, with the Lord, ought to be able to say: "I know my sheep and mine know me". "To know", in the idiom of sacred Scripture, never refers to merely exterior knowledge, like the knowledge of someone's telephone number. "Knowing" means being inwardly close to another person. It means loving him or her. We should strive to "know" men and women as God does and for God's sake; we should strive to walk with them along the path of God's friendship.

Let us return to our Psalm. There we read: "He leads me in right paths for his name's sake. Even though I walk through the darkest valley, I fear no evil; for you are with me; your rod and your staff – they comfort me" (23[22]:3ff.). The shepherd points out the right path to those entrusted to him. He goes before them and leads them. Let us put it differently: the Lord shows us the right way to be human. He teaches us the art of being a person. What must I do in order not to fall, not to squander my life in meaninglessness? This is precisely the question which every man and woman must ask and one which remains valid at every moment of one's life. How much darkness surrounds this question in our own day! We are constantly reminded of the words of Jesus, who felt compassion for the crowds because they were like a flock without a shepherd. Lord, have mercy on us too! Show us the way! From the Gospel we know this much: he is himself the way. Living with Christ, following him – this means finding the right way, so that our lives can be meaningful and so that one day we might say: "Yes, it was good to have lived". The people of Israel continue to be grateful to God because in the Commandments he pointed out the way of life. The great Psalm 119[118] is a unique expression of joy for this fact: we are not fumbling in the dark. God has shown us the way and how to walk aright. The message of the Commandments was synthesized in the life of Jesus and became a living model. Thus we understand that these rules from God are not chains, but the way which he is pointing out to us. We can be glad for them and rejoice that in Christ they stand before us as a lived reality. He himself has made us glad. By walking with Christ, we experience the joy of Revelation, and as priests we need to communicate to others our own joy at the fact that we have been shown the right way of life.

Then there is the phrase about the "darkest valley" through which the Lord leads us. Our path as individuals will one day lead us into the valley of the shadow of death, where no one can accompany us. Yet he will be there. Christ himself descended into the dark night of death. Even there he will not abandon us. Even there he will lead us. "If I sink to the nether world, you are present there", says Psalm 139 (138). Truly you are there, even in the throes of death, and hence our Responsorial Psalm can say: even there, in the darkest valley, I fear no evil. When speaking of the darkest valley, we can also think of the dark valleys of temptation, discouragement and trial through which everyone has to pass. Even in these dark valleys of life he is there. Lord, in the darkness of temptation, at the hour of dusk when all light seems to have died away, show me that you are there. Help us priests, so that we can remain beside the persons entrusted to us in these dark nights. So that we can show them your own light.

"Your rod and your staff – they comfort me": the shepherd needs the rod as protection against savage beasts ready to pounce on the flock; against robbers looking for prey. Along with the rod there is the staff which gives support and helps to make difficult crossings. Both of these are likewise part of the Church's ministry, of the priest's ministry. The Church too must use the shepherd's rod, the rod with which he protects the faith against those who falsify it, against currents which lead the flock astray. The use of the rod can actually be a service of love. Today we can see that it has nothing to do with love when conduct unworthy of the priestly life is tolerated. Nor does it have to do with love if heresy is allowed to spread and the faith twisted and chipped away, as if it were something that we ourselves had invented. As if it were no longer God's gift, the precious pearl which we cannot let be taken from us. Even so, the rod must always become once again the shepherd's staff – a staff which helps men and women to tread difficult paths and to follow the Lord.

At the end of the Psalm we read of the table which is set, the oil which anoints the head, the cup which overflows, and dwelling in the house of the Lord. In the Psalm this is an expression first and foremost of the prospect of the festal joy of being in God's presence in the temple, of being his guest, whom he himself serves, of dwelling with him. For us, who pray this Psalm with Christ and his Body which is the Church, this prospect of hope takes on even greater breadth and depth. We see in these words a kind of prophetic foreshadowing of the mystery of the Eucharist, in which God himself makes us his guests and offers himself to us as food – as that bread and fine wine which alone can definitively sate man's hunger and thirst. How can we not rejoice that one day we will be guests at the very table of God and live in his dwelling-place? How can we not rejoice at the fact that he has commanded us: "Do this in memory of me"? How can we not rejoice that he has enabled us to set God's table for men and women, to give them his Body and his Blood, to offer them the precious gift of his very presence. Truly we can pray together, with all our heart, the words of the Psalm: "Goodness and mercy shall follow me all the days of my life" (Ps 23[22]:6).

Finally, let us take a brief look at the two communion antiphons which the Church offers us in her liturgy today. First there are the words with which St John concludes the account of Jesus' crucifixion: "One of the soldiers pierced his side with a spear, and at once blood and water came out" (Jn 19:34). The heart of Jesus is pierced by the spear. Once opened, it becomes a fountain: the water and the blood which stream forth recall the two fundamental sacraments by which the Church lives: Baptism and the Eucharist. From the Lord's pierced side, from his open heart, there springs the living fountain which continues to well up over the centuries and which makes the Church. The open heart is the source of a new stream of life; here John was certainly also thinking of the prophecy of Ezechiel who saw flowing forth from the new temple a torrent bestowing fruitfulness and life (Ez 47): Jesus himself is the new temple, and his open heart is the source of a stream of new life which is communicated to us in Baptism and the Eucharist.

The liturgy of the Solemnity of the Sacred Heart of Jesus also permits another phrase, similar to this, to be used as the communion antiphon. It is taken from the Gospel of John: Whoever is thirsty, let him come to me. And let the one who believes in me drink. As the Scripture has said: "Out of his heart shall flow rivers of living water" (cf. Jn 7:37ff.) In faith we drink, so to speak, of the living water of God's Word. In this way the believer himself becomes a wellspring which gives living water to the parched earth of history. We see this in the saints. We see this in Mary, that great woman of faith and love who has become in every generation a wellspring of faith, love and life. Every Christian and every priest should become, starting from Christ, a wellspring which gives life to others. We ought to be offering life-giving water to a parched and thirst world. Lord, we thank you because for our sake you opened your heart; because in your death and in your resurrection you became the source of life. Give us life, make us live from you as our source, and grant that we too may be sources, wellsprings capable of bestowing the water of life in our time. We thank you for the grace of the priestly ministry. Lord bless us, and bless all those who in our time are thirsty and continue to seek. Amen.

III.
ADDRESSES

TO THE COMMUNITIES OF THE PONTIFICAL REGIONAL SEMINARIES OF THE MARCHES, APULIA AND ABRUZZI-MOLISE (ITALY)

Clementine Hall
Saturday, 29 November 2008

Sowers of the Word

I would now like to address you in particular, dear Seminarians, who are preparing to be workers in the Lord's vineyard. As the recent Assembly of the Synod of Bishops recalled, among the prioritized tasks of the presbyterate is that of scattering the Word of God in the field of the world in large handfuls. Like the seed in the Gospel parable, it actually seems very small but once it has sprouted it grows into a great shrub and bears abundant fruit (cf. Mt 13:31-32). The Word of God that you will be called to sow in large handfuls and that bears within it eternal life is Christ himself, the only one who can change the human heart and renew the world. But we might well ask ourselves: does contemporary man still feel the need for Christ and for his message of salvation?

In today's social context a certain culture seems to be showing us the face of a self-sufficient humanity desirous of accomplishing its own projects by itself, which chooses to be the sole author of its own destiny and consequently considers that God's presence is irrelevant; it therefore excludes him de facto from its choices and decisions. In a climate at times marked by a rationalism closed in on itself, that considers the practical sciences the only form of knowledge, the rest becomes completely subjective and consequently the religious experience also risks being perceived as a subjective choice, neither essential nor crucial for life. Today, of course, for these and other reasons, it has certainly become more difficult to believe, always more difficult to accept the Truth that is Christ, always more difficult to spend one's life for the cause of the Gospel. However, as the news reports daily, contemporary man often seems lost and worried about his future, in search of certainties and longing for reliable reference points. Moreover, as in every epoch, people in the third millennium need God and sometimes seek him even without realizing it. The task of Christians, and especially of priests, is to take in this deep yearning of the human heart and to offer to all, with the means and in the manner required by the needs of the times, the unchanging and therefore always alive and actual Word of eternal life that is Christ, Hope of the world.

With a view to this important mission that you will be called to carry out in the Church, the seminary years assume great value. This is a period designed for formation and discernment; years in which the priority must be the constant pursuit of a personal relationship with Jesus, an intimate experience of his love that is acquired first of all through prayer and through contact with the Sacred Scriptures, read, interpreted and meditated upon in the faith of the ecclesial community. In this Pauline Year, how can I fail to propose the Apostle Paul to you as a model to inspire you in your preparation for the apostolic ministry? His extraordinary experience on the road to Damascus transformed him from a persecutor of Christians to a witness of the Lord's Resurrection, ready to lay down his life for the Gospel. He had been a faithful observer of all the prescriptions of the Torah and the Jewish traditions but after his encounter with Jesus, he writes in his Letter to the Philippians, "whatever gain I had, I counted as loss for the sake of Christ". "For his sake", he added, "I have suffered the loss of all things, and count them as refuse, in order that I may gain Christ and be found in him" (cf. 3:7-9). Conversion did not eliminate what was good and true in his life but permitted him to interpret the wisdom and truth of the law and of the prophets in a new way and thus be enabled to converse with all, after the example of the divine Teacher.

In imitation of St Paul, dear Seminarians, never tire of encountering Christ in listening, in reading and in studying Sacred Scripture, in prayer and in personal meditation, in the liturgy and in every other daily activity. Your role is important in this regard, dear formators, called to be witnesses for your pupils, even before being teachers of evangelical life. Because of their own typical characteristics, Regional Seminaries can be privileged places for the formation of seminarians in diocesan spirituality, engraving this formation in the broader ecclesial and regional context with wisdom and balance. May your institutions also be "homes" that welcome vocations in order to impress an even greater impetus upon vocations ministry, taking special care of the world of youth and teaching them the great evangelical and missionary ideals.

Dear friends, as I thank you for your visit, I invoke upon each one of you the motherly protection of the Virgin Mother of Christ, whom the Advent liturgy presents to us as the model of one who watches while awaiting the glorious return of her divine Son. I confidently entrust you to her. Have frequent recourse to her intercession so that she may help you to keep alert and watchful. For my part, I assure you of my affection and my daily prayers, while I warmly bless you all.

From the Address given

TO THE MEMBERS OF THE CONGREGATION FOR THE CLERGY ON THE OCCASION OF THEIR PLENARY ASSEMBLY

Consistory Hall
Monday, 16 March 2009

The missionary identity of the Priest.

The theme you have chosen for this Plenary Assembly "The missionary identity of the priest in the Church as an intrinsic dimension of the exercise of the tria munera" suggests some reflections on the work of these days and the abundant fruit that it will certainly yield. If the whole Church is missionary and if every Christian, by virtue of Baptism and Confirmation *quasi ex officio* (cf. *Catechism of the Catholic Church,* n. 1305), receives the mandate to profess the faith publicly, the ministerial priesthood, also from this viewpoint, is ontologically distinct, and not only by rank, from the baptismal priesthood that is also known as the "common priesthood". In fact, the apostolic mandate "Go into all the world and preach the Gospel to the whole of creation" (Mk 16:15) is constitutive of the ministerial priesthood. This mandate is not, as we know, a mere duty entrusted to collaborators; its roots are deeper and must be sought further back in time.

The missionary dimension of the priesthood is born from the priest's sacramental configuration to Christ. As a conequence it brings with it a heartfelt and total adherence to what the ecclesial tradition has identified as *apostolica vivendi forma* (the apostolic form of life). This consists in participation in a "new life", spiritually speaking, in that "new way of life" which the Lord Jesus inaugurated and which the Apostles made their own. Through the imposition of the Bishop's hands and the consecratory prayer of the Church, the candidates become new men, they become "presbyters". In this light it is clear that the *tria munera* are first a gift and only consequently an office, first a participation in a life, and hence a *potestas*. Of course, the great ecclesial tradition has rightly separated sacramental efficacy from the concrete existential situation of the individual priest and so the legitimate expectations of the faithful are appropriately safeguarded. However, this correct doctrinal explanation takes nothing from the necessary, indeed indispensable, aspiration to moral perfection that must dwell in every authentically priestly heart.

Precisely to encourage priests in this striving for spiritual perfection on which, above all, the effectiveness of their ministry depends, I have decided to establish a special "Year for Priests" that will begin on 19 June and last until 19 June 2010. In fact, it is the 150th anniversary of the death of the Holy Curé d'Ars, John Mary Vianney, a true example of a pastor at the service of Christ's flock. It will be the task of your Congregation, in agreement with the diocesan Ordinaries and with the superiors of religious institutes to promote and to coordinate the various spiritual and pastoral initiatives that seem useful for making the importance of the priest's role and mission in the Church and in contemporary society ever more clearly perceived.

The priest's mission, as the theme of the Plenary Assembly emphasizes, is carried out "in the Church". This ecclesial communal, hierarchical and doctrinal dimension is absolutely indispensable to every authentic mission and, alone guarantees its spiritual effectiveness. The four aspects mentioned must always be recognized as intimately connected: the mission is "ecclesial" because no one proclaims himself in the first person, but within and through his own humanity every priest must be well aware that he is bringing to the world Another, God himself. God is the only treasure which ultimately people desire to find in a priest. The mission is "communional" because it is carried out in a unity and communion that only secondly has also important aspects of social visibility. Moreover, these derive essentially from that divine intimacy in which the priest is called to be expert, so that he may be able to lead the souls entrusted to him humbly and trustingly to the same encounter with the Lord. Lastly, the "hierarchical" and "doctrinal" dimensions suggest reaffirming the importance of the ecclesiastical discipline (the term has a connection with "disciple") and doctrinal training and not only theological, initial and continuing formation.

Awareness of the radical social changes that have occurred in recent decades must motivate the best ecclesial forces to supervise the formation of candidates for the ministry. In particular, it must foster the constant concern of Pastors for their principal collaborators, both by cultivating truly fatherly human relations and by taking an interest in their continuing formation, especially from the doctrinal and spiritual view-points. The mission is rooted in a special way in a good formation, developed in communion with uninterrupted ecclesial Tradition, without breaks or temptations of irregularity. In this sense, it is important to encourage in priests, especially in the young generations, a correct reception of the texts of the Second Ecumenical Vatican Council, interpreted in the light of the Church's entire fund of doctrine. It seems urgent to recover that awareness that has always been at the heart of the Church's mission, which impels priests to be present, identifiable and recognizable both for their judgement of faith, for their personal virtues as well as for the habit, in the contexts of culture and of charity.

As Church and as priests, we proclaim Jesus of Nazareth Lord and Christ, Crucified and Risen, Sovereign of time and of history, in the glad certainty that this truth coincides with the deepest expectations of the human heart. In the mystery of the Incarnation of the Word, that is, of the fact that God became man like us, lies both the content and the method of Christian proclamation. The true dynamic centre of the mission is here: in Jesus Christ, precisely. The centrality of Christ brings with it the correct appreciation of the ministerial priesthood, without which there would be neither the Eucharist, nor even the mission nor the Church herself. In this regard it is necessary to be alert to ensure that the "new structures" or pastoral organizations are not planned on the basis of an erroneous interpretation of the proper promotion of the laity for a time in which one would have "to do without" the ordained ministry, because in that case the presuppositions for a further dilution of the ministerial priesthood would be laid and possible presumed "solutions" might come dramatically to coincide with the real causes of contemporary problems linked to the ministry.

From the Address given

TO THE COMMUNITY OF THE PONTIFICAL ECCLESIASTICAL ACADEMY

Hall of the Popes
Saturday, 23 May 2009

'Cultivate a communion of love and life with the Lord.'

Dear priests, may you be, in the first place, men of intense prayer, who cultivate a communion of love and life with the Lord. Without this sound spiritual basis, how could you persevere in your ministry? Those who work in this way in the Lord's vineyard know that what they do with dedication, sacrifice and love is never wasted. And if at times we are given to taste the cup of loneliness, misunderstanding and suffering, if service seems at times a burden to us and the cross is sometimes heavy to carry, may the certainty that God knows how to make all things fruitful sustain and comfort us. We know that the dimension of the Cross, vividly symbolized in the parable of the ear of wheat which, having fallen to the ground dies to bear fruit an image that Jesus used shortly before his Passion is an essential part of every person's life and every apostolic mission. In every situation we must offer the joyful witness of our adherence to the Gospel, accepting the Apostle Paul's invitation to boast only of the Cross of Christ, with the sole ambition of completing in ourselves what is lacking in the Passion of the Lord, for the sake of his Body, that is the Church (cf. Col 1:24).

PASTORAL VISIT TO
SAN GIOVANNI ROTONDO

From the Address given during a

MEETING WITH THE PRIESTS, RELIGIOUS AND YOUTH

New Church of San Pio of Pietrelcina
Sunday, 21 June 2009

Saint Pio of Pietrelcina

Dear priests, the day before yesterday, the Solemnity of the Sacred Heart and a day of priestly holiness, we inaugurated the Year for Priests, during which we shall commemorate with veneration and affection the 150th anniversary of the death of St John Mary Vianney, the Holy Curé d'Ars. In the Letter I wrote for the occasion, I wanted to stress how important the holiness of priests is for the Church's life and mission. Like the Curé d'Ars, Padre Pio also reminds us of the dignity and responsibility of the priestly ministry. Who was not struck by the fervour with which he relived Christ's Passion in every Eucharistic celebration? In him, as in the Curé d'Ars, a total willingness to accept the faithful, especially sinners, flowed from love for the Eucharist. Furthermore, if in a turbulent and difficult epoch St John Mary Vianney sought in every possible way to enable his parishioners to rediscover the meaning and beauty of sacramental repentance, the holy Friar of the Gargano was consumed until the end of his life by his longing to care for souls and to convert sinners. How many people changed their way of living thanks to his patient priestly ministry; what long hours he spent in the confessional! Like the Curé d'Ars, it was his ministry as confessor itself that constituted this holy

Capuchin's distinctive feature and his greatest claim to glory. Consequently how can we fail to understand the importance of taking part devoutly in the Eucharistic celebration and of receiving the sacrament of Confession frequently? The sacrament of Penance in particular should be increasingly appreciated and priests must never resign themselves to seeing their confessionals deserted, or limit themselves to noting loss of interest in the faithful for this extraordinary source of serenity and peace.

Then there is another important lesson we can learn from Padre Pio's life: the value of and need for prayer. He would answer those who asked him to express an opinion of himself: "*I am only a poor friar who prays*". And effectively he prayed always and everywhere with humility, trust and perseverance. Here then is a key point, not only for the spirituality of the priest but also for that of every Christian, and especially for you, dear men and women religious, chosen to follow Christ more closely through the practice of the vows of poverty, chastity and obedience. One may sometimes be overcome by a certain discouragement at the weakening or even abandonment of faith which is recorded in our secularized societies. It is certainly necessary to find new channels for communicating the Gospel truth to the men and women of our time, but if the essential content of the Christian proclamation is always to remain the same, we must turn to its original source, to Jesus Christ who is "the same yesterday and today and for ever" (Heb 13:8). The human and spiritual life of Padre Pio teaches us that only a soul closely united with the Crucified One succeeds in communicating the joy and riches of the Gospel even to those who are remote.

Love for Christ is inevitably linked to love for Christ's Church, guided and enlivened by the power of the Holy Spirit, in which each one of us has a role and mission to carry out. Dear priests, dear men and women religious, the tasks entrusted to you and the charisms which you interpret may differ but may the spirit in which you carry them out always be the same so that your presence and action among the Christian people become an eloquent witness of God's primacy in your lives. Was it not perhaps precisely this that everyone perceived in St Pius of Pietrelcina?

GENERAL AUDIENCE

Saint Peter's Square
Wednesday, 24 June 2009

"Voice" of the Lord.

Dear Brothers and Sisters,

Last Friday, 19 June, the Solemnity of the Sacred Heart of Jesus and a Day traditionally dedicated to prayer for the sanctification of priests, I had the joy of inaugurating the Year for Priests which I established on the occasion of the 150th anniversary of the "birth in Heaven" of the Curé d'Ars, St John Baptist Mary Vianney. And on entering the Vatican Basilica for the celebration of Vespers, first by way of a symbolic gesture I paused in the Chapel of the Choir to venerate the relic of this holy pastor of souls: his heart. Why a Year for Priests? Why precisely in memory of the Holy Curé d'Ars who did not, apparently, achieve anything extraordinary?

Divine Providence has ensured that his figure be juxtaposed with that of St Paul. Indeed, while the Pauline Year, dedicated to the Apostle to the Gentiles an extraordinary evangelizer who made several missionary voyages in order to spread the Gospel is drawing to a close, this new Jubilee Year invites us to look at a poor peasant who became a humble parish priest and carried out his pastoral service in a small village. If the two saints differ widely because of the paths through life that characterized them one went from one region to the next to proclaim the Gospel, the other welcomed thousands and thousands of the faithful while remaining in his own tiny parish, something basic binds them together nevertheless; and it is their total identification with their own ministry, their communion with Christ, which made St Paul say "I have been crucified with Christ; it is no longer I who live, but Christ who lives in me" (Gal 2:20). And

117

St John Mary Vianney used to like to repeat: "if we had faith, we would see God hidden in the priest like a light behind glass or like wine mixed with water". The purpose of this Year for Priests, as I wrote in my Letter addressed to priests for this occasion, is therefore to encourage every priest in this striving for spiritual perfection on which, above all, the effectiveness of their ministry depends, and first and foremost to help priests and with them the entire People of God to rediscover and to reinforce their knowledge of the extraordinary, indispensable gift of Grace which the ordained minister represents for those who have received it, for the whole Church and for the world which would be lost without the Real Presence of Christ.

There is no doubt that the historical and social conditions in which the Curé d'Ars lived have changed and it is right to wonder how priests in today's globalized societies can imitate him by identifying with him in their own ministries. In a world in which the common vision of life includes less and less of the sacred, instead of which "functionality" becomes the only crucial element, the Catholic concept of the priesthood might risk losing its natural esteem, at times even within the ecclesial conscience. Two different conceptions of the priesthood are frequently compared and at times even set against one another, in theological milieus as well as in actual pastoral practice and the formation of the clergy. In this regard I pointed out several years ago that there is: "on the one hand a social and functional concept that defines the essence of the priesthood with the concept of "service': service to the community in the fulfilment of a function.... Moreover, there is the sacramental-ontological concept, which of course does not deny the priesthood's character of service but sees it anchored to the minister's existence and claims that this existence is determined by a gift granted by the Lord through the mediation of the Church, whose name is sacrament" (J. Ratzinger, *Ministero e vita del Sacerdote, in Elementi di Teologia fondamentale. Saggio su fede e ministero*, Brescia 2005, p. 165). The terminological shifting of the word "priesthood" to "service, ministry, assignment", is also a sign of this different conception. The primacy of the Eucharist, moreover, is linked to the former, the ontological-sacramental conception, in the dual term: "priesthood-sacrifice", whereas the primacy of the word and of the service of proclamation is held to correspond with the latter.

Clearly these two concepts are not contradictory and the tension which nevertheless exists between them may be resolved from within. Thus the Decree of the Second Vatican Council on the Ministry and Life of Priests, *Presbyterorum ordinis*, says: "For, through the apostolic proclamation of the Gospel, the People of God is called together and assembled so that when all who belong to this People have been sanctified by the Holy Spirit, they can offer themselves as "a sacrifice, living, holy, pleasing to God' (Rom 12:1). Through the ministry of priests the spiritual sacrifice of the faithful is made perfect in union with the sacrifice of Christ, the sole Mediator. Through the hands of priests and in the name of the whole Church, the Lord's sacrifice is offered in the Eucharist in an unbloody and sacramental manner until he himself returns" (n. 2).

Then let us ask ourselves: "What precisely does 'to evangelize' mean for priests? What does the 'primacy' of proclamation consist in?" Jesus speaks of the proclamation of the Kingdom of God as the true purpose of his coming into the world and his proclamation is not only a "discourse". At the same time it includes his action: the signs and miracles that he works show that the Kingdom comes into the world as a present reality which ultimately coincides with Jesus himself. In this sense it is only right to recall that even in the primacy of proclamation, the word and the sign are indivisible. Christian preaching does not proclaim "words", but the Word, and the proclamation coincides with the very Person of Christ, ontologically open to the relationship with the Father and obedient to his will. Thus, an authentic service to the Word requires of the priest that he strive for deeper self-denial, to the point that he can say, with the Apostle, "it is no longer I who live, but Christ who lives in me". The priest cannot consider himself "master" of the Word, but its servant. He is not the Word but, as John the Baptist, whose birth we are celebrating precisely today, proclaimed, he is the "voice" of the Word: "the voice of one crying in the wilderness: Prepare the way of the Lord, make his paths straight" (Mk 1:3).

For the priest, then, being the "voice" of the Word is not merely a functional aspect. On the contrary, it implies a substantial "losing of himself" in Christ, participating with his whole being in the mystery of Christ's death and Resurrection: his understanding, his freedom, his will and the offering of his body as a living sacrifice (cf. Rom 12:1-2). Only participation in Christ's sacrifice, in his kenosis, makes preaching authentic! And this is the way he must take with Christ to reach the point of being able to say to the Father, together with Christ: let "not what I will, but what you will" be done (Mk 14:36). Proclamation, therefore, always involves self-sacrifice, a prerequisite for its authenticity and efficacy.

As an *alter Christus*, the priest is profoundly united to the Word of the Father who, in becoming incarnate took the form of a servant, he became a servant (Phil 2:5-11). The priest is a servant of Christ, in the sense that his existence, configured to Christ ontologically, acquires an essentially relational character: he is *in* Christ, *for* Christ and *with* Christ, at the service of humankind. Because he belongs to Christ, the priest is radically at the service of all people: he is the minister of their salvation, their happiness and their authentic liberation, developing, in this gradual assumption of Christ's will, in prayer, in "being heart to heart" with him. Therefore this is the indispensable condition for every proclamation, which entails participation in the sacramental offering of the Eucharist and docile obedience to the Church.

The saintly Curé d'Ars would often say with tears in his eyes: "How dreadful it is to be a priest!". And he would add: "How a priest who celebrates Mass like an ordinary event is to be pitied! How unfortunate is a priest with no inner life!". May the Year for Priests lead all priests to identify totally with the Crucified and Risen Jesus so that, in imitation of St John the Baptist, they may be prepared to "shrink" that Christ may grow and that, in following the example of the Curé d'Ars, they feel constantly and profoundly the responsibility of their mission, which is the sign and presence of God's infinite mercy. Let us entrust to Our Lady, Mother of the Church, the Year for Priests which has just begun and all the priests of the world.

ANGELUS

The model of Saint Paul.

With the celebration of First Vespers of Saints Peter and Paul at which I shall preside this evening in the Basilica of St Paul Outside-the-Walls, the Pauline Year, established to mark the 2,000th anniversary of the birth of the Apostle of the Gentiles, is drawing to a close. It has been a true time of grace in which, through pilgrimages, catecheses, numerous publications and various initiatives, the figure of St Paul has been presented anew throughout the Church and his vibrant message has revived in Christian communities everywhere a passion for Christ and for the Gospel. Let us, therefore, thank God for the Pauline Year and for all the spiritual gifts that it has brought us.

Divine Providence disposed only a few days ago that on 19 June, the Solemnity of the Sacred Heart of Jesus, another special Year be inaugurated, the Year for Priests, on the occasion of the 150th anniversary of the death *dies natalis* of John Mary Vianney, the Holy Curé d'Ars. This is a further spiritual and pastoral incentive, which I am sure will not fail to bring numerous benefits to the Christian people and especially to the clergy. What is the purpose of the Year for Priests? As I wrote in my special Letter addressed to priests, it is meant to encourage the commitment of all priests to interior renewal for a stronger and more effective Gospel witness in today's world. In this regard the Apostle Paul is a splendid model to imitate, not so much in the practical details of his life which was truly extraordinary but rather in his love for Christ, in his zeal to proclaim the Gospel, in his dedication to the communities and in his elaboration of effective syntheses of pastoral theology. St

Paul is the example of a priest who identified totally with his ministry as the Holy Curé d'Ars would also be aware that he was carrying a priceless treasure, namely, the message of salvation, but in "earthen vessels" (cf. 2 Cor 4:7). Thus he is simultaneously strong and humble, deeply convinced that everything is God's doing, everything is his grace. "The love of Christ impels us", the Apostle writes, and this could well be the motto of every priest, whom the Spirit has "compelled" (cf. Acts 20:22) to be a faithful steward of the mysteries of God (cf. 1 Cor 4:1-2): the priest should belong completely to Christ and completely to the Church, to whom he is called to dedicate himself with undivided love like a faithful husband to his wife.

Dear friends, let us now invoke the intercession of the Virgin Mary, together with that of the Holy Apostles Peter and Paul, so that she may obtain from the Lord abundant Blessings for priests during this Year for Priests which has just begun. May Our Lady, whom St John Mary Vianney so deeply loved and made loved by his parishioners, help every priest to revive the gift of God that is in him by virtue of his Holy Ordination, so that he may grow in holiness and be prepared to bear witness, if necessary even to the point of martyrdom, to the beauty of his total and definitive consecration to Christ and to the Church.

GENERAL AUDIENCE

Saint Peter's Square
Wednesday, 1st July 2009

Faithfulness of Christ, faithfulness of priests

The celebration of First Vespers of the Solemnity of the Holy Apostles, Peter and Paul in the Basilica of St Paul-Outside-the-Walls on 28 June, as you know, brought to a close the Pauline Year commemorating the 2,000th anniversary of the birth of the Apostle to the Gentiles.

Let us thank the Lord for the spiritual fruit that this important initiative has brought to so many Christian communities. We may accept the Apostle's invitation to deepen our knowledge of the mystery of Christ as a precious heritage of the Pauline Year because he is at the heart and the centre of our personal and community existence. This is in fact the indispensable condition for a true spiritual and ecclesial renewal. As I emphasized during the first Eucharistic Celebration in the Sistine Chapel after my election as Successor of the Apostle Peter, it is precisely from full communion with Christ that "flows every other element of the Church's life: first of all, communion among all the faithful, the commitment to proclaiming and witnessing to the Gospel, the ardour of love for all, especially the poorest and lowliest". This applies to priests in the first place. For this reason let us thank God's Providence for offering us the possibility of celebrating the Year for Priests now. My heartfelt hope for every priest is that it will be an opportunity for inner renewal and, consequently, that it will firmly strengthen him in his commitment to his mission.

Just as during the Pauline Year our constant reference point was St Paul, so in the coming months we shall look in the first place to St John Mary Vianney, the Holy Curé d'Ars, recalling the 150th anniversary of his death. In the Letter I wrote to priests on this occasion, I wished to underline what shines brightest in the life of this humble minister of the altar: his "complete identification... with his ministry". He used to like to say that "a good shepherd, a pastor after God's heart, is the greatest treasure which the good Lord can grant to a parish, and one of the most precious gifts of divine mercy", and, almost not managing to understand the greatness of the gift and task entrusted to a poor human creature, he would sigh: "O, how great is the priest! ... If he realized what he is, he would die... God obeys him: he utters a few words and the Lord descends from heaven at his voice, to be contained within a small host".

In fact, precisely by considering the pairing of identity with mission each priest is able to be more aware of the need for that gradual identification with Christ which will guarantee him fidelity and the fruitfulness of Gospel witness. The very title of the Year for Priests *Faithfulness of Christ, faithfulness of priests* highlights the fact that the gift of divine grace precedes every possible human response and pastoral initiative. Thus, in the priest's life, missionary preaching and worship can never be separated, just as the ontological-sacramental identity and evangelizing mission must never be separated. Moreover, we might say that the purpose of every priest's mission is one of worship. Thus may all people offer themselves to God as a living sacrifice, holy and acceptable to him (cf. Rom 12:1), which in Creation itself, in people, becomes worship, praise of the Creator, receiving that love which they in turn are called to offer to each other in abundance. The early Christian communities were already clearly aware of this. St John Chrysostom said, for example, that the sacrament of the altar and the "sacrament of the brother" or "sacrament of the poor man", are two aspects of the same mystery. Love for one's neighbour, attention to justice and to the poor are not so much themes of a moral society as they are an expression of a sacramental conception of Christian morality. This is because, through the ministry of priests, the spiritual sacrifice of all the faithful is fulfilled in union with that of Christ, the one Mediator: a sacrifice that priests offer in an unbloody and sacramental way as they wait for the Lord to come again. This is the principal, essentially missionary and dynamic dimension of the priestly ministry and identity: through the proclamation of the Gospel they generate faith in those who do not yet believe, so that they may combine their sacrifice with Christ's through love of God and of one's neighbour.

Dear brothers and sisters, in the face of so much uncertainty and weariness that also arises in the exercise of the priestly ministry, the recovery of a clear and unequivocal opinion on the absolute primacy of divine grace is urgent, remembering what St Thomas Aquinas wrote: "The good of grace in one is greater than the good of nature in the whole universe" (*Summa Theologiae*, I-II, q. 113, a. 9, ad 2). The mission of each individual priest will therefore depend also and above all on knowledge of the sacramental reality of his "new being". His ever renewed enthusiasm for the mission depends on the certainty of his own identity not artificially and humanly constructed but freely and divinely given and received. And what I wrote in the Encyclical *Deus Caritas Est* also applies to priests: "Being Christian is not the result of an ethical choice or a lofty idea, but the encounter with an event, a person, which gives life a new horizon and a decisive direction" (n. 1).

Having received such an extraordinary gift of grace with their "consecration", priests become permanent witnesses of their encounter with Christ. Starting precisely from this inner awareness, they can fully carry out their "mission" through the proclamation of the word and the administration of the Sacraments. After the Second Vatican Council, an impression spread that there was a more pressing need in the mission of priests in our time; some thought that above all it was necessary for a new society to be built. The Gospel passage that we heard at the outset recalls instead the two essential elements of the priestly ministry. Jesus sends the Apostles out to proclaim the Gospel and gives them the power to expel evil spirits.

"Proclamation" and "power", that is, "word" and "sacrament", are therefore the two basic pillars of priestly service, over and above its possible multiple circumstances.

When the "diptych" of consecration and mission is not taken into account, it becomes truly difficult to understand the identity of the priest and his ministry in the Church. Indeed, who is the priest if not a man who has been converted and renewed by the Spirit, who lives on his personal relationship with Christ, ceaselessly making the Gospel criteria his own? Who is the priest if not a man of unity and truth, aware of his own limitations and at the same time of the extraordinary greatness, of the vocation he has received, namely that of helping to spread the Kingdom of God to the very ends of the earth? Yes! The priest is a man who belongs totally to the Lord, for it is God himself who has called him and establishes him in his apostolic service. For the very reason that he belongs completely to the Lord, he belongs completely to the people, for the people. During this Year for Priests that will last until the next Solemnity of the Sacred Heart, let us pray for all priests. Let us pray that in dioceses, parishes, religious and especially monastic communities, in associations and movements, in the various pastoral groups that exist throughout the world there may be an increase in prayer initiatives and in particular in Eucharistic Adoration for the sanctification of the clergy and for priestly vocations, in response to Jesus' invitation to pray "the Lord of the harvest to send out labourers into his harvest" (Mt 9:38). Prayer is the first commitment, the true path of sanctification for priests and the soul of an authentic "vocations ministry". Not only must the scarcity of ordinations to the priesthood in certain countries not discourage us, but it must also be an incentive to increase the number of places of silence and listening to the word, to better attend to spiritual direction and the sacrament of Confession. In this way God's voice, which always continues to call and to strengthen, may be heard and promptly followed by numerous young people. Those who pray are not afraid; those who pray are never alone; those who pray are saved! St John Mary Vianney is without a doubt the model of an existence made prayer. May Mary, Mother of the Church, help all priests to follow his example in order to be, like him, witnesses of Christ and apostles of the Gospel.

ADDRESS
TO PARTICIPANTS IN THE
EUROPEAN CONGRESS ON THE
PASTORAL CARE OF VOCATIONS

Clementine Hall
Saturday, 4 July 2009

*"Sowers of the Gospel of Vocation: a word that calls
and sends forth"*

I meet you with great pleasure, aware of the precious pastoral service that you carry out in the context of the promotion, animation and discernment of vocations. You have come to Rome to take part in a congress of reflection, comparison and sharing among the Churches of Europe on the theme: *"Sowers of the Gospel of Vocation: a word that calls and sends forth"* and it aims to imbue your commitment to vocations with new dynamism. The fostering of vocations is a pastoral priority for every diocese which assumes even greater value in the context of the Year for Priests that has just begun. I therefore warmly greet the Bishops Delegate for the pastoral care of vocations of the various Bishops' Conferences, as well as the directors of the national Vocations Centres, their collaborators and all of you present.

At the heart of your labours is the Gospel Parable of the Sower. The Lord scatters the seed of the word of God freely and with abundance but knowing that it may fall on poor soil, which will not allow a seed to mature because of dryness, or that its vital force may be extinguished, choked by thorn bushes. Yet the sower does not lose heart, for he knows that part of this seed is destined to find "good soil", namely, ardent hearts capable of receiving the word with willingness to help it mature through perseverance and yield fruit generously for the benefit of many.

The image of the soil can evoke the reality of the family, on the whole good; the sometimes arid and harsh environment of work; the days of suffering and tears. The earth is above all the heart of every person, especially of youth, to whom you address your service of listening and guidance: a heart that is often confused and disoriented, yet capable of containing unimaginable powers of generosity. It is like a bud ready to open to a life spent for the love of Jesus, able to follow him with the totality and the certainty that comes from having found the greatest treasure that exists. It is always and only the Lord who sows in human hearts. Only after the abundant and generous sowing of the word of God can one progress further along the paths of companionship and education, of formation and discernment. All this is linked to that tiny seed, the mysterious gift of divine Providence which releases from within an extraordinary force. In fact, it is the Word of God who brings about in himself what he says and desires.

There is another saying of Jesus' which uses the image of the seed, and which can accompany the Parable of the Sower: "Unless a grain of wheat falls into the earth and dies, it remains alone; but if it dies, it bears much fruit" (Jn 12:24). Here the Lord insists on the connection between the death of the seed and the "much fruit" that it will yield. The grain of wheat is he, Jesus. The fruit is having "life abundantly" (Jn 10:10), which he acquired for us through his Cross. This is also the logic and the true fruitfulness of every vocations ministry in the Church. Like Christ, the priest and the animator must be a "grain of wheat" who sacrifices itself to do the Father's will; who lives hidden from the clamour and the noise; who renounces the search for that visibility and grandiose image which today often become the criteria and even goals of life in a large part of our culture and which attract many young people.

Dear friends, be sowers of trust and hope. The sense of being lost that the youth of today often experience is indeed profound.

Human words are frequently without a future or prospects, and also lack meaning and wisdom. The attitude of frenetic impatience and of the inability to live through a period of waiting is spreading. Yet, this could be God's hour: his call, mediated by the power and efficacy of the word, generates a path of hope towards the fullness of life. The word of God can truly become light and strength, a spring of hope, it can plot a path that passes through Jesus, the "path" and the "way"; through his Cross, which is the fullness of love. This is the message that comes to us from the Pauline Year which has just ended. St Paul, won over by Christ, inspired and formed vocations, as can be seen clearly from the greetings of his Letters, in which dozens of proper names appear, that is, the faces of men and women who worked with him in service of the Gospel. This is also the message of the Year for Priests that has just begun: the Holy Curé d'Ars, John Mary Vianney who is the "beacon" of this new spiritual itinerary was a priest who devoted his life to the spiritual guidance of people, with humility and simplicity, "tasting and seeing" God's goodness in ordinary situations. He thus proved to be a true teacher in the ministry of consolation and vocational guidance. The Year for Priests therefore offers a beautiful opportunity to rediscover the profound sense of the vocations ministry, as well as the fundamental decisions on its method: simple and credible witness, communion, with itineraries organized and shared within the local Church, the daily routine which is a lesson in following the Lord in everyday life; listening, guided by the Holy Spirit, to orient youth in their search for God and for true happiness; and lastly truth, which alone can give rise to inner freedom.

Dear brothers and sisters, may the word of God become in each one of you a source of blessing, of consolation and of renewed trust, so that you may help many to "see" and "touch" that Jesus whom they welcomed as Teacher. May the Word of the Lord always dwell within you, renew in your hearts the light, love and peace that God alone can give, and make you capable of witnessing and proclaiming the Gospel, source of communion and love. With this hope, which I entrust to the intercession of Mary Most Holy, I warmly impart the Apostolic Blessing to you all.

From the

ANGELUS

Les Combes (Val D'Aosta)
Sunday, 26 July 2009

'Instruments of salvation'

Today, on this splendid Sunday, as the Lord shows us all the beauty of his Creation, the liturgy provides us with the Gospel passage at the beginning of Chapter Six of John's Gospel. It contains, first of all, the miracle of the loaves – when Jesus fed thousands of people with only five loaves of bread and two fish; then, the Lord's miracle when he walks on the waters of the lake during a storm; and finally, the discourse in which he reveals himself as "the Bread of Life". In recounting the "sign" of bread, the Evangelist emphasizes that Christ, before distributing the food, blessed it with a prayer of thanksgiving (cf. v. 11). The Greek term used is *eucharistein* and it refers directly to the Last Supper, though, in fact, John refers here not to the institution of the Eucharist but to the washing of the feet. The Eucharist is mentioned here in anticipation of the great symbol of the Bread of Life. In this Year for Priests, how can we fail to recall that we priests, especially, may see ourselves reflected in this Johannine text, identifying ourselves with the Apostles when they say: Where can we find bread for all these people? Reading about that unknown boy who has five barley loaves and two fish, we too spontaneously say: But what are they for such a multitude? In other words: Who am I? How can I, with my limitations, help Jesus in his mission? And the Lord gives the answer: By taking in his "holy and venerable" hands the little that they are, priests, we priests, become instruments of salvation for many, for everyone!

ANGELUS

Models of priestly devotion.

Dear brothers and sisters, the Year for Priests that we are celebrating is a precious opportunity to deepen our knowledge of the value of the mission of priests in the Church and in the world. In this regard, useful ideas for reflection can be found in remembering the saints whom the Church holds up to us daily. In these first days of the month of August, for example, we commemorate some who are real models of spirituality and priestly devotion. Yesterday was the liturgical Memorial of St Alphonsus Mary de' Liguori, a Bishop and Doctor of the Church, a great teacher of moral theology and a model of Christian and pastoral virtues who was ever attentive to the religious needs of the people. Today we are contemplating St Francis of Assisi's ardent love for the salvation of souls which every priest must always foster. In fact today is the feast of the "Pardon of Assisi", which St Francis obtained from Pope Honorious III in the year 1216, after having a vision while he was praying in the little church of the Portiuncula. Jesus appeared to him in his glory, with the Virgin Mary on his right and surrounded by many Angels. They asked him to express a wish and Francis implored a "full and generous pardon" for all those who would visit that church who "repented and confessed their sins". Having received papal approval, the Saint did not wait for any written document but hastened to Assisi and when he reached the Portiuncula announced the good news: "Friends, the Lord wants to have us all in Heaven!". Since then, from noon on 1 August to midnight on the second, it has been possible to obtain, on the usual conditions, a Plenary Indulgence, also for the dead, on visiting a parish church or a Franciscan one.

What can be said of St John Mary Vianney whom we shall commemorate on 4 August? It was precisely to commemorate the 150th anniversary of his death that I announced the Year for Priests. I promise to speak again of this humble parish priest who constitutes a model of priestly life not only for parish priests but for all priests at the Catechesis of the General Audience next Wednesday. Then on 7 August it will be the Memorial of St Cajetan da Thiene, who used to like to say: "it is not with sentimental love but rather with loving actions that souls are purified". And the following day, 8 August, the Church will point out as a model St Dominic, of whom it has been written that he only "opened his mouth either to speak to God in prayer or to speak of God". Lastly, I cannot forget to mention the great figure of Pope Montini, Paul VI, the 31st anniversary of whose death, here in Castel Gandolfo, occurs on 6 August. His life, so profoundly priestly and so rich in humanity, continues to be a gift to the Church for which we thank God. May the Virgin Mary, Mother of the Church, help priests to be totally in love with Christ, after the example of these models of priestly holiness.

GENERAL AUDIENCE

Papal Summer Residence,
Castel Gandolfo
Wednesday, 5 August 2009

St John Mary Vianney, the Curé d'Ars

In today's Catechesis I would like briefly to review the life of the Holy Curé of Ars. I shall stress several features that can also serve as an example for priests in our day, different of course from the time in which he lived, yet marked in many ways by the same fundamental human and spiritual challenges. Precisely yesterday was the 150th anniversary of his birth in Heaven. Indeed it was at two o'clock in the morning on 4 August 1859 that St John Baptist Mary Vianney, having come to the end of his earthly life, went to meet the heavenly Father to inherit the Kingdom, prepared since the world's creation for those who faithfully follow his teachings (cf. Mt 25:34). What great festivities there must have been in Heaven at the entry of such a zealous pastor! What a welcome he must have been given by the multitude of sons and daughters reconciled with the Father through his work as parish priest and confessor! I wanted to use this anniversary as an inspiration to inaugurate the Year for Priests, whose theme, as is well known, is "Faithfulness of Christ, Faithfulness of Priests". The credibility of witness depends on holiness and, once and for all, on the actual effectiveness of the mission of every priest.

John Mary Vianney was born into a peasant family in the small town of Dardilly on 8 May 1786. His family was poor in material possessions but rich in humanity and in faith. Baptized on the day of his birth, as was the good custom in those days, he spent so many years of his childhood and adolescence working in the fields and tending the flocks that at the age of seventeen he was still illiterate.

Nonetheless he knew by heart the prayers his devout mother had taught him and was nourished by the sense of religion in the atmosphere he breathed at home. His biographers say that since his earthly youth he sought to conform himself to God's will, even in the humblest offices. He pondered on his desire to become a priest but it was far from easy for him to achieve it. Indeed, he arrived at priestly ordination only after many ordeals and misunderstandings, with the help of far-sighted priests who did not stop at considering his human limitations but looked beyond them and glimpsed the horizon of holiness that shone out in that truly unusual young man. So it was that on 23 June 1815 he was ordained a deacon and on the following 13 August, he was ordained a priest. At last, at the age of 29, after numerous uncertainties, quite a few failures and many tears, he was able to walk up to the Lord's altar and make the dream of his life come true.

The Holy Curé of Ars always expressed the highest esteem for the gift he had received. He would say: "Oh! How great is the Priesthood! It can be properly understood only in Heaven... if one were to understand it on this earth one would die, not of fright but of love!" (Abbé Monnin, *Esprit du Curé d'Ars,* p. 113). Moreover, as a little boy he had confided to his mother: "If I were to become a priest, I would like to win many souls" (Abbé Monnin, *Procès de l'ordinaire,* p. 1064). And so he did. Indeed, in his pastoral service, as simple as it was extraordinarily fertile, this unknown parish priest of a forgotten village in the south of France was so successful in identifying with his ministry that he became, even in a visibly and universally recognizable manner, an *alter Christus,* an image of the Good Shepherd who, unlike the hired hand, lays down his life for his sheep (cf. Jn 10:11). After the example of the Good Shepherd, he gave his life in the decades of his priestly service. His existence was a living catechesis that acquired a very special effectiveness when people saw him celebrating Mass, pausing before the tabernacle in adoration or spending hour after hour in the confessional.

Therefore the centre of his entire life was the Eucharist, which he celebrated and adored with devotion and respect. Another fundamental characteristic of this extraordinary priestly figure was his diligent ministry of confession. He recognized in the practice of the sacrament of penance the logical and natural fulfilment of the priestly apostolate, in obedience to Christ's mandate: "if you forgive the sins of any, they are forgiven; if you retain the sins of any, they are retained" (cf. Jn 20:23). St John Mary Vianney thus distinguished himself as an excellent, tireless confessor and spiritual director. Passing "with a single inner impulse from the altar to the confessional", where he spent a large part of the day, he did his utmost with preaching and persuasive advice to help his parishioners rediscover the meaning and beauty of the sacrament of Penance, presenting it as an inherent demand of the Eucharistic presence (cf. *Letter to Priests for the inauguration of the Year for Priests*).

The pastoral methods of St John Mary Vianney might hardly appear suited to the social and cultural conditions of the present day. Indeed, how could a priest today imitate him in a world so radically changed? Although it is true that times change and many charisms are characteristic of the person, hence unrepeatable, there is nevertheless a lifestyle and a basic desire that we are all called to cultivate. At a close look, what made the Curé of Ars holy was his humble faithfulness to the mission to which God had called him; it was his constant abandonment, full of trust, to the hands of divine Providence. It was not by virtue of his own human gifts that he succeeded in moving peoples' hearts nor even by relying on a praiseworthy commitment of his will; he won over even the most refractory souls by communicating to them what he himself lived deeply, namely, his friendship with Christ. He was "in love" with Christ and the true secret of his pastoral success was the fervour of his love for the Eucharistic Mystery, celebrated and lived, which became love for Christ's flock, for Christians and for all who were seeking God. His testimony reminds us, dear brothers and sisters, that for every baptized person and especially for every priest the Eucharist is not merely an event with two protagonists, a dialogue between God and me. Eucharistic Communion aspires to a total transformation of one's life and forcefully flings open the whole human "I" of man and creates a new "we" (cf. Joseph Ratzinger, *La Comunione nella Chiesa,* p. 80).

Thus, far from reducing the figure of St John Mary Vianney to an example albeit an admirable one of eighteenth-century devotional spirituality, on the contrary one should understand the prophetic power that marked his human and priestly personality that is extremely timely. In post-revolutionary France which was experiencing a sort of "dictatorship of rationalism" that aimed at obliterating from society the very existence of priests and of the Church, he lived first in the years of his youth a heroic secrecy, walking kilometres at night to attend Holy Mass. Then later as a priest Vianney distinguished himself by an unusual and fruitful pastoral creativity, geared to showing that the then prevalent rationalism was in fact far from satisfying authentic human needs, hence definitively unliveable.

Dear brothers and sisters, 150 years after the death of the Holy Curé of Ars, contemporary society is facing challenges that are just as demanding and may have become even more complex. If in his time the "dictatorship of rationalism" existed, in the current epoch a sort of "dictatorship of relativism" is evident in many contexts. Both seem inadequate responses to the human being's justifiable request to use his reason as a distinctive and constitutive element of his own identity. Rationalism was inadequate because it failed to take into account human limitations and claims to make reason alone the criterion of all things, transforming it into a goddess; contemporary relativism humiliates reason because it arrives de facto at affirming that the human being can know nothing with certainty outside the positive scientific field. Today however, as in that time, man, "a beggar for meaning and fulfilment", is constantly in quest of exhaustive answers to the basic questions that he never ceases to ask himself.

The Fathers of the Second Vatican Council had very clearly in mind this "thirst for the truth" that burns in every human heart when they said that it is the task of priests "as instructors of the people in the faith" to see to the "formation of a genuine Christian community", that can "smooth the path to Christ for all men" and exercise "a truly motherly function" for them, "showing or smoothing the path towards Christ and his Church" for non-believers and for believers, while also "encouraging, supporting and strengthening believers for their spiritual struggles" (cf. *Presbyterorum Ordinis,* n. 6).

The teaching which in this regard the Holy Curé of Ars continues to pass on to us is that the priest must create an intimate personal union with Christ that he must cultivate and increase, day after day. Only if he is in love with Christ will the priest be able to teach his union, this intimate friendship with the divine Teacher to all, and be able to move people's hearts and open them to the Lord's merciful love. Only in this way, consequently, will he be able to instil enthusiasm and spiritual vitality in the communities the Lord entrusts to him. Let us pray that through the intercession of St John Mary Vianney, God will give holy priests to his Church and will increase in the faithful the desire to sustain and help them in their ministry. Let us entrust this intention to Mary, whom on this very day we invoke as Our Lady of the Snow.

ANGELUS

Charity which loves "to the end".

Like last Sunday, today too in the context of the Year for Priests that we are celebrating we shall pause to meditate on some of the men and women Saints that the liturgy commemorates in these days. Except for the Virgin Clare of Assisi, who was consumed with divine love in her daily sacrifice of prayer and community life, the others are martyrs, two of whom were killed in the concentration camp at Auschwitz: St Teresa Benedicta of the Cross, Edith Stein, who, born into the Jewish faith and won over by Christ as an adult, became a Carmelite nun and sealed her existence with martyrdom; and St Maximilian Kolbe, a son of Poland and of St Francis of Assisi, a great apostle of Mary Immaculate. We shall then encounter other splendid figures, martyrs of the Church of Rome, such as Pope St Pontianus, St Hippolytus, a priest, and St Lawrence the Deacon. What marvellous models of holiness the Church presents to us! These saints are witnesses of that charity which loves "to the end", which does not take into account a wrong suffered but instead combats it with good (cf. 1 Cor 13:4-8). From them we can learn especially we priests the evangelical heroism that impels us to give our life fearlessly for the salvation of souls. Love triumphs over death!

All the saints, but especially martyrs, are witnesses of God, who is Love: *Deus Caritas est.* The Nazi concentration camps, like all extermination camps, can be considered extreme symbols of evil, of hell that opens on earth when man forgets God and supplants him, usurping his right to decide what is good and what is evil, to give life and death. However, this sad phenomenon is unfortunately not limited to concentration camps. Rather, they are the culmination of an extensive and widespread reality, often with shifting boundaries. The Saints whom I have briefly recalled lead us to reflect on the profound divergences that exist between atheistic humanism and Christian humanism. This antithesis permeates the whole of history but with the contemporary nihilism, at the end of the second millennium, it has reached a crucial point, as great literary figures and thinkers have perceived and as events have amply demonstrated. On the one hand, there are philosophies and ideologies, but there are also always more ways of thinking and acting that exalt freedom as the unique principle of the human being, as an alternative to God, and which in this way transform the human being into a god, but an erroneous god who makes arbitrariness his own system of behaviour. On the other hand, we have the Saints who, in practising the Gospel of charity, account for their hope. They show the true Face of God who is Love and, at the same time, the authentic face of man, created in the divine image and likeness.

Dear brothers and sisters, let us pray the Virgin Mary to help all of us and in the first place priests to be holy like these heroic witnesses of faith and of self-dedication to the point of martyrdom. And charity in truth is the only credible and exhaustive response one can offer to the profound human and spiritual crisis of the contemporary world.

GENERAL AUDIENCE

Papal Summer Residence,
Castel Gandolfo
Wednesday, 12 August 2009

The Blessed Virgin Mary and the priesthood

The celebration of the Solemnity of the Assumption of the Blessed Virgin Mary, next Saturday, is at hand and we are in the context of the Year for Priest. I therefore wish to speak of the link between Our Lady and the priesthood. This connection is deeply rooted in the Mystery of the Incarnation. When God decided to become man in his Son, he needed the freely-spoken "yes" of one of his creatures. God does not act against our freedom. And something truly extraordinary happens: God makes himself dependent on the free decision, the "yes" of one of his creatures; he waits for this "yes". St Bernard of Clairvaux explained dramatically in one of his homilies this crucial moment in universal history when Heaven, earth and God himself wait for what this creature will say.

Mary's "yes" is therefore the door through which God was able to enter the world, to become man. So it is that Mary is truly and profoundly involved in the Mystery of the Incarnation, of our salvation. And the Incarnation, the Son's becoming man, was the beginning that prepared the ground for the gift of himself; for giving himself with great love on the Cross to become Bread for the life of the world. Hence sacrifice, priesthood and Incarnation go together and Mary is at the heart of this mystery.

Let us now go to the Cross. Before dying, Jesus sees his Mother beneath the Cross and he sees the beloved son. This beloved son is certainly a person, a very important individual, but he is more; he is an example, a prefiguration of all beloved disciples, of all the people called by the Lord to be the "beloved disciple" and thus also particularly of priests. Jesus says to Mary: "Woman, behold, your son!" (Jn 19:26). It is a sort of testament: he entrusts his Mother to the care of the son, of the disciple. But he also says to the disciple: "Behold, your mother!" (Jn 19:27). The Gospel tells us that from that hour St John, the beloved son, took his mother Mary "to his own home". This is what it says in the [English] translation; but the Greek text is far deeper, far richer. We could translate it: he took Mary into his inner life, his inner being, "*eis tà ìdia*", into the depths of his being. To take Mary with one means to introduce her into the dynamism of one's own entire existence it is not something external and into all that constitutes the horizon of one's own apostolate. It seems to me that one can, therefore, understand how the special relationship of motherhood that exists between Mary and priests may constitute the primary source, the fundamental reason for her special love for each one of them. In fact, Mary loves them with predilection for two reasons: because they are more like Jesus, the supreme love of her heart, and because, like her, they are committed to the mission of proclaiming, bearing witness to and giving Christ to the world. Because of his identification with and sacramental conformation to Jesus, Son of God and Son of Mary, every priest can and must feel that he really is a specially beloved son of this loftiest and humblest of Mothers.

The Second Vatican Council invites priests to look to Mary as to the perfect model for their existence, invoking her as "Mother of the supreme and eternal Priest, as Queen of Apostles, and as Protectress of their ministry". The Council continues, "priests should always venerate and love her, with a filial devotion and worship" (cf. *Presbyterorum Ordinis,* n. 18). The Holy Curé d'Ars, whom we are remembering in particular in this Year, used to like to say: "Jesus Christ, after giving us all that he could give us, wanted further to make us heirs to his most precious possession, that is, his Holy Mother (B. Nodet, *Il pensiero e l'anima del Curato d'Ars,* Turin 1967, p. 305). This applies for every Christian, for all of us, but in a special way for priests. Dear brothers and sisters, let us pray that Mary will make all priests, in all the problems of today's world, conform with the image of her Son Jesus, as stewards of the precious treasure of his love as the Good Shepherd. Mary, Mother of priests, pray for us!

SOLEMNITY OF THE ASSUMPTION OF THE BLESSED VIRGIN MARY

ANGELUS

Courtyard of the Papal Summer Residence,
Castel Gandolfo
Saturday, 15 August 2009

'Man was created for Heaven.'

In the heart of the month of August, a holiday period for many families and also for me, the Church celebrates the Solemnity of the Assumption of the Blessed Virgin. This is a privileged opportunity to meditate on the ultimate meaning of our existence, helped by today's Liturgy which invites us to live in this world oriented to eternal happiness in order to share in the same glory as Mary, the same joy as our Mother (cf. Opening Prayer). Let us, therefore, turn our gaze to Our Lady, Star of Hope, who illumines us on our earthly journey, and follow the example of the Saints who turned to her in every circumstance. You know that we are celebrating the Year for Priests in remembrance of the Holy Curé d'Ars, and I would like to draw from the thoughts and testimonies of this holy country parish priest some ideas for reflection that will be able to help all of us especially us priests to strengthen our love and veneration for the Most Holy Virgin.

His biographers claim that St John Mary Vianney spoke to Our Lady with devotion and, at the same time, with trust and spontaneity. "The Blessed Virgin", he used to say, "is immaculate and adorned with all the virtues that make her so beautiful and pleasing to the Blessed Trinity" (B. Nodet, *Il pensiero e l'anima del Curato d'Ars*, Turin 1967, p. 303). And further: "The heart of this good Mother is nothing but love and mercy, all she wants is to see us happy. To be heard, it suffices to address oneself to her" (ibid., p. 307). The priest's zeal shines through these words. Motivated by apostolic longing, he rejoiced in speaking to his faithful of Mary and never tired of doing so. He could even present a difficult mystery like today's, that of the Assumption, with effective images, such as, for example: "Man was created for Heaven. The devil broke the ladder that led to it. Our Lord, with his Passion, made another.... The Virgin Most Holy stands at the top of the ladder and holds it steady with both hands" (ibid.).

The Holy Curé d'Ars was attracted above all by Mary's beauty, a beauty that coincides with her being Immaculate, the only creature to have been conceived without a shadow of sin. "The Blessed Virgin", he said, "is that beautiful Creature who never displeased the good Lord" (ibid. p. 306). As a good and faithful pastor, he first of all set an example also in this filial love for the Mother of Jesus by whom he felt drawn toward Heaven. "Were I not to go to Heaven", he exclaimed, "how sorry I should be! I should never see the Blessed Virgin, this most beautiful creature!" (ibid., p. 309). Moreover, on several occasions he consecrated his parish to Our Lady, recommending that mothers in particular do the same, every morning, with their children. Dear brothers and sisters, let us make our own the sentiments of the Holy Curé d'Ars. And with his same faith let us turn to Mary, taken up into Heaven, in a special way entrusting to her the priests of the whole world.

GENERAL AUDIENCE

Wednesday, 19 August 2009

Saint John Eudes

Today is the liturgical Memorial of St John Eudes, a tireless apostle of the devotion to the Sacred Hearts of Jesus and Mary who lived in France in the seventeenth century that was marked by opposing religious phenomena and serious political problems. It was the time of the Thirty Years' War, which devastated not only a large part of Central Europe but also souls. While contempt for the Christian faith was being spread by certain currents of thought which then prevailed, the Holy Spirit was inspiring a spiritual renewal full of fervour with important figures such as de Bérulle, St Vincent de Paul, St Louis-Marie Grignon de Montfort and St John Eudes. This great "French school" of holiness also included St John Mary Vianney. Through a mysterious design of Providence, my venerable Predecessor Pius XI canonized John Eudes and the Curé d'Ars together, on 31 May 1925, holding up to the whole world two extraordinary examples of priestly holiness.

In the context of the Year for Priests, I want to dwell on the apostolic zeal of St John Eudes, which he focused in particular on the formation of the diocesan clergy. The saints are true interpreters of Sacred Scripture. In the experience of their lives the saints have verified the truth of the Gospel; thus they introduce us into a knowledge and understanding of the Gospel. In 1563 the Council of Trent issued norms for the establishment of diocesan seminaries and for the formation of priests, since the Council was well aware that the whole crisis of the Reformation was also conditioned by the inadequate formation of priests who were not properly prepared for the priesthood either intellectually or spiritually, in their hearts or in their minds. This was in 1563; but since the application and realization of the norms was delayed both in Germany and in France, St John Eudes saw the consequences of this omission. Prompted by a lucid awareness of the grave need for spiritual assistance in which souls lay because of the inadequacy of the majority of the clergy, the Saint, who was a parish priest, founded a congregation specifically dedicated to the formation of priests. He founded his first seminary in the university town of Caen, a particularly appreciated experience which he very soon extended to other dioceses. The path of holiness, which he took himself and proposed to his followers, was founded on steadfast trust in the love that God had revealed to humanity in the priestly Heart of Christ and in the maternal Heart of Mary. In those times of cruelty, of the loss of interiority, he turned to the heart to speak to the heart, a saying of the Psalms very well interpreted by St Augustine. He wanted to recall people, men and women and especially future priests, to the heart by showing them the priestly Heart of Christ and the motherly Heart of Mary. Every priest must be a witness and an apostle of this love for Christ's Heart and Mary's Heart. And here we come to our own time.

Today too people feel in need of priests who witness to God's infinite mercy with a life totally "conquered" by Christ and who learn to do this in the years of their seminary training. After the Synod in 1990 Pope John Paul II published the Apostolic Exhortation *Pastores Dabo Vobis* in which he returned to and updated the norms of the Council of Trent and stressed above all the necessary continuity between the priest's initial and continuing formation. For him this is a true starting point for an authentic reform of the life and apostolate of priests. It is also the key to preventing the "new evangelization" from being merely an attractive slogan and to ensuring that it is expressed in reality. The foundations laid in seminary formation constitute that indispensable "*humus spirituale*" in which "to learn Christ", letting oneself be gradually configured to him, the one and only High Priest and Good Shepherd. The seminary period should therefore be seen as the actualization of the moment when the

Lord Jesus, after calling the Apostles and before sending them out to preach, asks them to be with him (cf. Mk 3:14). When St Mark recounts the calling of the Twelve Apostles he says that Jesus had a twofold purpose: firstly that they should be with him, and secondly, that they should be sent out to preach. Yet, in being with him always, they really proclaim Christ and bring the reality of the Gospel to the world.

During this Year for Priests I ask you, dear brothers and sisters, to pray for priests and for all those who are preparing to receive the extraordinary gift of the ministerial priesthood. I address to you all and thus I conclude the exhortation of St John Eudes who said to priests: "Give yourselves to Jesus in order to enter the immensity of his great Heart which contains the Heart of his Holy Mother and the hearts of all the Saints and lose yourselves in this abyss of love, charity, mercy, humility, purity, patience, submission and holiness" (*Coeur admirable,* III, 2).

VIDEO MESSAGE
TO PARTICIPANTS IN
THE INTERNATIONAL RETREAT
FOR PRIESTS

Ars, 27 September – 3 October 2009

"The joy of priesthood: consecrated for the salvation of the world."

As you can easily imagine, I would have been extremely happy to be with you on this international retreat for priests on the theme: "The joy of priesthood: consecrated for the salvation of the world". A large number of you are taking part and you have the benefit of Cardinal Christoph Schönborn's teaching. I greet him cordially together with the other preachers and Bishop Guy-Marie Bagnard of Belley-Ars. I must be content with addressing this recorded message to you, but please believe that through these words I am speaking to each one of you in the most personal way possible because, as St Paul says: "I hold you in my heart, for you are all partakers with me of grace" (Phil 1:7).

St John Mary Vianney emphasized the indispensable role of the priest when he said: "A good pastor, a pastor according to the heart of God, is the greatest treasure that the good Lord can give to a parish and one of the most precious gifts of divine mercy" (*Le Curé d'Ars, Pensées,* presented by Abbé Bernard Nodet, Desclée de Brouwer, Foi Vivante, 2000, p. 101). In this *Year for Priests* we are all called to explore and to rediscover the greatness of the sacrament which has configured us for ever to Christ the High Priest and has "consecrated" us all "in truth" (Jn 17:19).

Chosen from among men, the priest continues to be one of them and is called to serve them by giving them the life of God.

151

It is he who "continues the work of redemption on earth" (Nodet, p. 98). Our priestly vocation is a treasure that we bear in earthen vessels (cf. 2 Cor 4:7). St Paul expressed with happiness the infinite distance that exists between our vocation and the poverty of the responses we can give to God. From this point of view, a secret bond unites the Pauline Year with the Year for Priests. Let us keep present in our ears and in the depths of our hearts the moving and trusting exclamation of the Apostle who said: "When I am weak, then I am strong" (2 Cor 12:10). Awareness of this weakness opens us to intimacy with God who gives us strength and joy. The more the priest perseveres in friendship with God, the more he will continue the Redeemer's work on this earth (cf. Nodet, p. 98). The priest does not exist for himself, he exists for everyone (cf. Nodet, p. 100).

That is precisely where one of the greatest challenges of our time lies. Indeed, today more than ever the priest, a man of the divine word and of the sacred, must be a man of joy and hope. To people who can no longer conceive that God is pure Love, he will always affirm that life is worth living and that Christ gives it its full meaning because he loves human beings, he loves them all. The religion of the Curé d'Ars is a religion of joy, not a morbid quest for mortification as has sometimes been believed: "Our happiness is too great; no, no, we shall never understand it" (Nodet, p. 110), he would say, and further: "when we are travelling and see a bell-tower, this view should quicken our heart beat, just as the sight of the roof of her beloved's dwelling place quickens the bride's heart beat" (*ibid.*). Here I would like to greet with very special affection all those of you who have pastoral responsibility for several bell-towers and spend yourselves without counting the cost to keep up the sacramental life in your respective communities. The Church is immensely grateful to you all! Do not lose heart but continue to pray and to have prayers said that numerous young men will be ready to respond to the call of Christ who never stops wanting to increase the number of his apostles to reap the harvest in his fields.

Dear priests, think too of the extreme diversity of the ministries you exercise in the service of the Church. Think of the great number of Masses you have celebrated or will celebrate, making Christ really present on the altar each time. Think of the innumerable absolutions you have given and will give, enabling a sinner to be forgiven. Then you perceive the infinite fruitfulness of the sacrament of Orders. In the space of a moment your hands, your lips became the hands and lips of God. You bear Christ within you; through grace, you have entered the Holy Trinity. Just as the saintly Curé said: "if we had faith, we would see God hidden in the priest like a light behind glass or like wine mixed with water" (Nodet, p. 97). This consideration should lead to harmonizing relations between priests so as to create a priestly community, as St Peter exhorted (cf. 1 Pet 2:9), in order to build up the body of Christ and build up yourselves in love (cf. Eph 4:11-16).

The priest is the man of the future: it is he who has taken seriously Paul's words: "If then you have been raised with Christ, seek the things that are above" (Col 3:1). What he does on earth is in the order of the means ordered to the last things. The Mass is this one point of union between the means and the End because it already enables us to contemplate, under the humble appearances of bread and wine, the Body and Blood of the One we shall adore for eternity. The holy Curé's simple, concentrated sentences on the Eucharist help us perceive more clearly the riches of this unique moment in the day when we experience an encounter that is life-giving for ourselves and for each one of the faithful. "The happiness that exists in saying Mass", he wrote, "will only be properly understood in Heaven" (Nodet, page 104).

I therefore encourage you to strengthen your faith and that of your faithful in the sacrament you celebrate, which is the source of true joy. The Saint of Ars wrote: "The priest must feel the same joy (as the Apostles) in seeing Our Lord whom he holds in his hands" (*ibid.*). In giving thanks for what you are and for what you do, I repeat to you: "Nothing will ever replace the ministry of priests at the heart of the Church" (*Homily, Mass on the Esplanade des Invalides,* Paris, 13 September 2008). Living witnesses of the power of God at work in human weakness, consecrated for the salvation of the world, you remain, my dear brothers, chosen by Christ himself in order to be, through him, salt of the earth and light of the world. At this spiritual retreat may you have a profound experience of the "inexpressible closeness" (St Augustine, *Les Confessions,* III, 6, 11 BA 13, p. 383) in order to be perfectly united to Christ so as to proclaim his Love around you and to be wholly committed to the service of the sanctification of all the members of the People of God. As I entrust you to the Virgin Mary, Mother of Christ and of priests, I impart my Apostolic Blessing to you all.

GENERAL AUDIENCE

Saint Peter's Square
Wednesday, 7 October 2009

St John Leonardi

The day after tomorrow, 9 October, will be the 400th anniversary of the death of St John Leonardi, Founder of the religious order of Clerics Regular of the Mother of God. He was canonized on 17 April 1938 and chosen as Patron of Pharmacists on 8 August 2006. He is also remembered for his great missionary zeal. Together with Mons. Juan Bautista Vives and Martín de Funes, a Jesuit, he planned and contributed to founding a specific Congregation of the Holy See for the missions, *Propaganda Fide,* which has forged thousands of priests down the centuries, many of them martyrs. Thus he was a luminous priestly figure whom I like to point out as an example to all presbyters in this Year for Priests. He died in 1609 from influenza, contracted while he was doing all he could to minister to those stricken by the epidemic in the Campitelli neighbourhood of Rome.

John Leonardi was born in 1541 at Diecimo in the Province of Lucca. The youngest of seven siblings, his adolescence was marked by the rhythm of faith lived in a healthy, hard-working family, as well as by regular visits to a workshop in his home town that made and sold essences and medicines. When John was 17, his father enrolled him in an ordinary apothecary's course in Lucca, aiming to make him a future pharmacist, indeed an apothecary, as it was then termed. For about 10 years young John attended this course, alert and hardworking, but when, in accordance with the legislation of the ancient Republic of Lucca he earned the official recognition that would authorize him to open his own apothecary's shop, he started wondering whether the moment had not come to carry out a plan he had always had at heart. After mature reflection he decided to train for the priesthood. Thus, having left the apothecary's shop and having acquired an adequate theological formation, he was ordained a priest and, on the day of Epiphany 1572, celebrated his first Mass. However, he never lost his interest in medicine, because he felt that the professional mediation of the pharmacist would permit him to fulfil his vocation to the full, one in which he could pass on to men and women, by means of a holy life, "*the medicine of God*", which is the Crucified and Risen Jesus Christ, the "measure of all things".

Inspired by the conviction that all human beings need this medicine more than anything else, St John Leonardi sought to make the personal encounter with Jesus Christ his fundamental *raison d'être*. "It is necessary to start afresh from Christ", he liked to repeat again and again. The primacy of Christ over all things became for him the concrete criterion of judgement and action and the vital principle of his priestly activity, which he exercised while a vast and widespread movement of spiritual renewal was taking place in the Church, thanks to the flourishing of new religious institutes and the luminous witness of Saints such as Charles Borromeo, Philip Neri, Ignatius of Loyola, Joseph Calasanctius, Camillus de Lellis and Aloysius Gonazaga. He dedicated himself enthusiastically to the apostolate among boys through the Confraternity of Christian Doctrine, gathering around him a group of young men with whom, on 1 September 1574, he founded the Congregation of Reformed Priests of the Blessed Virgin, later called the Order of Clerics Regular of the Mother of God. He recommended his disciples to keep "before their eyes and minds only the honour, service and glory of Jesus Christ Crucified", and, as a good pharmacist used to administering doses, he added using a precise reference: "lift up your hearts a little higher to God and with him measure all things".

Motivated by apostolic zeal, in May 1605 he sent Pope Paul V, who had just been elected, a *Petition* in which he suggested the criteria for an authentic renewal of the Church. Observing that it is "necessary for those who aspire to the reform of human morals to seek especially and above all things, the glory of God", he added that they must shine out "for their integrity of life and the excellence of their morals so that, rather than constraining people, they gently draw them to reform".

He remarked that "any one who wishes to carry out a serious religious and moral reform must first of all, like a good doctor, make an attentive diagnosis of the evils besetting the Church, thereby to be able to prescribe the most appropriate remedy for each one of them". And he noted that "likewise the renewal of the Church must be brought about in her leaders and in their subordinates, both above and below. It must be started by those in charge and extended to their subjects". For this reason, while asking the Pope to promote a "universal reform of the Church", he concerned himself with the Christian formation of the people and especially of children, to be educated "from their earliest years... in the purity of Christian faith and holy morals".

Dear brothers and sisters, the luminous figure of this Saint invites priests in the first place, and all Christians, to strive constantly for "the high standard of Christian living", which means holiness, naturally each one in accordance with his own state. Indeed, authentic ecclesial renewal can only stem from faithfulness to Christ. In those years, on the cultural and social threshold between the 16th and 17th centuries, the premises of the contemporary culture of the future began to be outlined. It was characterized by an undue separation between faith and reason that produced, among its negative effects, the marginalization of God, with the illusion of the possible and total autonomy of man who chooses to live "as though God did not exist". This is the crisis of modern thought, which I have frequently had the opportunity to point out and which often leads to forms of relativism. John Leonardi perceived what the real medicine for these spiritual evils was and summed it up in the expression: "Christ first of all", Christ at the centre of the heart, at the centre of history and of the cosmos. And, St John said forcefully, humanity stands in extreme need of Christ because he is our "measure". There is no area that cannot be touched by his power; there is no evil that cannot find a remedy in him, no problem that is not resolved in him. "Either Christ or nothing!". This was his recipe for every type of spiritual and social reform.

There is another aspect of St John Leonardi's spirituality that I would like to emphasize. On various occasions he reasserted that the living encounter with Christ takes place in his Church, holy but frail, rooted in history and in its sometimes obscure unfolding, where wheat and weeds grow side by side (cf. Mt 13:30), yet always the sacrament of salvation. Since he was clearly aware that the Church is God's field (cf. Mt 13:24), St John was not shocked at her human weaknesses. To combat the weeds he chose to be good wheat: that is, he decided to love Christ in the Church and to help make her, more and more, a transparent sign of Christ. He saw the Church very realistically, her human frailty, but he also saw her as being "God's field", the instrument of God for humanity's salvation. And this was not all. Out of love for Christ he worked tirelessly to purify the Church, to make her more beautiful and holy. He realized that every reform should be made within the Church and never against the Church. In this, St John Leonardi was truly extraordinary and his example is ever timely. Every reform, of course, concerns her structures, but in the first place must have an effect in believers' hearts. Only Saints, men and women who let themselves be guided by the divine Spirit, ready to make radical and courageous decisions in the light of the Gospel, renew the Church and make a crucial contribution to building a better world.

Dear brothers and sisters, St John Leonardi's life was illumined throughout by the splendour of the "Holy Face" of Jesus, preserved and venerated in the Cathedral Church of Lucca, which has become an eloquent symbol and an indisputable synthesis of the faith that enlivened him.

Conquered by Christ, like the Apostle Paul, he pointed out to his followers and continues to point out to all of us, the Christocentric ideal for which "it is necessary to strip oneself of every personal interest and look only to the service of God", keeping "before the eyes of the mind only the honour, service and glory of Jesus Christ Crucified". Besides the Face of Christ, St John fixed his gaze on the motherly face of Mary. The One whom he chose to be Patroness of his Order was for him a teacher, sister and mother, and he experienced her constant protection. May the example and intercession of this "fascinating man of God" be a reference and an encouragement, particularly in this Year for Priests, for priests and for all Christians to live their own vocation with passionate enthusiasm.

From the

ADDRESS
OF HIS HOLINESS BENEDICT XVI
TO THE MEMBERS OF THE
ROMAN CURIA AND
PAPAL REPRESENTATIVES FOR
THE TRADITIONAL EXCHANGE
OF CHRISTMAS GREETINGS

Clementine Hall
Monday, 21 December 2009

'The grandeur of small things.'

Another year full of important events for the Church and for the world is drawing to a close. As I look back upon this year with great gratitude, I would like at this moment to mention just a few key points for the life of the Church. From the Pauline Year we have moved on to the Year for Priests. From the impressive figure of the Apostle to the Gentiles who, struck by the light of the Risen Christ and by his call, took the Gospel to the peoples of the world, we have passed to the humble Curé of Ars, who spent his whole life in the little village that had been entrusted to him and yet, precisely in the humility of his service, made God's reconciling goodness visible throughout the world. Starting with these two figures we can see the great breadth of the priestly ministry, the grandeur of small things, and how, through the seemingly insignificant service of one individual, God can achieve great things, purifying and renewing the world from within...

Finally, once again, a word about the Year for Priests. As priests we are available to all: to those who know God at first hand and to those for whom he is the Unknown. We all need to become acquainted with him ever anew, and we need to seek him constantly in order to become true friends of God. How, in the end, can we get to know God other than through those people who are friends of God? The inmost core of our priestly ministry consists of our being Christ's friends (cf. Jn 15:15), friends of God through whom others may also discover God's closeness.

CONFERRAL OF HONORARY CITIZENSHIP OF FREISING – FEDERAL REPUBLIC OF GERMANY

From the

ADDRESS

Clementine Hall
Saturday, 16 January 2010

In my life biography, in the biography of my heart, if I may, the City of Freising has played a very special role. In this City I received the formation that has marked my life ever since. Thus, in a certain way, Freising is always present in me and I in it. And as you noted, Mr Mayor, the inclusion in my coat-of-arms of the Moor and Bear of Freising shows the whole world how closely I belong to it. Then the fact that I am also now legally a citizen of Freising, is the crowning point and I am profoundly glad.

On this occasion a whole horizon of images and memories wells up within me. You have mentioned some of them, dear Mr Mayor. I would like to take up certain points. To start with there is 3 January 1946. After a long wait, the time came at last when the Seminary of Freising could open its doors to all who were returning home. Indeed, it was still a hospital for former prisoners-of-war, but we were then able to begin. That moment marked a turning point in our lives: being on the path to which we felt called. In today's context we lived in a very "old-fashioned" way without comforts. We were in dormitories, study halls and so forth, but we were happy and not only because we had at last escaped the wretchedness and threats of war and Nazi domination, but also because we were free and,

162

especially, because we had set out on the path to which we felt called. We knew that Christ was stronger than the tyranny, than the power of the Nazi ideology and its mechanisms of oppression. We knew that time and the future belong to Christ and we knew that he had called us and that he needed us, that there was a need for us. We knew that the people of those changed times were waiting for us, they were waiting for priests to arrive with a new impetus of faith to build the house of the living God. On this occasion I must also raise a small hymn of praise to the old athenaeum to which I belonged, first as a student and then as a teacher. Some were very erudite, and some were even known internationally, but what, to my mind, was most important was that they were not only scholars but also teachers, people who not only offered the first-fruits of their specialization but were concerned to give the students the essential, the healthy bread they needed in order to receive faith from within. And it was important that we, if I may now say we, did not feel like individual experts but rather that we were part of a whole, that each one of us was working for theology as a whole; that our work had to make visible the logic of faith as unity and thereby increase our ability to account for our faith, as St Peter said (cf. 1 Pet 3:15), so as to pass it on in a new epoch with new challenges.

The second image that I would like to mention is the day of my ordination to the priesthood. The Cathedral was always the centre of our life, just as at the seminary where we were one family. And it was Fr Höck who made us a real family. The Cathedral was the centre of it and for our entire life represented the unforgettable day of our priestly ordination. Three moments are particularly deeply impressed within me. First of all, lying stretched out on the ground during the litany of the saints. In lying prostrate on the ground, one becomes newly aware of all one's poverty and asks oneself: am I truly capable of it? And at the same time the names of all the saints of history and the entreaty of the faithful ring out: "Hear us; help them". In this way the awareness grows that, yes, I am weak and inadequate but I am not alone, there are others with me, the entire community of the saints is with me. They accompany me and thus I can make this journey and become a companion and guide for others. The second moment, the imposition of hands by the elderly, venerable Cardinal Faulhaber who laid his hands upon me, upon all of us, in a profound and intense manner and the knowledge that it was the Lord who was laying his hands upon me and saying: "you belong to me, you do not simply belong to yourself, I want you, you are at my service"; but also the awareness that this imposition of hands is a grace, that it does not only create obligations, but above all is a gift, that he is with me and that his love protects and accompanies me. Then there was also the old rite in which the power to forgive sins was conferred at a separate moment. It began when the Bishop, pronouncing the Lord's words, said: "No longer do I call you servants... but... friends". And I knew we knew that this is not only a quotation from John 15 but a timely word that the Lord is addressing to me now. He accepts me as a friend; I am in this friendly relationship; he has given me his trust and I can work within this friendship and make others friends of Christ.

GENERAL AUDIENCE

Paul VI Audience Hall
Wednesday, 27 January 2010

St Francis of Assisi

It has been said that Francis represents an *alter Christus*, that he was truly a living icon of Christ. He has also been called "the brother of Jesus". Indeed, this was his ideal: to be like Jesus, to contemplate Christ in the Gospel, to love him intensely and to imitate his virtues. In particular, he wished to ascribe interior and exterior poverty with a fundamental value, which he also taught to his spiritual sons. The first Beatitude of the Sermon on the Mount "Blessed are the poor in spirit, for theirs is the kingdom of heaven" (Mt 5:3) found a luminous fulfilment in the life and words of St Francis. Truly, dear friends, the saints are the best interpreters of the Bible. As they incarnate the word of God in their own lives, they make it more captivating than ever, so that it really speaks to us. The witness of Francis, who loved poverty as a means to follow Christ with dedication and total freedom, continues to be for us too an invitation to cultivate interior poverty in order to grow in our trust of God, also by adopting a sober lifestyle and a detachment from material goods.

Francis' love for Christ expressed itself in a special way in the adoration of the Blessed Sacrament of the Eucharist. In the *Fonti Francescane* (Writings of St Francis) one reads such moving expressions as: "Let everyone be struck with fear, let the whole world tremble, and let the heavens exult, when Christ, the Son of the living God, is present on the altar in the hands of a priest. Oh stupendous dignity! O humble sublimity, that the Lord of the universe, God and the Son of God, so humbles himself that for our salvation he hides himself under an ordinary piece of bread" (Francis of Assisi, *Scritti*, Editrici Francescane, Padova 2002, 401).

In this Year for Priests, I would also like to recall a piece of advice that Francis gave to priests: "When you wish to celebrate Mass, in a pure way, reverently make the true sacrifice of the Most Holy Body and Blood of our Lord Jesus Christ" (Francis of Assisi, *Scritti*, 399). Francis always showed great deference towards priests, and asserted that they should always be treated with respect, even in cases where they might be somewhat unworthy personally. The reason he gave for this profound respect was that they receive the gift of consecrating the Eucharist. Dear brothers in the priesthood, let us never forget this teaching: the holiness of the Eucharist appeals to us to be pure, to live in a way that is consistent with the Mystery we celebrate.

ADDRESS
TO THE BISHOPS OF
THE EPISCOPAL CONFERENCE
OF ENGLAND AND WALES
ON THEIR "AD LIMINA" VISIT

Consistory Hall
Monday, 1st February 2010

John Henry Cardinal Newman

Much attention has rightly been given to Newman's scholarship and to his extensive writings, but it is important to remember that he saw himself first and foremost as a priest. In this *Annus Sacerdotalis*, I urge you to hold up to your priests his example of dedication to prayer, pastoral sensitivity towards the needs of his flock, and passion for preaching the Gospel. You yourselves should set a similar example. Be close to your priests, and rekindle their sense of the enormous privilege and joy of standing among the people of God as *alter Christus*. In Newman's words, "Christ's priests have no priesthood but His … what they do, He does; when they baptize, He is baptizing; when they bless, He is blessing" (*Parochial and Plain Sermons*, VI 242). Indeed, since the priest plays an irreplaceable role in the life of the Church, spare no effort in encouraging priestly vocations and emphasizing to the faithful the true meaning and necessity of the priesthood. Encourage the lay faithful to express their appreciation of the priests who serve them, and to recognize the difficulties they sometimes face on account of their declining numbers and increasing pressures. The support and understanding of the faithful is particularly necessary when parishes have to be merged or Mass times adjusted. Help them to avoid any temptation to view the clergy as mere functionaries but rather to rejoice in the gift of priestly ministry, a gift that can never be taken for granted.

From the

ADDRESS
TO THE BISHOPS OF
THE EPISCOPAL CONFERENCE
OF SCOTLAND ON THEIR
"AD LIMINA" VISIT

Friday, 5 February 2010

'Sanctify the world.'

It is a happy coincidence that the *Year for Priests*, which the whole Church is currently celebrating, marks the four hundredth anniversary of the priestly ordination of the great Scottish martyr St John Ogilvie. Rightly venerated as a faithful servant of the Gospel, he was truly outstanding in his dedication to a difficult and dangerous pastoral ministry, to the point of laying down his life. Hold him up as an example for your priests today. I am glad to know of the emphasis you place on continuing formation for your clergy, especially through the initiative "Priests for Scotland". The witness of priests who are genuinely committed to prayer and joyful in their ministry bears fruit not only in the spiritual lives of the faithful, but also in new vocations. Remember, though, that your commendable initiatives to promote vocations must be accompanied by sustained catechesis among the faithful about the true meaning of priesthood. Emphasize the indispensable role of the priest in the Church's life, above all in providing the Eucharist by which the Church herself receives life. And encourage those entrusted with the formation of seminarians to do all they can to prepare a new generation of committed and zealous priests, well equipped humanly, academically and spiritually for the task of ministry in the twenty-first century.

Hand in hand with a proper appreciation of the priest's role is a correct understanding of the specific vocation of the laity. Sometimes a tendency to confuse *lay apostolate* with *lay ministry* has led to an inward-looking concept of their ecclesial role. Yet the Second Vatican Council's vision is that wherever the lay faithful live out their baptismal vocation – in the family, at home, at work – they are actively participating in the Church's mission to sanctify the world. A renewed focus on *lay apostolate* will help to clarify the roles of clergy and laity and so give a strong impetus to the task of evangelizing society.

GENERAL AUDIENCE

Paul VI Audience Hall
Wednesday, 10 February 2010

St Anthony of Padua

Anthony, in the school of Francis, always put Christ at the centre of his life and thinking, of his action and of his preaching. This is another characteristic feature of Franciscan theology: Christocentrism. Franciscan theology willingly contemplates and invites others to contemplate the mysteries of the Lord's humanity, the man Jesus, and in a special way the mystery of the Nativity: God who made himself a Child and gave himself into our hands, a mystery that gives rise to sentiments of love and gratitude for divine goodness.

Not only the Nativity, a central point of Christ's love for humanity, but also the vision of the Crucified One inspired in Anthony thoughts of gratitude to God and esteem for the dignity of the human person, so that all believers and non-believers might find in the Crucified One and in his image a life-enriching meaning. St Anthony writes: "Christ who is your life is hanging before you, so that you may look at the Cross as in a mirror. There you will be able to know how mortal were your wounds, that no medicine other than the Blood of the Son of God could heal. If you look closely, you will be able to realize how great your human dignity and your value are... Nowhere other than looking at himself in the mirror of the Cross can man better understand how much he is worth" (*Sermones Dominicales et Festivi* III, pp. 213-214).

In meditating on these words we are better able to understand the importance of the image of the Crucified One for our culture, for our humanity that is born from the Christian faith.

Precisely by looking at the Crucified One we see, as St Anthony says, how great are the dignity and worth of the human being. At no other point can we understand how much the human person is worth, precisely because God makes us so important, considers us so important that, in his opinion, we are worthy of his suffering; thus all human dignity appears in the mirror of the Crucified One and our gazing upon him is ever a source of acknowledgement of human dignity.

Dear friends, may Anthony of Padua, so widely venerated by the faithful, intercede for the whole Church and especially for those who are dedicated to preaching; let us pray the Lord that he will help us learn a little of this art from St Anthony. May preachers, drawing inspiration from his example, be effective in their communication by taking pains to combine solid and sound doctrine with sincere and fervent devotion. In this Year for Priests, let us pray that priests and deacons will carry out with concern this ministry of the proclamation of the word of God, making it timely for the faithful, especially through liturgical homilies. May they effectively present the eternal beauty of Christ, just as Anthony recommended: "If you preach Jesus, he will melt hardened hearts; if you invoke him he will soften harsh temptations; if you think of him he will enlighten your mind; if you read of him he will satifsfy your intellect" (*Sermones Dominicales et Festivi* III, p. 59).

From the Address

TO PARTICIPANTS IN THE COURSE ON THE INTERNAL FORUM ORGANIZED BY THE APOSTOLIC PENITENTIARY

Clementine Hall
Thursday, 11 March 2010

'A dialogue of salvation.'

As I said in the Letter for the inauguration of the Year, "We priests should feel that the following words, which he [the Curé d'Ars] put on the lips of Christ, are meant for each of us personally: "I will charge my ministers to proclaim to sinners that I am ever ready to welcome them, that my mercy is infinite". From the Holy Curé d'Ars we can learn to put our unfailing trust in the sacrament of Penance, to set it once more at the centre of our pastoral concerns, and to take up the "'dialogue of salvation' which it entails" (*L'Osservatore Romano English edition,* 24 June 2009, p. 4).

Where did the heroism and fruitfulness with which St John Mary Vianney lived his ministry as a confessor stem from? First of all from an intense personal penitential dimension. His knowledge of his own limitations and his need to have recourse to Divine Mercy to ask forgiveness, to convert his heart and to be sustained on the journey to holiness are fundamental in the life of a priest. Only those who have first experienced its greatness can be convinced preachers and administrators of God's mercy.

173

Every priest becomes a minister of Penance through his ontological configuration to Christ, the Eternal High Priest, who reconciles humanity with the Father; so the priest is charged with the responsibility of faithfully administering the Sacrament of Reconciliation.

We live in a cultural context marked by the hedonistic and relativistic mindset that tends to delete God from the horizon of life and does not encourage the acquisition of a clear set of values to refer to that would help one to discern good from evil and develop a proper sense of sin.

This situation makes even more urgent the service of stewards of Divine Mercy. We must not forget, in fact, that a sort of vicious circle exists between the clouding of the experience of God and the loss of the sense of sin. However, if we look at the cultural context in which St John Mary Vianney lived we see that in various aspects it was not so very unlike our own. In his time too, in fact, there was a mentality hostile to faith, expressed by forces that even sought to prevent the exercise of the ministry. In this circumstance, the Holy Curé d'Ars "chose the Church as his home", in order to lead people to God.

He lived radically the spirit of prayer, his personal and intimate relationship with Christ, the celebration of Holy Mass, Eucharistic Adoration and evangelical poverty, appearing to his contemporaries such a conspicuous sign of God's presence that he impelled a great many penitents to come to his confessional.

In the conditions of freedom in which it is now possible to exercise the priestly ministry, priests must live the response to their vocation "in a lofty manner", for only those who become every day a living and clear presence of the Lord can awaken in the faithful a sense of sin, impart courage and give rise to the desire for God's forgiveness.

Dear confrères, it is necessary to return to the confessional as a place in which to celebrate the Sacrament of Reconciliation, but also as a place in which "to dwell" more often, so that the faithful may find compassion, advice and comfort, feel that they are loved and understood by God and experience the presence of Divine Mercy beside the Real Presence in the Eucharist.

The discussed "crisis" of the Sacrament of Penance, frequently calls into question priests first of all and their great responsibility to teach the People of God the radical requirements of the Gospel. In particular, it asks them to dedicate themselves generously to hearing sacramental confessions; to guide the flock courageously so that it does not conform to the mindset of this world (cf. Rom 12:2) but may even be able to make decisions that run counter to the tide, avoiding adjustments and compromises.

For this reason it is important that priests have a constant aspiration to ascetism, nourished by communion with God, and that they tirelessly dedicate themselves to keeping up to date in the study of moral theology and the human sciences.

St John Mary Vianney knew how to establish a true and proper "dialogue of salvation" with his penitents, showing them the beauty and greatness of the Lord's kindness and awakening that desire for God and for Heaven of which the Saints are the first heralds.

He said: "The Good Lord knows everything; even before you make your confession he already knows that you will sin again and yet he forgives you. How great is the Love of our God, who goes so far as to voluntarily forget the future, in order to forgive us" (Monnin A., *Il Curato d'Ars. Vita di Gian-Battista-Maria Vianney,* Vol. I, Turin 1870, p. 130).

It is the priest's task to encourage that experience of a "dialogue of salvation", which, born from the certainty of being loved by God, helps the human being to recognize his sin and gradually to enter that stable dynamic of conversion of heart which leads to radical renouncement of evil and to a life in accordance with God (cf. *Catechism of the Catholic Church,* n. 1431).

Dear priests, what an extraordinary ministry the Lord has entrusted to us! Just as in the celebration of the Eucharist he places himself in the hands of the priest to continue to be present among his People, similarly, in the Sacrament of Reconciliation he entrusts himself to the priest so that men and women may experience the embrace with which the father welcomed back the prodigal son, restoring his filial dignity and fully re-establishing him as his heir (cf. Lk 15:11-32).

May the Virgin Mary and the Holy Curé d'Ars help us to experience in our lives the length and breadth and height and depth of the Love of God (cf. Eph 3:18-19), in order to be faithful and generous stewards. I warmly thank you all and willingly impart my Blessing to you.

TO PARTICIPANTS IN THE CONFERENCE ORGANIZED BY THE CONGREGATION FOR THE CLERGY

Hall of Blessing
Friday, 12 March 2010

Priestly identity.

The theme of priestly identity… is crucial to the exercise of the priestly ministry, today and in the future. In an epoch like our own, so "polycentric" and inclined to blur every conception of identity, deemed by many contrary to freedom and democracy, it is important to keep clearly in mind the theological particularity of the Ordained Ministry to avoid succumbing to the temptation to reduce it to the prevalent cultural categories.

In a context of widespread secularization, which is gradually excluding God from the public sphere and tendentially also from the common social conscience, the priest often appears "foreign" to the common perception. This is precisely because of the most fundamental aspects of his ministry, such as, being a man of the sacred, removed from the world to intercede on behalf of the world and being appointed to this mission by God and not by men (cf. Heb 5:1).

For this reason it is important to overcome dangerous forms of reductionism. In recent decades these have used categories that are functionalist rather than ontological and have introduced the priest almost as a "social worker", at the risk of betraying Christ's Priesthood itself.

Just as the hermeneutics of continuity are proving ever more urgent for a satisfactory understanding of the Second Vatican

177

Council's texts, likewise a hermeneutic we might describe as "of priestly continuity" appears necessary. This has come down to our day, starting from Jesus of Nazareth, Lord and Christ, and passing through the 2,000 years of the history of greatness and holiness, of culture and devotion which the Priesthood has written in the world.

Dear brother priests, in the time in which we live it is particularly important that the call to participate in the one Priesthood of Christ in the ordained Ministry flourishes in the "charism of prophecy": there is a great need for priests who speak of God to the world and who present God to the world; men who are not swayed by transient cultural trends but are capable of living authentically that freedom which alone the certainty of belonging to God can give.

As your Convention has clearly emphasized, the most necessary prophecy today is that of faithfulness, which, based on Christ's Faithfulness to humanity, leads through the Church and the ministerial Priesthood to living one's own priesthood in total adherence to Christ and to the Church. Indeed, the priest no longer belongs to himself but, because of the sacramental seal he has received (cf. *Catechism of the Catholic Church,* nn. 1563, 1582), is the "property" of God. The priest's "belonging to Another", must become recognizable to all, through a transparent witness.

In the way of thinking, speaking, and judging events of the world, of serving and loving, of relating to people, also in his habits, the priest must draw prophetic power from his sacramental belonging, from his profound being.

Consequently he must do all he can to separate himself from the predominant mindset that tends not to associate the minister's value with his being but with his function alone, thereby underestimating the work of God, which affects the profound identity of the priest as a person, configuring him to himself once and for all (cf. ibid., n. 1583).

The horizon of the ontological belonging to God also constitutes the proper framework for understanding and reaffirming, in our day too, the value of sacred celibacy which in the Latin Church is a charism required for Sacred Orders (cf. *Presbyterorum Ordinis,* n. 16) and is held in very great consideration in the Eastern Churches (cf. *CCEO,* can. 373).

It is an authentic prophecy of the Kingdom, a sign of consecration with undivided heart to the Lord and to "the affairs of the Lord" (1 Cor 7:32), the expression of their gift of self to God and to others (cf. *Catechism of the Catholic Church,* n. 1579).

The priest's vocation is thus most exalted and remains a great mystery, even to us who have received it as a gift. Our limitations and weaknesses must prompt us to live out and preserve with deep faith this precious gift with which Christ has configured us to him, making us sharers in his saving Mission. Indeed, our comprehension of the ministerial priesthood is bound to faith and requires, ever more forcefully, a radical continuity between seminary formation and continuing formation. The prophetic life, without compromises, with which we serve God and the world, proclaiming the Gospel and celebrating the Sacraments, will encourage the advent of the Kingdom of God already present and the growth of the People of God in faith.

Dear priests, the men and women of our time ask us only to be truly priests and nothing more. The lay faithful will find in a great many other people what they humanly need, but in the priest alone will they be able to find the word of God that must always be on his lips (cf. *Presbyterorum Ordinis,* n. 4); the Mercy of the Father, abundantly and freely bestowed in the Sacrament of Reconciliation; the Bread of new Life, "true food given to men" (cf. Hymn of the Office of the Solemnity of *Corpus Christi* of the Roman Rite).

Let us ask God, through the intercession of the Blessed Virgin Mary and of St John Mary Vianney to obtain that we may thank him every day for the great gift of our vocation and that we may live our Priesthood with full and joyous faithfulness.

GENERAL AUDIENCE

Saint Peter's Square
Wednesday, 14 April 2010

The Ordained Ministry – teaching, sanctifying and governing.

In this Easter Season that brings us to Pentecost and also ushers us into the celebrations for the closure of the Year for Priests, scheduled for this coming 9-11 June, I am eager to devote a few more reflections to the topic of the ordained Ministry, elaborating on the fruitful realities of the priest's configuration to Christ the Head in the exercise of the *tria munera* that he receives: namely, the three offices of teaching, sanctifying and governing.

In order to understand what it means for the priest to act *in persona Christi Capitis,* in the person of Christ, the Head and to realize what consequences derive from the duty of representing the Lord, especially in the exercise of these three offices, it is necessary first of all to explain what "representation" means. The priest represents Christ. What is implied by "representing" someone? In ordinary language it usually means being delegated by someone to be present in his place, to speak and act in his stead because the person he represents is absent from the practical action. Let us ask ourselves: does the priest represent the Lord in this way? The answer is no, because in the Church Christ is never absent, the Church is his living Body and he is the Head of the Church, present and active within her. Christ is never absent, on the contrary he is present in a way that is untrammelled by space and time through the event of the Resurrection that we contemplate in a special way in this Easter Season.

Therefore the priest, who acts *in persona Christi Capitis* and representing the Lord, never acts in the name of someone who is absent but, rather, in the very Person of the Risen Christ, who makes himself present with his truly effective action. He really acts today and brings about what the priest would be incapable of: the consecration of the wine and the bread so that they may really be the Lord's presence, the absolution of sins. The Lord makes his own action present in the person who carries out these gestures. These three duties of the priest which Tradition has identified in the Lord's different words about mission: teaching, sanctifying and governing in their difference and in their deep unity are a specification of this effective representation. In fact, they are the three actions of the Risen Christ, the same that he teaches today, in the Church and in the world. Thereby he creates faith, gathers together his people, creates the presence of truth and really builds the communion of the universal Church; and sanctifies and guides.

The first duty of which I wish to speak today is the *munus docendi,* that is, the task of teaching. Today, in the midst of the educational emergency, the *munus docendi* of the Church, exercised concretely through the ministry of each priest, is particularly important. We are very confused about the fundamental choices in our life and question what the world is, where it comes from, where we are going, what we must do in order to do good, how we should live and what the truly pertinent values are. Regarding all this, there are numerous contrasting philosophies that come into being and disappear, creating confusion about the fundamental decisions on how to live; because collectively we no longer know from what and for what we have been made and where we are going. In this context the words of the Lord who took pity on the throng because the people were like sheep without a shepherd came true (cf. Mk 6:34). The Lord had noticed this when he saw the thousands of people following him in the desert because, in the diversity of the currents of that time, they no longer knew what the true meaning of Scripture was, what God was saying. The Lord, moved by compassion, interpreted God's word, he himself is the Word of God, and thus provided an orientation. This is the function *in persona Christi* of the priest: making present, in the confusion and bewilderment of our times, the light of God's Word, the light that is Christ himself in this our world. Therefore the priest does not teach his own ideas, a philosophy that he himself has invented, that he has discovered or likes; the priest does not speak of himself, he does not speak for himself, to attract admirers, perhaps, or create a party of his own; he does not say his own thing, his own inventions but, in the medley of all the philosophies, the priest teaches in the name of Christ present, he proposes the truth that is Christ himself, his word and his way of living and of moving ahead. What Christ said of himself applies to the priest: "My teaching is not mine" (Jn 7:16); Christ, that is, does not propose himself but, as the Son he is the voice, the Word of the Father. The priest too must always speak and act in this way: "My teaching is not mine, I do not spread my own ideas or what I like, but I am the mouthpiece and heart of Christ and I make present this one, shared teaching that has created the universal Church and creates eternal life".

This fact, namely that the priest does not invent, does not create or proclaim his own ideas, since the teaching he announces is not his own but Christ's does not mean, however, that he is neutral, as if he were a spokesman reading a text that he does not, perhaps, make his own. In this case too the model of Christ who said: "I do not come from myself and I do not live for myself but I come from the Father and live for the Father" applies. Therefore, in this profound identification, Christ's teaching is that of the Father and he himself is one with the Father. The priest who proclaims Christ's word, the faith of the Church, and not his own ideas, must also say: "I do not live by myself and for myself, but I live with Christ and by Christ and therefore all that Christ said to us becomes my word even if it is not mine". The priest's life must be identified with Christ and, in this manner, the word that is not his own becomes, nevertheless, a profoundly personal word. On this topic St Augustine, speaking of priests said: "And as for us, what are we?

Ministers (of Christ), his servants; for what we distribute to you is not ours but we take it from his store. And we too live of it, because we are servants like you" (*Sermo 229/E,* 4).

The teaching that the priest is called to offer, the truth of the faith, must be internalized and lived in an intense personal and spiritual process so that the priest really enters into a profound inner communion with Christ himself. The priests believes, accepts and seeks to live, first of all as his own, all that the Lord taught and that the Church has passed on in that process of identification with his own ministry of which St John Mary Vianney is an exemplary witness (cf. *Letter for the inauguration of the Year for Priests*). "For in charity itself we are all listening to him, who is our One Master in heaven" (*En.* in Ps 131:1, 7).

Consequently the priest's voice may often seem to be "the voice of one crying in the wilderness" (Mk 1:3), but his prophetic power consists precisely in this: in never being conformist, in never conforming to any dominant culture or mindset but, rather, in showing the one newness that can bring about an authentic and profound renewal of the human being, that is, that Christ is the Living One, he is the close God, the God who works in the life and for the life of the world and gives us the truth, the way to live.

In the careful preparation of Sunday preaching, without excluding weekday preaching, in imparting catechetical formation in schools, in academic institutions and, in a special way, through that unwritten book which is his own life, the priest is always an "educator", he teaches; yet not with the presumption of one who imposes his own truth but on the contrary with the humble, glad certainty of someone who has encountered the Truth, who has been grasped and transformed by it, hence cannot but proclaim it. In fact, no one can choose the priesthood on his own, it is not a means of obtaining security in life or achieving a social position: no one can give it to him nor can he seek it by himself. The priesthood is the response to the Lord's call, to his will, in order to become a herald of his truth, not a personal truth but of his truth.

Dear brother priests, the Christian people ask to hear from our teachings the genuine ecclesial doctrine, through which they can renew their encounter with Christ who gives joy, peace and salvation. In this regard Sacred Scripture, the writings of the Fathers and Doctors of the Church, the *Catechism of the Catholic Church* are indispensable reference points in the exercise of the *munus docendi,* so essential for conversion, the development of faith and the salvation of humankind. "Priestly ordination... means... to be immersed in the Truth" (*Homily at the Chrism Mass,* Holy Thursday, 9 April 2009), that Truth which is not merely a concept or a collection of ideas to be assimilated and passed on but, rather, is the Person of Christ with whom, for whom and in whom to live and thus, necessarily, the timeliness and comprehensibility of the proclamation are also born. Only this knowledge of a Truth that became a Person in the Incarnation of the Son justifies the missionary mandate: "Go into all the world and preach the Gospel to the whole creation" (Mk 16:15). Only if it is the Truth is it intended for every creature, it is not the imposition of some thing but openness of heart to what the creature has been created for.

Dear Brothers and Sisters, the Lord has entrusted a great task to priests: to be heralds of his word, of the Truth that saves; to be his voice in the world to bring what serves the true good of souls and the authentic path of faith (cf. 1 Cor 6:12). May St John Mary Vianney be an example to all priests. He was a man of great wisdom and heroic fortitude in resisting the cultural and social pressures of his time in order to lead souls to God: simplicity, fidelity and immediacy were the essential features of his preaching, the transparency of his faith and of his holiness. The Christian People was edified by him and as happens for genuine teachers in every epoch recognized in him the light of the Truth. In him it recognized, ultimately, what should always be recognizable in a priest: the voice of the Good Shepherd.

GENERAL AUDIENCE

Saint Peter's Square
Wednesday, 28 April 2010

Saint Leonard Murialdo and Saint Joseph Cottolengo

We are moving towards the end of the Year for Priests and, on this last Wednesday of April, I would like to talk to you about two holy priests who were exemplary in the gift of themselves to God, in their witness of charity, lived in and for the Church, and to their needier brethren: St Leonard Murialdo and St Joseph Benedict Cottolengo. We are commemorating the 110th anniversary of the death of the former and the 40th anniversary of his canonization, and the celebrations for the second centenary of the priestly ordination of the latter are beginning.

Murialdo was born in Turin on 26 October 1828: it was the Turin of St John Bosco and likewise of St Joseph Cottolengo, a land made fruitful by so many examples of holiness among lay people and priests. Leonard was the eighth child of a simple family. As a boy, together with his brother, he entered the College of the Piarist Fathers of Savona for the elementary classes, middle school and secondary school. There he encountered teachers trained in a pious atmosphere, based on serious catechesis with regular devotional practices. Nevertheless in adolescence he went through a profound existential and spiritual crisis that led him to go home sooner than expected and to conclude his studies in Turin, where he enrolled in the two-year philosophy course. His "return to the light" occurred as he recounts after several months with the grace of a general confession in which he rediscovered God's immense mercy. Then, at the age of seventeen, he took the decision to become a priest, as a loving response to God who had grasped him with his love. Leonard Murialdo was ordained on 20 September 1851. Precisely in that period, as a catechist of the *Oratorio* of the Guardian Angel, he came to the attention of Don Bosco who appreciated his qualities and convinced him to accept the directorship of the new *Oratorio di San Luigi*, in Porta Nuova, which he held until in 1865. There Fr Leonard also came into contact with the grave problems of the poorest classes. He visited their homes, developing a deep social, educational and apostolic sensitivity which led him subsequently to undertake a wide range of projects for youth. Catecheses, school and recreational activities were the foundation of his educational method in the *Oratorio*. Don Bosco still wanted Leonard with him on the occasion of the Audience that Blessed Pius IX granted to him in 1858.

In 1873, Fr Leonard founded the Congregation of St Joseph whose aim from the start was the formation of youth, especially the poorest and most neglected. Turin at that time was marked by the vigorously flourishing works and charitable activities promoted by Murialdo until his death on 30 March 1900.

I would like to emphasize that the heart of Murialdo's spirituality was his conviction of the merciful love of God, a Father ever good, patient and generous, who reveals the grandeur and immensity of his mercy with forgiveness. St Leonard did not experience this reality at an intellectual level but rather in his life, through his vivid encounter with the Lord. He always considered himself a man whom God in his mercy had pardoned. He therefore experienced a joyful feeling of gratitude to the Lord, serene awareness of his own limitations, the ardent desire for penance, and the constant and generous commitment to conversion. He saw his whole life not only enlightened, guided and supported by this love but continuously immersed in God's infinite mercy. He wrote in his *Spiritual Testament*: "Your mercy surrounds me, O Lord... Just as God is always and everywhere, so there is always and everywhere love, mercy is always and everywhere". Remembering the crisis he had been through in his youth, he noted: "The good Lord wanted to make his kindness and generosity shine out in a completely special way. Not only did he readmit me to his friendship, but he called me to make a decision of predilection: he called me to the priesthood, even only a few months after I had returned to him". Thus St Leonard lived his priestly vocation as a gift of God's mercy, freely given, with a sense of gratitude, joy and love. He wrote further: "God has chosen me! He has called me, he has even forced upon me the honour, glory, and ineffable happiness of being his minister, of being "another Christ'.... And where was I when you sought me, my God? At the bottom of the abyss! I was there, and there God came to find me; there he made me hear his voice".

Underlining the greatness of the mission of the priest who must "continue the work of redemption, the great work of Jesus Christ, the work of the Saviour of the world" namely, the work of "saving souls", St Leonard always reminded himself and his brethren of the responsibility of a life consistent with the sacrament received. Love of God and love for God: this was the force that impelled him on his journey to holiness, the law of his priesthood, the deepest meaning of his apostolate among poor youths and the source of his prayer. St Leonard Murialdo abandoned himself with trust to Providence, generously doing the divine will, in touch with God and dedicating himself to poor young people. In this way he combined contemplative silence with the tireless zeal of action, fidelity to every day tasks with ingenious initiatives, fortitude in difficulty with peace of mind. This was his path of holiness in order to live the commandment of love for God and for his neighbour.

St Joseph Benedict Cottolengo, who lived 40 years before Murialdo the Founder of the work which he himself called the "Little House of Divine Providence" and which today is also called "Cottolengo" embodied this same spirit of charity. Next Sunday, during my Pastoral Visit to Turin, I shall have the opportunity to venerate the remains of this Saint and to meet the residents of the "Little House".

Joseph Benedict Cottolengo was born in Bra, a small town in the Province of Cuneo, on 3 May 1786. The eldest of twelve, six of whom died in infancy, he showed great sensitivity to the poor from childhood. He embraced the way of the priesthood, setting an example to two of his brothers. The years of his youth coincided with the Napoleonic period and the consequent hardships in both the religious and social contexts. Cottolengo became a good priest much sought after by penitents and, in the Turin of that time, a preacher of spiritual exercises and conferences for university students who always met with noteworthy success. At the age of 32, he was appointed canon of the *Santissima Trinità,* a congregation of priests whose task was to officiate in the *Corpus Domini* Church and to ensure the decorum of the city's religious ceremonies, but he felt uneasy in this situation. God was preparing him for a special mission and, precisely with an unexpected and decisive encounter, made him realize what was to be his future destiny in the exercise of the ministry.

The Lord always sets signs on our path to guide us according to his will to our own true good. This also happened to Cottolengo, dramatically, on Sunday morning, 2 September 1827. The diligence from Milan arrived in Turin, more crowded than ever. Crammed into it was a whole French family. The mother, with five children, was at an advanced stage of pregnancy and had a high temperature. After traipsing to various hospitals, this family found lodgings in a public dormitory but the woman's situation was serious and some people went in search of a priest. By a mysterious design they came across Cottolengo and it was precisely he who, heavy hearted, accompanied this young mother to her death, amid the distress of the entire family. Having carried out this painful task, with deep anguish he went to the Blessed Sacrament and knelt in prayer: "My God, why? Why did you want me to be a witness? What do you want of me? Something must be done!". He got to his feet and had all the bells rung and the candles lit and, gathering in the church those who were curious, told them:

"The grace has been granted! The grace has been granted!". From that time Cottolengo was transformed: all his skills, especially his financial and organizational ability, were used to give life to projects in support of the neediest.

In his undertaking he was able to involve dozens and dozens of collaborators and volunteers. Moving towards the outskirts of Turin to expand his work, he created a sort of village, in which he assigned a meaningful name to every building he managed to build: "House of Faith", "House of Hope", "House of Charity". He adopted a "familystyle", establishing true and proper communities of people with volunteers, men and women religious and lay people, who joined forces in order to face and overcome the difficulties that arose. Everyone in that Little House of Divine Providence had a precise task: work, prayer, service, teaching or administration. The healthy and the sick shared the same daily burden. With time religious life could be specifically planned in accordance with particular needs and requirements. Cottolengo even thought of setting up his own seminary to provide specific formation for the priests of his Work. He was always ready to follow and serve Divine Providence and never questioned it. He would say: "I am a good for nothing and I don't even know what to make of myself. But Divine Providence certainly knows what it wants. It is only up to me to support it. Let us go ahead *in Domino*". To his poor and the neediest, he would always call himself "the labourer of Divine Providence".

He also chose to found, beside the small citadels, five monasteries of contemplative sisters and one of hermits, and considered them among his most important achievements. They were a sort of "heart" which was to beat for the entire Work. He died on 30 April 1842, with these words on his lips: *"Misericordia, Domine; Misericordia, Domine.* Good and Holy Providence... Blessed Virgin, it is now up to you". The whole of his life, as a newspaper of the time said, was "an intense day of love".

Dear friends, these two holy priests, a few of whose characteristics I have described, carried out their ministry with the total gift of their lives to the poorest, the neediest and the lowliest, always finding the deep roots, the inexhaustible source for their action in their relationship with God. They drew from his love in the profound conviction that it is impossible to exercise charity without living in Christ and in the Church. May their intercession and example continue to illumine the ministry of the many priests who spend themselves generously for God and for the flock entrusted to them, and help each one give himself joyfully and generously to God and neighbour.

GENERAL AUDIENCE

Saint Peter's Square
Wednesday, 5 May 2010

Munus sanctificandi

Last Sunday, on my Pastoral Visit to Turin, I had the joy of pausing in prayer before the Holy Shroud, joining the more than two million pilgrims who have been able to contemplate it during the solemn Exposition of these days. That sacred Cloth can nourish and foster faith and reinvigorate Christian devotion because it is an incentive to go to the Face of Christ, to the Body of the Crucified and Risen Christ, to contemplate the Paschal Mystery, the heart of the Christian Message. We, dear Brothers and Sisters, are living members of the Body of the Risen Christ, alive and active in history (cf. Rom 12:5), each one in accordance with the role, that is, the task the Lord has wished to entrust to each one of us. Today, in this *Catechesis*, I would like to return to the specific tasks of priests, which tradition claims are essentially three: teaching, sanctifying and governing. In one of our previous Catecheses I spoke on the first of these three duties: teaching, the proclamation of the truth, the proclamation of God revealed in Christ or, in other words the prophetic task of putting the person in touch with the truth, of helping him to know the essential of his life, of reality itself.

Today I would like to reflect with you briefly on the priest's second duty, that of sanctifying people, above all through the sacraments and the worship of the Church. Here we must ask ourselves first of all: what does the word "Holy" mean? The answer is: "Holy" is God's specific quality of being, namely, absolute truth, goodness, love, beauty pure light. Thus sanctifying a person means putting him or her in touch with

191

God, with this being light, truth, pure love. It is obvious that such contact transforms the person. The ancients had this firm conviction: no one can see God without dying instantly. The power of truth and light is too great! If the human being touches this absolute current, he cannot survive. On the other hand there is also the conviction: without a minimal contact with God man cannot live. Truth, goodness and love are fundamental conditions of his being. The question is: how can man find that contact with God, which is fundamental, without dying overpowered by the greatness of his divine being? The Church's faith tells us that God himself creates this contact that gradually transforms us into true images of God.

Thus we have once again arrived at the priest's task of "sanctifying". No man on his own, relying on his own power, can put another in touch with God. An essential part of the priest's grace is the gift, the task of creating this contact. This is achieved in the proclamation of God's word in which his light comes to meet us. It is achieved in a particularly concentrated manner in the Sacraments. Immersion in the Paschal Mystery of the death and Resurrection of Christ takes place in Baptism, is reinforced in Confirmation and Reconciliation and is nourished by the Eucharist, a sacrament that builds the Church as the People of God, Body of Christ, Temple of the Holy Spirit (cf. John Paul II, Apostolic Exhortation *Pastores Gregis*, n. 32). Thus it is Christ himself who makes us holy, that is, who draws us into God's sphere. However, as an act of his infinite mercy, he calls some "to be" with him (cf. Mk 3:14) and to become, through the Sacrament of Orders, despite their human poverty, sharers in his own priesthood, ministers of this sanctification, stewards of his mysteries, "bridges" to the encounter with him and of his mediation between God and man and between man and God (cf. *Presbyterorum Ordinis*, n. 5).

In recent decades there have been tendencies that aim to give precedence, in the priest's identity and mission, to the dimension of proclamation, detaching it from that of sanctification; it is often said that it would be necessary to go beyond a merely sacramental pastoral ministry. Yet, is it possible to exercise the priestly ministry authentically by "going beyond" the sacramental ministry? What exactly does it mean for priests to evangelize, in what does the professed "primacy of proclamation" consist? As the Gospels report, Jesus says that the proclamation of the Kingdom of God is the goal of his mission; this proclamation, however, is not only a "discourse" but at the same time includes his action; the signs and miracles that Jesus works show that the Kingdom comes as a present reality and in the end coincides with his very Person, with his gift of himself, as we heard today in the Gospel Reading. And the same applies for the ordained ministry: he, the priest, represents Christ, the One sent by the Father, he continues his mission, through the "word" and the "sacrament", in this totality of body and soul, of sign and word. Referring to priests in a letter to Bishop Honoratus of Thiabe, St Augustine says: "Let those, therefore, who are servants of Christ, his ministers in word and sacrament, do what he has commanded or permitted" (Letter 228, 2). It is necessary to reflect on whether, in some cases, having under-estimated the faithful exercise of the *munus sanctificandi* might not have represented a weakening of faith itself in the salvific efficacy of the sacraments, and ultimately in the actual action of Christ and of his Spirit, through the Church, in the world.

Who, therefore, saves the world and man? The only answer we can give is: Jesus of Nazareth, Lord and Christ, Crucified and Risen. And where is the Mystery of the death and Resurrection of Christ that brings about salvation? In Christ's action through the Church, and in particular in the sacrament of the Eucharist, which makes the redemptive sacrificial offering of the Son of God present in the sacrament of Reconciliation in which from the death of sin one returns to new life, and in every other sacramental act of sanctification (cf. *Presbyterorum Ordinis,* n. 5). It is therefore important to encourage an appropriate catechesis to help the faithful understand the value of the sacraments; but it is likewise necessary, after the example of the Holy Curé d'Ars, to be available, generous and attentive in giving the brothers and sisters the treasures of grace that God has placed in our hands, and of which we are not the "masters" but rather caretakers and stewards. Especially in this time of ours, in which, on the one hand it seems that faith is weakening, and, on the other, a profound need and a widespread quest for spirituality are emerging, it is essential that every priest remember that in his mission the missionary proclamation and worship and the sacraments are never separate and encourage a healthy sacramental ministry, to form the People of God and to help it experience to the full the Liturgy, the Church's worship and the sacraments as freely given gifts of God, free and effective gestures of his saving action.

As I recalled in the Holy Chrism Mass this year: "At the centre of the Church's worship is the notion of "sacrament'. This means that it is not primarily we who act, but God comes first to meet us through his action, he looks upon us and he leads us to himself.... God touches us through material things... that he takes up into his service, making them instruments of the encounter between us and himself" (Chrism Mass, 1 April 2010). The truth according to which in the Sacrament "it is not primarily we who act" (*ibid.*), also concerns and must concern priestly awareness: each priest knows well that he is an instrument necessary to God's saving action but also that he is always only an instrument. This awareness must make priests humble and generous in the administration of the Sacraments, in respect of the canonical norms, but also in the deep conviction that their mission is to ensure that all people, united to Christ, may offer themselves to God as a living sacrifice, holy and acceptable to him (cf. Rom 12:1). St John Mary Vianney, once again, is exemplary with regard to the *munus sanctificandi* and the correct interpretation of the sacramental ministry; one day, to a man who was saying that he had no faith and wished to ask him about it, the parish priest answered: "Oh! My friend, you are not really speaking to the right person, I do not know how to reason... but if you need some comfort, sit there... (and he pointed to the ever present stool in the confessional) and believe me, many others have sat there before you and have had nothing to regret" (cf. Monnin, A., *Il Curato d'Ars, Vita di Gian-Battista-Maria Vianney,* Vol. I, Turin 1870, pp. 163-164).

Dear priests, experience the Liturgy and worship with joy and love: it is an action which the Risen One carries out with the power of the Holy Spirit in us, with us and for us. I would like to renew the invitation made recently to "return to the confessional as a place in which to celebrate the Sacrament of Reconciliation, but also as a place in which "to dwell' more often, so that the faithful may find compassion, advice and comfort, feel that they are loved and understood by God and experience the presence of Divine Mercy beside the Real Presence in the Eucharist" (*Address to participants in the course on the Internal Forum organized by the Apostolic Penitentiary,* 11 March 2010). And I would also like to ask each priest to celebrate and to live intensely the Eucharist which is at the heart of the duty of sanctifying; it is Jesus who wants to be with us, to live in us, to give himself to us, to show us God's infinite mercy and tenderness; it is the one sacrifice of the love of Christ who makes himself present, who makes himself real among us and arrives at the throne of Grace, at God's presence... embraces humanity... and unites us with him (cf. *Discourse to the Parish Priests of the Diocese of Rome,* 18 February 2010). And the priest is called to be a minister of this great Mystery, in the Sacrament and in life. If "the great ecclesial tradition has rightly separated sacramental efficacy from the concrete existential situation of the individual priest and so the legitimate expectations of the faithful are appropriately safeguarded", this correct doctrinal explanation takes nothing "from the necessary, indeed indispensable aspiration to moral perfection that must dwell in every authentically priestly heart": there is also an example of faith and the testimony of holiness, that the People of God rightly expect from its Pastors (cf. *Benedict XVI, Address to the Plenary Assembly of the Congregation for the Clergy,* 16 March 2009). And it is in the celebration of the Holy Mysteries that the priest finds the root of his holiness (cf. *Presbyterorum Ordinis,* nn. 12-13).

Dear Friends, may you be aware of the great gift that priests are for the Church and for the world; through their ministry the Lord continues to save men, to make himself present, to sanctify. May you be able to thank God and above all be close to your priests with prayer and support, especially in difficulty, so that there may be more and more Pastors in accordance with the Heart of God. Many thanks.

From the Address

TO THE BISHOPS
OF THE BELGIUM ON THEIR
"AD LIMINA" VISIT

Saturday, 8 May 2010

St Damien de Veuster

A significant event, for the present and for the future, was the Canonization of Fr Damien de Veuster. This new Saint speaks to the consciences of Belgians. Has he not been designated the most outstanding son of the nation of all time? His greatness, lived in the total gift of himself to his brother lepers, to the point of catching the contagious disease and dying of it, lies in his inner wealth, his constant prayer and his union with Christ, whom he saw present in his brothers and sisters and to whom, as Christ did, he gave himself without reserve. In this Year for Priests, it is right to hold up his example as a priest and a missionary. The fall in the number of priests must not be perceived as an inevitable process. The Second Vatican Council said forcefully that the Church cannot do without the ministry of priests. It is therefore necessary and urgent to give the ministry of priests its right place and to recognize is irreplaceable sacramental character. This results in the need for a broad and serious vocations apostolate that is based on the exemplarity and holiness of priests, on attention to the seeds of a vocation present in many young people and on assiduous and trusting prayer, as Jesus recommended (cf. Mt 9:37).

I address a cordial and grateful greeting to all priests and consecrated people, often overburdened by work and desirous of the support and friendship of their Bishop and their confreres, without forgetting the older priests who have devoted their whole life to serving God and their brethren. Nor do I forget the missionaries as a whole. May all priests, men and women religious and lay people of Belgium receive my encouragement and the expression of my gratitude, and may they not forget that Christ alone calms every storm (cf. Mt 8:25-26) and restores strength and courage (cf. Mt 11:28-30 and Mt 14:30-32) in order to lead a holy life in full fidelity to their ministry, to their consecration to God and to Christian witness.

The Constitution *Sacrosanctum concilium* stresses that it is in the Liturgy that the mystery of the Church is made manifest in its grandeur and its simplicity (cf. Introduction, n. 2). Thus it is important that priests take care in liturgical celebrations, particularly the Eucharist, to ensure that they permit a profound communion with the Living God, Father, Son and Holy Spirit. It is necessary that celebrations take place with respect for the Church's liturgical tradition, with the active participation of the faithful, according to each one's specific role, uniting personally with Christ's Paschal Mystery.

In your reports you show that you are attending to the formation of lay people with a view to their increasingly effective incorporation in the animation of temporal realities. This is a praiseworthy programme that is born from the vocation of every baptized person, configured to Christ the priest, prophet and king. It is right to discern all the possibilities that stem from the common vocation to holiness and the apostolic commitment of lay people, with respect for the essential distinction between the ministerial priesthood and the common priesthood of the faithful. All the members of the Catholic community, but in a particular way the lay faithful, are called to witness openly to their faith and to be leaven in society, while respecting both a healthy laicism in the public institutions and the other religious denominations. This witness cannot be limited to the personal encounter alone but must also acquire the characteristics of a public proposal, respectful but legitimate, of the values inspired by Christ's Gospel message.

APOSTOLIC JOURNEY OF
POPE BENEDICT XVI TO PORTUGAL
ON THE OCCASION OF THE TENTH
ANNIVERSARY OF THE BEATIFICATION
OF JACINTA AND FRANCISCO,
YOUNG SHEPHERDS OF FÁTIMA

MEETING WITH THE BISHOPS OF PORTUGAL

From the

ADDRESS

Conference Hall of the
"Casa Nossa Senhora do Carmo" – Fátima
Thursday, 13 May 2010

In this Year for Priests now drawing to a close, rediscover, dear brothers, the role of the Bishop as father, especially with regard to your priests. For all too long the responsibility of authority as a service aimed at the growth of others and in the first place of priests, has been given second place. Priests are called to serve, in their pastoral ministry, and to be part of a pastoral activity of communion or oneness, as the Conciliar Decree *Presbyterorum Ordinis* reminds us, "No priest is sufficiently equipped to carry out his mission alone and as it were single-handed. He can only do so by joining forces with other priests, under the leadership of those who govern the Church" (No. 7). This is not a matter of turning back to the past, nor of a simple return to our origins, but rather of a recovery of the fervour of the origins, of the joy of the initial Christian experience, and of walking beside Christ like the disciples of Emmaus on the day of Easter, allowing his word to warm our hearts and his "broken bread" to open our eyes to the contemplation of his face. Only in this way will the fire of charity blaze strongly enough to impel every Christian to become a source of light and life in the Church and among all men and women.

BENEDICT XVI

GENERAL AUDIENCE

Saint Peter's Square
Wednesday, 26 May 2010

Munus regendi

The Year for Priests, is drawing to a close; therefore I began to talk in the last Catecheses about the essential tasks of the priest: to teach, to sanctify and to govern. I have already given two Catecheses, one on the ministry of sanctification, the Sacraments above all, and one on that of teaching. So it remains for me today to speak of the priest's mission to govern, to guide – with the authority of Christ, not his own, the portion of the People that God has entrusted to him.

How can we comprehend in our modern day culture a dimension of this kind that implies the concept of authority and has its origins in the Lord's own mandate to tend his flock? What is authority really, for us Christians? The cultural, political and historical experiences of the recent past, above all the dictatorships in Eastern and Western Europe in the 20th century, have made contemporary man suspicious of this concept. A suspicion which is often expressed in a conviction that it is necessary to eliminate every kind of authority does not come exclusively from man, and is not regulated and controlled by him. But it is precisely in reviewing those regimes which in the last century disseminated terror and death, that we are forcibly reminded that authority, in every circumstance, when it is exercised without reference to the Transcendent, if it neglects the Supreme Authority, which is God, inevitably finishes by turning against man. It is important, therefore, to recognize that human authority is never an end in itself but always and only a means and that, necessarily and in every age, the end is the person, created by God with his own inviolable dignity and called to relate to his Creator, both along the path of his earthly journey and in eternal life; it is an authority exercised in responsibility before God, before the Creator. An authority whose sole purpose is understood to be to serve the true good of the person and to be a glass through which we can see the one and supreme Good, which is God. Not only is it not foreign to man, but on the contrary, it is a precious help on our journey towards a total fulfilment in Christ, towards salvation.

The Church is called and commits herself to exercise this kind of authority which is service and exercises it not in her own name, but in the name of Jesus Christ, who received from his Father all authority both in Heaven and on Earth (cf. Mt 28:18) Christ tends his flock through the Pastor of the Church, in fact: it is he who guides, protects and corrects them, because he loves them deeply. But the Lord Jesus, the supreme Shepherd of our souls, has willed that the Apostolic College, today the Bishops, in communion with the Successor of Peter and the priests, their most precious collaborators, to participate in his mission of taking care of God's People, of educating them in the faith and of guiding, inspiring and sustaining the Christian community, or, as the Council puts it, "to see to it... that each member of the faithful shall be led in the Holy Spirit to the full development of his own vocation in accordance with Gospel preaching, and to sincere and active charity" and to exercise that liberty with which Christ has set us free (cf. *Presbyterorum Ordinis*, 6). Every Pastor, therefore, is a means through whom Christ himself loves men: it is through our ministry, dear priests, it is through us that the Lord reaches souls, instructs, guards and guides them. St Augustine, in his *Commentary on the Gospel of St John*, says: "let it therefore be a commitment of love to feed the flock of the Lord" (cf. 123, 5); this is the supreme rule of conduct for the ministers of God, an unconditional love, like that of the Good Shepherd, full of joy, given to all, attentive to those close to us and solicitous for those who are distant (cf. St Augustine, *Discourse* 340, 1; *Discourse* 46, 15), gentle towards the weakest, the little ones, the simple, the sinners, to manifest the infinite mercy of God with the reassuring words of hope (cf. *ibid., Epistle*, 95, 1).

Even if this pastoral task is founded on the Sacraments, its efficacy is not independent of the personal existence of the priest. In order to be a priest according to the heart of God (cf. Jer 3:15) it is necessary that not only the mind, but also the freedom and the will be deeply rooted in living friendship with Christ, a clear awareness of the identity received in Priestly Ordination, an unconditional readiness to lead the flock entrusted to him where the Lord desires and not in the direction which might, apparently, seem easier or more convenient. This requires, above all, a continuous and progressive willingness to allow Christ himself to govern the sacerdotal life. In fact, no one is really able to feed Christ's flock, unless he lives in profound and true obedience to Christ and the Church, and the docility of the people towards their priests depends on the docility of the priests towards Christ; for this reason the personal and constant encounter with the Lord, profound knowledge of him and the conformation of the individual will to Christ's will is always at the root of the pastoral ministry .

During the last decades, we have heard the adjective "pastoral" used almost as if it were in opposition to the concept of "hierarchical", and in the same way the idea of "communion" has also been set against it. At this point it may be useful to make a brief comment on the word "hierarchy", which is the traditional designation of the structure of sacramental authority within the Church, ordered according to the three levels of the Sacrament of Holy Orders, episcopate, presbyterate, diaconate: The concept of "hierarchy" carries, in public opinion, an element of subordination and of judgement; therefore to many the concept of hierarchy appears to be in contrast with the flexibility and vitality of the pastoral meaning and also appears contrary to the humility of the Gospel. However, this is a misunderstanding of the meaning of hierarchy, which arose in historical times from abuses of authority and careerism. But these are, in fact, abuses, and have nothing to do with the essential meaning of "hierarchy" itself. Common opinion holds that "hierarchy" is something connected with dominion and therefore cannot correspond to the real sense of the Church, that is unity in the love of Christ. But, as I have said, this is a mistaken interpretation, which has its origins in the abuses of the past, but does not correspond to the real meaning of hierarchy. Let us begin with the word. The word hierarchy is generally said to mean "sacred dominion", yet the real meaning is not this, but rather "sacred origin", that is to say: this authority does not come from man himself, but it has its origins in the sacred, in the Sacrament; so it subjects the person in second place to the vocation, to the mystery of Christ; it makes of the individual a servant of Christ, and only as a servant of Christ can he govern and guide for Christ and with Christ. Therefore he who enters into the Sacred Order of the Sacrament, the "hierarchy", is not an autocrat but he enters into a new bond of obedience to Christ: he is tied to Christ in communion with the other members of the Sacred Order, the Priesthood. Nor can the Pope, reference point for all the Pastors and for the communion of the Church, do what he likes; on the contrary, the Pope is the custodian of obedience to Christ, to his word summed up in the "*regula fidei*", in the Creed of the Church, and must lead the way in obedience to Christ and to his Church. Thus hierarchy implies a triple bond: in the first place the bond with Christ and with the order given by Our Lord to his Church; then the bond with the other Pastors in the one communion of the Church; and lastly, the bond with the faithful who are entrusted to the individual, in the order of the Church.

Therefore it is clear that communion and hierarchy are not contrary to each other, but they influence each other. Together they form one thing (hierarchical communion). The Pastor fulfils his role precisely when he guides and protects his flock and sometimes prevents it from scattering. Except in a vision which is clearly and explicitly supernatural, the task of governing which belongs to the priest is incomprehensible. On the contrary, sustained by a sincere desire for the salvation of each believer, he is particularly precious and necessary, also in our time. If the aim is to spread the message of Christ and to lead men and women towards a saving encounter with him, so that they may have life, then the task of guiding appears as a service lived in pure giving, for the edification of the flock in truth and holiness, often going against the tide, and remembering that he who is greater must act as the lesser, and he who governs as he who serves (cf. *Lumen Gentium*, n. 27).

Where can a priest today find the strength for such an exercise of his ministry, in full fidelity to Christ and to the Church, and complete devotion to his flock? There is only one answer: in Christ the Lord. Jesus' way of governing was not through dominion, but in the humble and loving service of the Washing of the feet, and the kingship of Christ over the Universe is not an earthly triumph, but reaches its highest point on the wood of the Cross, which becomes a judgement for the world and a point of reference for the exercising of that authority which is the true expression of pastoral charity. The saints, among them St John Mary Vianney, carried out with love and devotion the task of caring for the portion of God's People entrusted to them, showing themselves to be strong and determined men with the single aim of promoting the true good of souls, and capable of paying a price in person, even to martyrdom, in order to remain faithful to the truth and justice of the Gospel.

Dear priests, "tend the flock of God that is your charge, not by constraint but willingly... being examples to the flock" (1 Pet 5:2). Therefore, do not be afraid to lead to Christ each one of the brethren whom he has entrusted to you, certain that every word and every action will bear fruit if they come from obedience to God's will: know how to live in appreciating the merits and in recognition of the limits of the culture in which we find ourselves, with the firm assurance that the proclamation of the Gospel is the greatest service to render to man. In fact, there is no greater good, in this earthly life, than to lead people to God, to reawaken faith, to lift the person out of his inertia and desperation, to give the hope that God is near and directs our personal histories and that of the world: this, in the ultimate analysis, is the deep and final meaning of the task of governing that the Lord has given to us. To form Christ in believers, through that process of sanctification that is a conversion of criteria, scale of values, and patterns of behaviour, to allow Christ to live in every one of the faithful. St Paul sums up his pastoral action in these words, "my little children, with whom I am again in travail until Christ be formed in you" (Gal 4:19).

Dear brothers and sisters, I should like to invite you to pray for me, the Successor of Peter, who have a specific task in governing the Church of Christ, as have all your Bishops and priests. Pray that we may know how to take care of all the sheep, including those that are lost, that make up the flock entrusted to us. You, dear priests, I cordially invite to the closing celebrations of the Year for Priests, to be held on the 9th, 10th, and 11th June, here in Rome: we shall meditate on conversion and on mission, on the gift of the Holy Spirit and on the relationship with Mary Most Holy, and we shall renew our priestly promises, sustained by all the People of God. Thank you!

IV.
LECTIO DIVINA

VISIT TO THE PONTIFICAL ROMAN MAJOR SEMINARY IN HONOUR OF THE MEMORIAL OF OUR LADY OF TRUST

LECTIO DIVINA

Chapel of the Seminary
Friday, 12 February 2010

Every year it is a great joy to me to be with the seminarians of the Diocese of Rome, young men who are preparing themselves to respond to the Lord's call to be labourers in his vineyard and priests of his mystery. This is the joy of seeing that the Church lives, that the Church's future is also present in our region and, precisely, also in Rome.

In this Year for Priests let us be particularly attentive to the Lord's words about our service. The Gospel Passage that has just been read speaks indirectly but profoundly of our sacrament, of our call to be in the Lord's vineyard, to be servants of his mystery.

In this brief passage we find certain key words that give an idea of the proclamation that the Lord wishes to make with this text. "Abide": in this short passage we find the word "abide" ten times. We then find the new commandment: "Love one another as I have loved you" , "No longer do I call you servants... but friends", "bear fruit"; and lastly, "Ask, and it will be given you... that your joy may be full". Let us pray to the Lord that he may help us enter into the meaning of his words, that these words may penetrate our hearts, thus becoming in us the way and life, with us and through us.

The first words are: "Abide in me... in my love". Abiding in the Lord is fundamental as the first topic of this passage. Abide:

where? In love, in the love of Christ, in being loved and in loving the Lord. The whole of chapter 15 explains where we are to abide, because the first eight verses explain and present the Parable of the Vine: "I am the vine, you are the branches". The vine is an Old Testament image that we find in both the Prophets and the Psalms and it has a double meaning: it is a parable for the People of God which is his vineyard. He planted a vine in this world, he tended this vine, he tended his vineyard, he protected his vineyard and what was his intention? It was of course to produce fruit, to harvest the precious gift of grapes, of good wine.

And thus the second meaning appears: wine is a symbol, the expression of the joy of love. The Lord created his people to find the answer to his love. This image of the vine, of the vineyard thus has a spousal meaning, it is an expression of the fact that God seeks his creature's love, through his Chosen People he wants to enter into a relationship of love, a spousal relationship with the world.

Then, however, history proved to be a history of infidelity: instead of precious grapes, only small "inedible fruits" are produced. The response of this great love is not forthcoming, this unity, this unconditional union between man and God in the communion of love does not come about, man withdraws into himself, he wants to keep himself to himself, he wants to have God for himself, he wants the world for himself. Consequently the vineyard is devastated, the boar from the forest and all the enemies arrive and the vineyard becomes a wilderness.

But God does not give up. God finds a new way of reaching a free, irrevocable love, the fruit of this love, the true grape: God becomes man, and thus he himself becomes the root of the vine, he himself becomes the vine and so the vine becomes indestructible. This people of God cannot be destroyed for God himself has entered it, he has put down roots in this land. The new People of God is truly founded in God himself who becomes man and thus calls us to be the new vine in him and to abide in him, to dwell in him.

Let us also bear in mind that in chapter 6 of John's Gospel we find the Discourse of the Bread that becomes the great Discourse on the Eucharistic mystery. In this chapter 15 we have the Discourse on the Vine: the Lord does not speak explicitly of the Eucharist. Naturally, however, behind the mystery of the wine is the reality that he has made himself fruit and wine for us, that his Blood is the fruit of the love born from the earth for ever and, in the Eucharist, this Blood becomes our blood, we are renewed, we receive a new identity because Christ's Blood becomes our blood. Thus we are related to God in the Son and, in the Eucharist, this great reality of life in which we are branches joined to the Son and thereby in union with eternal love becomes our reality.

"Abide": abide in this great mystery, abide in this new gift of the Lord that has made us a people in itself, in his Body and with his Blood. It seems to me that we must meditate deeply on this mystery, that is, that God makes himself Body, one with us; Blood, one with us; that we may abide in this mystery in communion with God himself, in this great history of love that is the history of true happiness. In meditating on this gift God made himself one of us and at the same time he made us all one, a single vine we must also begin to pray so that this mystery may penetrate our minds and hearts ever more deeply and that we may be ever more capable of living the greatness of the mystery and thus begin to put this imperative: "abide" into practice.

If we continue to read this Gospel passage attentively, we also find a second imperative: "abide", and "observe my commandments". "Observe" only comes second. "Abide" comes first, at the ontological level, namely that we are united with him, he has given himself to us beforehand and has already given us his love, the fruit. It is not we who must produce the abundant fruit; Christianity is not moralism, it is not we who must do all that God expects of the world but we must first of all enter this ontological mystery: God gives himself. His being, his loving, precedes our action and, in the context of his Body, in the context of being in him, being identified with him and ennobled with his Blood, we too can act with Christ.

Ethics are a consequence of being: first the Lord gives us new life, this is the great gift. Being precedes action and from this being action then follows, as an organic reality, for we can also be what we are in our activity. Let us thus thank the Lord for he has removed us from pure moralism; we cannot obey a prescribed law but must only act in accordance with our new identity. Therefore it is no longer obedience, an external thing, but rather the fulfilment of the gift of new life.

I say it once again: let us thank the Lord because he goes before us, he gives us what we must give, and we must then be, in the truth and by virtue of our new being, protagonists of his reality. Abiding and observing: observing is the sign of abiding and abiding is the gift that he gives us but which must be renewed every day of our lives.

Next comes this new commandment: "love one another as I have loved you". There is no greater love than this, "that a man lay down his life for his friends". What does this mean? Here too it is not a question of moralism. Some might say: "It is not a new commandment; the commandment to love one's neighbour as oneself already exists in the Old Testament". Others say: "This love should be even more radicalized; this love of others must imitate Christ who gave himself for us; it must be a heroic love, to the point of the gift of self". In this case, however, Christianity would be a heroic moralism. It is true that we must reach the point of this radicalism of love which Christ showed to us and gave for us, but here too the true newness is not what we do, the true newness is what he did: the Lord gave us himself, and the Lord gave us the true newness of being members of his Body, of being branches of the vine that he is. Therefore, the newness is the gift, the great gift, and from the gift, from the newness of the gift, also follows, as I have said, the new action.

St Thomas Aquinas says this very succinctly when he writes: "The New Law is the grace of the Holy Spirit" (*Summa Theologiae,* I-IIae, q.106 a. 1). The New Law is not another commandment more difficult than the others: the New Law is a gift, the New Law is the presence of the Holy Spirit imparted to us in the sacrament of Baptism, in Confirmation, and given to us every day in the Most Blessed Eucharist. The Fathers distinguished here between *"sacramentum"* and *"exemplum"*. *"Sacramentum"* is the gift of the new being, and this gift also becomes an example for our action, but *"sacramentum"* precedes it and we live by the sacrament. Here we see the centrality of the sacrament which is the centrality of the gift.

Let us proceed in our reflection. The Lord says: "No longer do I call you servants, for the servant does not know what his master is doing; but I have called you friends, for all that I have heard from my Father I have made known to you". No longer servants who obey orders, but friends who know, who are united in the same will, in the same love. Hence the newness is that God has made himself known, that God has shown himself, that God is no longer the unknown God, sought but not found or only perceived from afar. God has shown himself: in the Face of Christ we see God, God has made himself "known", and has thereby made us his friends. Let us think how, in humanity's history, in all the archaic religions, it is known that there is a God. This knowledge is deeply rooted in the human heart, the knowledge that God is one, that deities are not "the" God. Yet this God remains very distant, he does not seem to make himself known, he does not make himself loved, he is not a friend, but is remote. Religions, therefore, were not very concerned with this God, concrete life was concerned with the spirits that we meet every day and with which we must reckon daily. God remained distant.

Then we see the great philosophical movement: let us think of Plato and Aristotle who began to understand that this God is the *agathon,* goodness itself, that he is the *eros* that moves the world; yet this remains a human thought, it is an idea of God that comes close to the truth but it is an idea of ours and God remains the hidden God.

A Regensburg professor recently wrote to me, a professor of physics who had read my Discourse to the University very late. He wrote to tell me that he could not agree, or not fully, with my logic. He said: "Of course, the idea is convincing that the rational structure of the world demands a creative reason that made this rationality which is not explained by itself". And he continued: "But if a demiurge can exist", this is how he put it, "a demiurge seems to me certain by what you say, I do not see that there is a God who is good, just and merciful. I can see that there is a reason that precedes the rationality of the cosmos, but I cannot see the rest". Thus God remains hidden to him. It is a reason that precedes our reasoning, our rationality, the rationality of being, but eternal love does not exist, the great mercy that gives us life does not exist.

And here, in Christ, God showed himself in his total truth, he showed that he is reason and love, that eternal reason is love and thus creates. Unfortunately, today too, many people live far from Christ, they do not know his face and thus the eternal temptation of dualism, which is also hidden in this professor's letter, is constantly renewed, in other words perhaps there is not only one good principle but also a bad principle, a principle of evil; perhaps the world is divided and there are two equally strong realities and the Good God is only part of the reality. Today, even in theology, including Catholic theology, this thesis is being disseminated: that God is not almighty. Thus an apology is sought for God who would not, therefore, be responsible for the great store of evil we encounter in the world. But what a feeble apology! A God who is not almighty! Evil is not in his hands! And how could we possibly entrust ourselves to this God? How could we be certain of his love if this love ended where the power of evil began?

However, God is no longer unknown: in the Face of the Crucified Christ we see God and we see true omnipotence, not the myth of omnipotence. For us human beings, almightiness, power, is always identified with the capacity to destroy, to do evil. Nevertheless the true concept of omnipotence that appears in Christ is precisely the opposite: in him true omnipotence is loving to the point that God can suffer: here his true omnipotence is revealed, which can even go as far as a love that suffers for us. And thus we see that he is the true God and the true God, who is love, is power: the power of love. And we can trust ourselves to his almighty love and live in this, with this almighty love.

I think we should always meditate anew on this reality, that we should thank God because he has shown himself, because we know his Face, we know him face to face; no longer like Moses who could only see the back of the Lord. This too is a beautiful idea of which St Gregory of Nyssa said: "Seeing only his back, means that we must always follow Christ". But at the same time God showed us his Countenance with Christ, his Face. The curtain of the temple was torn. It opened, the mystery of God is visible. The first commandment that excludes images of God because they might only diminish his reality is changed, renewed, taking another form. Today we can see God's Face in Christ the man, we can have an image of Christ and thus see who God is.

I think that those who have understood this, who have been touched by this mystery, that God has revealed himself, that the curtain of the temple has been torn asunder, that he has shown his Face, find a source of permanent joy. We can only say "thank you. Yes, now we know who you are, who God is and how to respond to him". And I think that this joy of knowing God who has shown himself, to the depths of his being, also embraces the joy of communicating this: those who have understood this, who live touched by this reality, must do as the first disciples did when they went to their friends and brethren saying: "We have found the one of whom the Prophets spoke. He is present now". Mission is not an external appendix to the faith but rather the dynamism of faith itself. Those who have seen, who have encountered Jesus, must go to their friends and tell them:

"We have found him, he is Jesus, the One who was Crucified for us."

Then, continuing, the text says: "I chose you and appointed you that you should go and bear fruit and that your fruit should abide". With this we return to the beginning, to the image, to the Parable of the Vine: it is created to bear fruit. And what is the fruit? As we have said, the fruit is love. In the Old Testament, with the Torah as the first stage of God's revelation of himself, the fruit was understood as justice, that is, living in accordance with the Word of God, living in accordance with God's will, hence, living well.

This continues but at the same time is transcended: true justice does not consist in obedience to a few norms, rather it is love, creative love that finds in itself the riches and abundance of good. Abundance is one of the key words of the New Testament. God himself always gives in abundance. In order to create man, he creates this abundance of an immense cosmos; to redeem man he gives himself, in the Eucharist he gives himself. And anyone who is united with Christ, who is a branch of the Vine and who abides by this law does not ask: "Can I still do this or not?", "Should I do this or not?". Rather, he lives in the enthusiasm of love that does not ask: "Is this still necessary or is it forbidden?", but simply, in the creativity of love, wants to live with Christ and for Christ and give his whole self to him, thus entering into the joy of bearing fruit. Let us also bear in mind that the Lord says: "I chose you and appointed you that you should go": this is the dynamism that dwells in Christ's love; to go, in other words not to remain alone for me, to see my perfection, to guarantee eternal beatification for me, but rather to forget myself, to go as Christ went, to go as God went from the immensity of his majesty to our poverty, to find fruit, to help us, to give us the possibility of bearing the true fruit of love. The fuller we are of this joy in having discovered God's Face, the more real will the enthusiasm of love in us be and it will bear fruit.

And finally, we come to the last words in this passage: "Whatever you ask the Father in my name, he may give it to you": a brief catechesis on prayer that never ceases to surprise us. Twice in this chapter 15 the Lord says: "ask whatever you will, and it shall be done for you", and he says it once more in chapter 16. And we want to say: "But no, Lord it is not true". There are so many good and deeply-felt prayers of mothers who pray for a dying child which are not heard, so many prayers that something good will happen and the Lord does not grant it. What does this promise mean? In chapter 16 the Lord offers us the key to understanding it: he tells us what he gives us, what all this is, *chara,* joy. If someone has found joy he has found all things and sees all things in the light of divine love. Like St Francis, who wrote the great poem on creation in a bleak situation, yet even there, close to the suffering Lord, he rediscovered the beauty of being, the goodness of God and composed this great poem.

It is also useful to remember at the same time some verses of Luke's Gospel, in which the Lord, in a parable, speaks of prayer, saying, "If you then, who are evil, know how to give good gifts to your children, how much more will the heavenly Father give the Holy Spirit to those who ask him!". The Holy Spirit, in the Gospel according to Luke, is joy, in John's Gospel he is the same reality: joy is the Holy Spirit and the Holy Spirit is joy or, in other words from God we do not ask something small or great, from God we invoke the divine gift, God himself; this is the great gift that God gives us: God himself. In this regard we must learn to pray, to pray for the great reality, for the divine reality, so that God may give us himself, may give us his Spirit and thus we may respond to the demands of life and help others in their suffering. Of course he teaches us the "Our Father". We can pray for many things. In all our needs we can pray: "Help me!". This is very human and God is human, as we have seen; therefore it is right to pray God also for the small things of our daily lives.

However, at the same time, prayer is a journey, I would say flight of stairs: we must learn more and more what it is that we can pray for and what we cannot pray for because it is an expression of our selfishness. I cannot pray for things that are harmful for others, I cannot pray for things that help my egoism, my pride. Thus prayer, in God's eyes, becomes a process of purification of our thoughts, of our desires. As the Lord says in the Parable of the Vine: we must be pruned, purified, every day; living with Christ, in Christ, abiding in Christ, is a process of purification and it is only in this process of slow purification, of liberation from ourselves and from the desire to have only ourselves, that the true journey of life lies and the path of joy unfolds.

As I have already said, all the Lord's words have a sacramental background. The fundamental background for the Parable of the Vine is Baptism: we are implanted in Christ; and the Eucharist: we are one loaf, one body, one blood, one life with Christ. Thus this process of purification also has a sacramental background: the sacrament of Penance, of Reconciliation, in which we accept this divine pedagogy which day by day, throughout our life, purifies us and increasingly makes us true members of his Body. In this way we can learn that God responds to our prayers, that he often responds with his goodness also to small prayers, but often, too, he corrects them, transforms them and guides them so that we may at last and really be branches of his Son, of the true vine, members of his Body.

Let us thank God for the greatness of his love, let us pray that he may help us to grow in his love and truly to abide in his love.

MEETING WITH THE PARISH PRIESTS
OF THE DIOCESE OF ROME

LECTIO DIVINA

Hall of Blessings
Thursday, 18 February 2010

It is always a very joyful as well as an important tradition for me to be able to begin Lent with my Presbyterium, the Priests of Rome. Thus, as the local Church of Rome but also as the universal Church, we can start out on this essential journey with the Lord towards the Passion, towards the Cross, the Easter journey.

Let us meditate this year on the passages from the Letter to the Hebrews that have just been read. The Author of this Letter introduced a new way of understanding the Old Testament as a Book that speaks of Christ. The previous tradition had seen Christ above all, essentially, in the key of the Davidic promise, the promise of the true David, of the true Solomon, of the true King of Israel, the true King since he was both man and God. And the inscription on the Cross truly proclaimed this reality to the world: now there is the true King of Israel, who is King of the world, the King of the Jews hangs on the Cross. It is a proclamation of the kingship of Jesus, of the fulfilment of the messianic expectation of the Old Testament which, at the bottom of their hearts, is shared by all men and women who await the true King who will bring justice, love and brotherhood.

However, the author of the Letter to the Hebrews discovered a citation which until then had gone unnoticed: Psalm 110 [109]:4 "You are a priest for ever after the order of Melchizedek". This means that not only does Jesus fulfil the Davidic promise, the expectation of the true King of Israel and of the world, but he also makes the promise of the real Priest come true. In a part of the Old Testament and especially in Qumran there are two separate lines of expectation: of the King and of the Priest. In discovering this verse, the Author of the Letter to the Hebrews realized that the two promises are united in Christ: Christ is the true King, the Son of God in accordance with Psalm 2:7, from which he quotes but he is also the true Priest.

Thus the whole of the religious world, the whole reality of sacrifices, of the priesthood that is in search of the true priesthood, the true sacrifice, finds in Christ its key, its fulfilment. And with this key it can reinterpret the Old Testament and show precisely that also the religious law abolished after the destruction of the Temple was actually moving towards Christ. Hence it was not really abolished but renewed, transformed, so that in Christ all things might find their meaning. The priesthood thus appears in its purity and in its profound depth.

In this way the Letter to the Hebrews presents the theme of the priesthood of Christ, of Christ the priest, at three levels: the priesthood of Aaron, that of the Temple; Melchizedek; and Christ himself as the true priest. Indeed, the priesthood of Aaron, in spite of being different from Christ's priesthood, in spite of being, so to speak, solely a quest, a journey in the direction of Christ, is nevertheless a "journey" towards Christ and in this priesthood the essential elements are already outlined. Then Melchizedek we shall return to this point who is a pagan. The pagan world enters the Old Testament. It enters as a mysterious figure, without father or mother the Letter to the Hebrews says it simply appears, and in this figure can be seen the true veneration of the Most High God, of the Creator of the Heavens and of the earth. Thus the pagan world too experiences the expectation and profound prefiguration of Christ's mystery. In Christ himself everything is recapitulated, purified and led to its term, to its true essence.

Let us now look at the individual elements concerning the priesthood as best we can. We learn two things from the Law, from the priesthood of Aaron, the Author of the Letter to the Hebrews says: if he is truly to be a mediator between God and man, a priest must be man. This is fundamental and the Son of God was made man precisely in order to be a priest, to be able to fulfil the priest's mission. He must be man – we shall come back to this point – but he is unable, on his own, to make himself a mediator for God. The priest needs divine authorization, institution, and only by belonging to both spheres, the divine and the human, can he be a mediator, can he be a "bridge". This is the priest's mission: to combine, to link these two realities that appear to be so separate, that is, the world of God far from us, often unknown to the human being and our human world. The priest's mission is to be a mediator, a bridge that connects, and thereby to bring human beings to God, to his redemption, to his true light, to his true life.

As the first point, therefore, the priest must be on God's side. Only in Christ is this need, this prerequisite of mediation, fully brought about. This Mystery was therefore necessary: the Son of God is made man so that he may be the true bridge for us, the true mediation. Others must have at least an authorization from God, or in the Church's case, the Sacrament, that is they must introduce our being into the being of Christ, into divine being. Only with the Sacrament, this divine act that makes us priests in communion with Christ, can we accomplish our mission. And this seems to me a first point for our meditation: the importance of the Sacrament. No one can become a priest by himself; God alone can attract me, can authorize me, can introduce me into participation in Christ's mystery; God alone can enter my life and take me by the hand. This aspect of divine giving, of divine precedence, of divine action that we ourselves cannot bring about and our passivity being chosen and taken by the hand by God is a fundamental point we must enter into. We must always return to the Sacrament, to this gift in which

God gives me what I will never be able to give; participation, communion with divine being, with the priesthood of Christ.

Let us also make this reality a practical factor in our life: if this is how it is, a priest must really be a man of God, he must know God intimately and know him in communion with Christ and so we must live this communion; and the celebration of Holy Mass, the prayer of the Breviary, all our personal prayers are elements of being with God, of being men of God. Our being, our life and our heart must be fixed in God, in this point from which we must not stir. This is achieved and reinforced day after day with short prayers in which we reconnect with God and become, increasingly, men of God who live in his communion and can thus speak of God and lead people to God.

The other element is that the priest must be man, human in all senses. That is, he must live true humanity, true humanism; he must be educated, have a human formation, human virtues; he must develop his intelligence, his will, his sentiments, his affections; he must be a true man, a man according to the will of the Creator, of the Redeemer, for we know that the human being is wounded and the question of "what man is" is obscured by the event of sin that hurt human nature even to the quick. Thus people say: "he lied" "it is human"; "he stole" "it is human"; but this is not really being human. Human means being generous, being good, being a just person, it means true prudence and wisdom. Therefore emerging with Christ's help from this dark area in our nature so as to succeed in being truly human in the image of God is a lifelong process that must begin in our training for the priesthood. It must subsequently be achieved, however, and continue as long as we live. I think that basically these two things go hand in hand: being of God and with God and being true man, in the true sense meant by the Creator when he formed this creature that we are.

To be man: the Letter to the Hebrews stresses our humanity; we find this surprising for it says: "He can deal gently with the ignorant and wayward, since he himself is beset with weakness" (5:2). And then even more forcefully "In the days of his flesh,

Jesus offered up prayers and supplications, with loud cries and tears, to him who was able to save him from death, and he was heard for his godly fear" (5:7). For the Letter to the Hebrews, the essential element of our being human is being compassionate, suffering with others: this is true humanity. It is not sin because sin is never solidarity but always tears solidarity apart, it is living life for oneself instead of giving it. True humanity is real participation in the suffering of human beings. It means being a compassionate person *metriopathèin,* the Greek text says that is, being at the core of human passion, really bearing with others the burden of their suffering, the temptation of our time: "God, where are you in this world?".

The humanity of the priest does not correspond to the Platonic or Aristotelian ideal which claims that the true man is the one who lives in contemplation of the truth alone and so is blessed happy because he only has friendship with beautiful things, with divine beauty, while "the work" is left to others. This is a hypothesis; whereas here it is implied that the priest enter, like Christ, into human wretchedness, carry it with him, visit those who are suffering and look after them and, not only outwardly but also inwardly, take upon himself, recapitulate in himself the "passion" of his time, of his parish, of the people entrusted to his care. This is how Christ showed his true humanity. Of course, his Heart was always fixed on God, he always saw God, he was always in intimate conversation with him. Yet at the same time he bore the whole being, the whole of human suffering entered the Passion. In speaking, in seeing people who were lowly, who had no pastor, he suffered with them. Moreover, we priests cannot withdraw to an *Elysium.* Let us rather be immersed in the passion of this world and with Christ's help and in communion with him, we must seek to transform it, to bring it to God.

Precisely this should be said, with the following really stimulating text: "Jesus offered up prayers and supplications, with loud cries and tears" (Heb 5:7). This is not only a reference to the hour of anguish on the Mount of Olives but sums up the whole history of the Passion that embraces Jesus' entire life.

Tears: Jesus wept by the tomb of Lazarus, he was truly moved inwardly by the mystery of death, by the terror of death. People forgive the brother, as in this case, the mother and the son, the friend: all the dreadfulness of death that destroys love, that destroys relationships, that is a sign of our finiteness, our poverty. Jesus is put to the test and he confronts this mystery in the very depths of his soul in the sorrow that is death and weeps. He weeps before Jerusalem, seeing the destruction of the beautiful city because of disobedience; he weeps, seeing all the destruction of the world's history; he weeps, seeing that people destroy themselves and their cities with violence and with disobedience.

Jesus weeps with loud cries. We know from the Gospels that Jesus cried out from the Cross: "My God, my God, why have you forsaken me?" (Mk 15:34; cf. Mt 27:46) and cried out once again at the end. And this cry responds to a fundamental dimension of the Psalm: in the terrible moments of human life many Psalms are a loud cry to God: "Help us, hear us!". On this very day, in the Breviary, we prayed like this: God, where are you? "You have made us like sheep for slaughter" (Ps 44[43]:11 [rsv]). A cry of suffering humanity! And Jesus, who is the true subject of the Psalms, truly bears this cry of humanity to God, to God's ears: "help us and hear us!". He transforms the whole of suffering humanity, taking it to himself in a cry to God to hear him.

Thus we see that in this very way he brings about the priesthood, the function of mediator, bearing in himself, taking on in himself the sufferings and passion of the world, transforming it into a cry to God, bringing it before the eyes and to the hands of God and thus truly bringing it to the moment of redemption.

In fact the Letter to the Hebrews says that "he offered up prayers and supplications", "loud cries and tears" (5:7). It is a correct translation of the verb *prosphèrein*. This is a religious word and expresses the act of offering human gifts to God, it expresses precisely the act of offering, of sacrifice. Thus with these religious terms applied to the prayers and tears of Christ, it shows that Christ's tears, his anguish on the Mount of Olives, his cry on the Cross, all his suffering are nothing in comparison with his important mission. In this very way he makes his sacrifice, he becomes the priest. With this "offered", *prosphèrein,* the Letter to the Hebrews says to us: this is the fulfilment of his priesthood, thus he brings humanity to God, in this way he becomes mediator, he becomes priest.

We say, rightly, that Jesus did not offer God some thing. Rather, he offered himself and made this offering of himself with the very compassion that transforms the suffering of the world into prayer and into a cry to the Father. Nor, in this sense, is our own priesthood limited to the religious act of Holy Mass in which everything is placed in Christ's hands but all of our compassion to the suffering of this world so remote from God is a priestly act, it is *prosphèrein,* it is offering up. In this regard, in my opinion, we must understand and learn how to accept more profoundly the sufferings of pastoral life, because priestly action is exactly this, it is mediation, it is entering into the mystery of Christ, it is communication with the mystery of Christ, very real and essential, existential and then sacramental.

A second term in this context is important. It is said that by means of this obedience Christ is made perfect, in Greek *teleiothèis* (cf. Heb 5:8-9). We know that throughout the Torah, that is, in all religious legislation, the word *tèleion,* used here, means priestly ordination. In other words the Letter to the Hebrews tells us that precisely by doing this Jesus was made a priest, and his priesthood was fulfilled. Our sacramental priestly ordination should be brought about and achieved existentially but also Christologically, and through precisely this, should bring the world with Christ and to Christ and, with Christ, to God: thus we really become priests, *teleiothèis.* Therefore the priest is not a thing for a few hours but is fulfilled precisely in pastoral life, in his sufferings and his weaknesses, in his sorrows and also in his joys, of course. In this way we increasingly become priests in communion with Christ.

Finally the Letter to the Hebrews sums up all this compassion in the word *hypakoèn,* obedience: it is all obedience. This is an unpopular word in our day. Obedience appears as an alienation, a servile attitude. One does not enjoy one's own freedom, one's freedom is subjected to another's will, hence one is no longer free but determined by another, whereas self-determination, emancipation, would be true human existence. Instead of the word "obedience", as an anthropological keyword we would like the term "freedom". Yet, on considering this problem closely, we see that these two things go together: Christ's obedience is the conformity of his will with the will of the Father; it is bringing the human will to the divine will, to the conformation of our will with God's will.

In his interpretation of the Mount of Olives, of the anguish expressed precisely in Jesus' prayer, "not my will but your will", St Maximus Confessor described this process that Christ carries in himself as a true man, together with the human nature and will; in this act "not my will but your will" Jesus recapitulates the whole process of his life, of leading, that is, natural human life to divine life and thereby transforming the human being. It is the divinization of the human being, hence the redemption of the human being, because God's will is not a tyrannical will, is not a will outside our being but is the creative will itself; it is the very place where we find our true identity.

God created us and we are ourselves if we conform with his will; only in this way do we enter into the truth of our being and are not alienated. On the contrary, alienation occurs precisely by disregarding God's will, for in this way we stray from the plan for our existence; we are no longer ourselves and we fall into the void. Indeed, obedience, namely, conformity to God, the truth of our being, is true freedom, because it is divinization. Jesus, in bearing the human being, being human in himself and with himself, in conformity with God, in perfect obedience, that is, in the perfect conformation between the two wills, has redeemed us and redemption is always this process of leading the human will to communion with the divine will. It is

a process for which we pray every day: "May your will be done"
And let us really pray the Lord to help us see closely that this is
freedom and thus enter joyfully into this obedience and into
"taking hold of" human beings in order to bring them by our
own example, by our humility, by our prayer, by our pastoral
action into communion with God.

Continuing our reading, a sentence of difficult interpretation
follows. The Author of the Letter to the Hebrews says that Jesus
prayed loudly, with cries and tears, to God who could save him
from death and that in his total abandonment he is heard (cf.
5:7). Here let us say: "No, it is not true, his prayer went unheard,
he is dead". Jesus prayed to be released from death, but he was
not released, he died a very cruel death. Harnack, a liberal
theologian, therefore wrote: "Here a *not* is missing", it must be
written "He was not heard", and Bultmann accepted this
interpretation. Yet this is a solution that is not an exegesis but
rather a betrayal of the text. "Not" does not appear in any of the
manuscripts but "he was heard"; so we must learn to understand
what "being heard" means, in spite of the Cross.

I see three levels on which to understand these words. At a
first level the Greek text may be translated as: "he was redeemed
from his anguish", and in this sense Jesus is heard. This would
therefore be a hint of what St Luke tells us: an angel strengthened
him (cf. Lk 22:43), in such a way that after the moment of
anguish he was able to go, straight away and fearlessly towards
his hour, as the Gospels describe it to us, especially that of John.
This would be being heard in the sense that God gives him
the strength to bear the whole of this burden and so he was
heard. Yet to me it seems that this answer is not quite enough.
Being heard, in the fullest sense Fr Vanhoye emphasized, would
mean "he was redeemed from death", however not for the
moment, for that moment, but for ever, in the Resurrection:
God's true response to the prayer to be saved from death is
the Resurrection and humanity is saved from death precisely in
the Resurrection which is the true healing of our suffering and
of the terrible mystery of death.

Already present here is a third level of understanding: Jesus' Resurrection is not only a personal event. I think it would be helpful to keep in mind the brief text in which St John, in chapter 12 of his Gospel, presents and recounts, in a very concise manner, the event on the Mount of Olives. Jesus says: "Now is my soul troubled" (Jn 12:27) and, in all the anguish of the Mount of Olives, what shall I say? "Father, save me from this hour... Father glorify your name" (cf. Jn 12:27-28). This is the same prayer that we find in the Synoptic Gospels: "all things are possible to you... your will be done (cf. Mt 26:42; Mk 14:36; Lk 22:42) which in Johannine language appears: either as "save me" or "glorify" [your name]. And God answers: "I have glorified it, and I will glorify it again" (cf. Jn 12:28). This is the response, it is God hearing him: I will glorify the Cross; it is the presence of divine glory because it is the supreme act of love. On the Cross Jesus is raised above all the earth and attracts the earth to him; on the Cross the "*Kabod*" now appears, the true divine glory of God who loves even to the Cross and thus transforms death and creates the Resurrection.

Jesus' prayer was heard in the sense that his death truly becomes life, it becomes the place where he redeems the human being, where he attracts the human being to himself. If the divine response in John says: "I will glorify" you, it means that this glory transcends and passes through the whole of history over and over again: from your Cross, present in the Eucharist, it transforms death into glory. This is the great promise that is brought about in the Blessed Eucharist which ever anew opens the heavens. Being a servant of the Eucharist is, therefore, a depth of the priestly mystery.

Another brief word, at least about Melchizedek. He is a mysterious figure who enters Sacred History in Genesis 14. After Abraham's victory over several kings, Melchizedek, King of *Salem*, of Jerusalem, appears and brings out bread and wine. This uncommented and somewhat incomprehensible event appears only in Psalm 110 [109] as has been said, but it is clear that Judaism, Gnosticism and Christianity then wished to reflect profoundly on these words and created their interpretations. The Letter to the Hebrews does not speculate but reports only what Scripture says and there are various elements: he is a king of righteousness, he dwells in peace, he is king where peace reigns, he venerates and worships the Most High God, the Creator of Heaven and earth, and he brings out bread and wine (cf. Heb 7:1-3; Gen 14:18-20). It is not mentioned here that the High Priest of the Most High God, King of Peace, worships God, Creator of Heaven and earth with bread and wine. The Fathers stressed that he is one of the holy pagans of the Old Testament and this shows that even from paganism there is a path that leads to Christ. The criteria are: worshipping God Most High, the Creator, fostering righteousness and peace and venerating God in a pure way. Thus, with these fundamental elements, paganism too is on its way to Christ, and in a certain way, makes Christ's light present.

In the Roman canon after consecration we have the prayer *supra quae* that mentions certain prefigurations of Christ, his priesthood and his sacrifice: Abel, the first martyr, with his lamb; Abraham, whose intention is to sacrifice his son Isaac, replaced by the lamb sent by God; and Melchizedek, High Priest of God Most High who brings out bread and wine. This means that Christ is the absolute newness of God and at the same time is present in the whole of history, through history, and history goes to encounter Christ. And not only the history of the Chosen People, which is the true preparation desired by God, in which is revealed the mystery of Christ, but also in paganism the mystery of Christ is prepared, paths lead from it toward Christ who carries all things within him.

This seems to me important in the celebration of the Eucharist: here is gathered together all human prayer, all human desire, all true human devotion, the true search for God that is fulfilled at last in Christ. Lastly, it should be said that the Heavens are now open, worship is no longer enigmatic, in relative signs, but true. For Heaven is open and people do not offer some thing, rather, the human being becomes one with God and this is true worship. This is what the Letter to the Hebrews says: "Our priest... is seated at the right hand of the throne... in the sanctuary, the true tent which is set up... by the Lord" (cf. 8:1-2).

Let us return to the point that Melchizedek is King of *Salem*. The whole Davidic tradition refers to this, saying: "Here is the place, Jerusalem is the place of the true worship, the concentration of worship in Jerusalem dates back to the times of Abraham, Jerusalem is the true place for the proper veneration of God".

Let us take another step: the true Jerusalem, God's *Salem,* is the Body of Christ, the Eucharist is God's peace with humankind. We know that in his Prologue, St John calls the humanity of Jesus the tent of God, *eskènosen en hemìn* (cf. Jn 1:14). It was here that God himself pitched his tent in the world, and this tent, this new, true Jerusalem is at the same time on earth and in Heaven because this Sacrament, this sacrifice, is ceaselessly brought about among us and always arrives at the throne of Grace, at God's presence. Here is the true Jerusalem, at the same time heavenly and earthly, the tent which is the Body of God, which as a risen Body always remains a Body and embraces humanity. And, at the same time, since it is a risen Body, it unites us with God. All this is constantly brought about anew in the Eucharist. We, as priests, are called to be ministers of this great Mystery, in the Sacrament and in life. Let us pray the Lord that he grant us to understand this Mystery ever better, that he make us live this mystery ever better and thus to offer our help so that the world may be opened to God, so that the world may be redeemed. Thank you.

The Holy Father drew inspiration for his "lectio divina" from the following passages from the Letter to the Hebrews:

Heb 5:1-10
Heb 7:26-28
Heb 8:1-2

(*L'Osservatore Romano*, 24 February 2010)

V.
MESSAGES

MESSAGE
FOR THE 46th WORLD DAY
OF PRAYER FOR VOCATIONS

Fourth Sunday of Easter, 3 May 2009

Faith in the divine initiative – the human response.

On the occasion of the next World Day of prayer for vocations to the priesthood and to the consecrated life, which will be celebrated on 3 May 2009, the Fourth Sunday of Easter, I want to invite all the People of God to reflect on the theme: *Faith in the divine initiative – the human response.* The exhortation of Jesus to his disciples: "Pray therefore the Lord of the harvest to send out labourers into his harvest" (Mt 9:38) has a constant resonance in the Church. Pray! The urgent call of the Lord stresses that prayer for vocations should be continuous and trusting. The Christian community can only really "have ever greater faith and hope in God's providence" (*Sacramentum Caritatis*, 26) if it is enlivened by prayer.

The vocation to the priesthood and to the consecrated life constitutes a special gift of God which becomes part of the great plan of love and salvation that God has for every man and woman and for the whole of humanity. The Apostle Paul, whom we remember in a special way during this Pauline Year dedicated to the Two-thousandth anniversary of his birth, writing to the Ephesians says, "Blessed be the God and Father of our Lord Jesus Christ, who has blessed us in Christ with every spiritual blessing in the heavenly places, even as he chose us in him before the foundation of the world, that we should be holy and blameless before him" (Eph 1:3-4). In the universal call to holiness, of particular relevance is God's initiative of choosing some to follow his Son Jesus Christ more closely, and to be his privileged ministers and witnesses. The divine

Master personally called the Apostles "to be with him, and to be sent out to preach and have authority to cast out demons" (Mk 3:14-15); they, in turn, gathered other disciples around them as faithful collaborators in this mission. In this way, responding to the Lord's call and docile to the movement of the Holy Spirit, over the centuries, countless ranks of priests and consecrated persons placed themselves totally at the service of the Gospel in the Church. Let us give thanks to God, because even today he continues to call together workers into his vineyard. While it is undoubtedly true that a worrisome shortage of priests is evident in some regions of the world, and that the Church encounters difficulties and obstacles along the way, we are sustained by the unshakable certitude that the one who firmly guides her in the pathways of time towards the definitive fulfilment of the Kingdom is he, the Lord, who freely chooses persons of every culture and of every age and invites them to follow him according to the mysterious plans of his merciful love.

Our first duty, therefore, is to keep alive in families and in parishes, in movements and in apostolic associations, in religious communities and in all the sectors of diocesan life this appeal to the divine initiative with unceasing prayer. We must pray that the whole Christian people grows in its trust in God, convinced that the "Lord of the harvest" does not cease to ask some to place their entire existence freely at his service so as to work with him more closely in the mission of salvation. What is asked of those who are called, for their part, is careful listening and prudent discernment, a generous and willing adherence to the divine plan, and a serious study of the reality that is proper to the priestly and religious vocations, so as to be able to respond responsibly and with conviction.

The *Catechism of the Catholic Church* rightly reminds us that God's free initiative requires a free response on the part of men and women; a positive response which always presupposes acceptance of and identification with the plan that God has for everyone; a response which welcomes the Lord's loving initiative and becomes, for the one who is called, a binding moral imperative, an offering of thanksgiving to God and a total cooperation with the plan which God carries out in history (cf. n. 2062).

Contemplating the mystery of the Eucharist, which expresses in a sublime way the free gift of the Father in the Person of his Only Begotten Son for the salvation of mankind, and the full and docile readiness of Christ to drink to the dregs the "cup" of the will of God (cf. Mt 26:39), we can more readily understand how "*faith in the divine initiative*" models and gives value to the "*human response*". In the Eucharist, that perfect gift which brings to fulfilment the plan of love for the redemption of the world, Jesus offers himself freely for the salvation of mankind. "The Church", my beloved predecessor John Paul II wrote, "has received the Eucharist from Christ her Lord not as a gift – however precious – among so many others, but as the *gift par excellence*, for it is the gift of himself, of his person in his sacred humanity, as well as the gift of his saving work" (*Ecclesia de Eucharistia*, 11).

It is priests who are called to perpetuate this salvific mystery from century to century until the Lord's glorious return, for they can contemplate, precisely in the Eucharistic Christ, the eminent model of a "vocational dialogue" between the free initiative of the Father and the faithful response of Christ. In the celebration of the Eucharist it is Christ himself who acts in those whom he chooses as his ministers; he supports them so that their response develops in a dimension of trust and gratitude that removes all fear, even when they experience more acutely their own weakness (cf. Rom 8:26-28), or indeed when the experience of misunderstanding or even of persecution is most bitter (cf. Rom 8:35-39).

The awareness of being saved by the love of Christ, which every Mass nourishes in the faithful and especially in priests, cannot but arouse within them a trusting self-abandonment to Christ who gave his life for us. To believe in the Lord and to accept his gift, therefore, leads us to entrust ourselves to Him with thankful hearts, adhering to his plan of salvation. When this does happen, the one who is "called" voluntarily leaves everything and submits himself to the teaching of the divine Master; hence a fruitful dialogue between God and man begins, a mysterious encounter between the love of the Lord who calls and the freedom of man who responds in love, hearing the words of Jesus echoing in his soul, "You did not choose me, but I chose you and appointed you that you should go and bear fruit and that your fruit should abide" (Jn 15:16).

This intertwining of love between the divine initiative and the human response is present also, in a wonderful way, in the vocation to the consecrated life. The Second Vatican Council recalls, "The evangelical counsels of chastity dedicated to God, poverty and obedience are based upon the words and examples of the Lord. They were further commanded by the apostles and Fathers of the Church, as well as by the doctors and pastors of souls. The counsels are a divine gift, which the Church received from its Lord and which it always safeguards with the help of His grace" (*Lumen Gentium*, 43).

Once more, Jesus is the model of complete and trusting adherence to the will of the Father, to whom every consecrated person must look. Attracted by him, from the very first centuries of Christianity, many men and women have left families, possessions, material riches and all that is humanly desirable in order to follow Christ generously and live the Gospel without compromise, which had become for them a school of deeply rooted holiness. Today too, many undertake this same demanding journey of evangelical perfection and realise their vocation in the profession of the evangelical counsels. The witness of these our brothers and sisters, in contemplative monasteries, religious institutes and congregations of apostolic life, reminds the people of God of "that mystery of the Kingdom of God is already at work in history, even as it awaits its full realization in heaven" (*Vita Consecrata*, 1).

Who can consider himself worthy to approach the priestly ministry? Who can embrace the consecrated life relying only on his or her own human powers? Once again, it is useful to reiterate that the response of men and women to the divine call, whenever they are aware that it is God who takes the initiative and brings His plan of salvation to fulfilment, is never patterned after the timid self-interest of the worthless servant who, out of fear, hid the talent entrusted to him in the ground (cf. Mt 25: 14-30), but rather expresses itself in a ready adherence to the Lord's invitation, as in the case of Peter who, trusting in the Lord' word, did not hesitate to let down the net once more even after having toiled all night and catching nothing (cf. Lk 5:5). Without in any sense renouncing personal responsibility, the free human response to God thus becomes "co-responsibility", responsibility in and with Christ, through the action of his Holy Spirit; it becomes communion with the One who makes it possible for us to bear much fruit (cf. Jn 15:5).

An emblematic human response, full of trust in God's initiative, is the generous and unmitigated "Amen" of the Virgin of Nazareth, uttered with humble and decisive adherence to the plan of the Most High announced to her by God's messenger (cf. Lk 1:38). Her prompt "Yes" allowed Her to become the Mother of God, the Mother of our Saviour. Mary, after this first "fiat", had to repeat it many times, even up to the culminating moment of the crucifixion of Jesus, when "standing by the cross of Jesus" as the Evangelist John notes, she participated in the dreadful suffering of her innocent Son. And it was from the cross, that Jesus, while dying, gave her to us as Mother and entrusted us to her as sons and daughters (cf. Jn 19:26-27); she is especially the Mother of priests and consecrated persons. I want to entrust to her all those who are aware of God's call to set out on the road of the ministerial priesthood or consecrated life.

Dear friends, do not become discouraged in the face of difficulties and doubts; trust in God and follow Jesus faithfully and you will be witnesses of the joy that flows from intimate union with him. Imitating the Virgin Mary whom all genera-tions proclaim as blessed because she believed (cf. Lk 1:48), commit yourselves with every spiritual energy, to realise the heavenly Father's plan of salvation, cultivating in your heart, like her, the ability to be astonished and to adore him who is mighty and does "great things", for Holy is his name (cf. Lk 1:49).

From the Vatican, 20 January 2009

MESSAGE
FOR THE 47th WORLD DAY
OF PRAYER FOR VOCATIONS

Fourth Sunday of Easter, 25 April 2010

Witness Awakens Vocations

The 47th World Day of Prayer for Vocations, to be celebrated on the Fourth Sunday of Easter – Good Shepherd Sunday – 25 April 2010, gives me the opportunity to offer for your meditation a theme which is most fitting for this Year for Priests: *Witness Awakens Vocations.* The fruitfulness of our efforts to promote vocations depends primarily on God's free action, yet, as pastoral experience confirms, it is also helped by the quality and depth of the personal and communal witness of those who have already answered the Lord's call to the ministerial priesthood and to the consecrated life, for their witness is then able to awaken in others a desire to respond generously to Christ's call. This theme is thus closely linked to the life and mission of priests and of consecrated persons. Hence I wish to invite all those whom the Lord has called to work in his vineyard to renew their faithful response, particularly in this Year for Priests which I proclaimed on the 150th anniversary of the death of St John Mary Vianney, the Curé of Ars, an ever-timely model of a priest and a pastor.

In the Old Testament the prophets knew that they were called to witness by their own lives to the message they proclaimed, and were prepared to face misunderstanding, rejection and persecution. The task which God entrusted to them engaged them fully, like a "burning fire" in the heart, a fire that could not be contained (cf. Jer 20:9). As a result, they were prepared to hand over to the Lord not only their voice, but their whole existence. In the fullness of time, Jesus, sent by

238

the Father (cf. Jn 5:36), would bear witness to the love of God for all human beings, without distinction, with particular attention to the least ones, sinners, the outcast and the poor. Jesus is the supreme Witness to God and to his concern for the salvation of all. At the dawn of the new age, John the Baptist, by devoting his whole life to preparing the way for Christ, bore witness that the promises of God are fulfilled in the Son of Mary of Nazareth. When John saw Jesus coming to the river Jordan where he was baptizing, he pointed him out to his disciples as "the lamb of God, who takes away the sin of the world" (Jn 1:29). His testimony was so effective that two of his disciples, "hearing him say this, followed Jesus" (Jn 1:37).

Similarly the calling of Peter, as we read in the Evangelist John, occurred through the witness of his brother Andrew, who, after meeting the Master and accepting his invitation to stay with him, felt the need to share immediately with Peter what he discovered by "staying" with the Lord: "We have found the Messiah (which means Christ). He then brought him to Jesus" (Jn 1:41-42). This was also the case for Nathanael, Bartholomew, thanks to the witness of yet another disciple, Philip, who joyfully told him of his great discovery: "We have found him of whom Moses in the law and also the prophets wrote, Jesus of Nazareth, the son of Joseph" (Jn 1:45). God's free and gracious initiative encounters and challenges the human responsibility of all those who accept his invitation to become, through their own witness, the instruments of his divine call. This occurs in the Church even today: the Lord makes use of the witness of priests who are faithful to their mission in order to awaken new priestly and religious vocations for the service of the People of God. For this reason, I would like to mention three aspects of the life of a priest which I consider essential for an effective priestly witness.

A fundamental element, one which can be seen in every vocation to the priesthood and the consecrated life, is friendship with Christ. Jesus lived in constant union with the Father and this is what made the disciples eager to have the same experience; from him they learned to live in communion and unceasing dialogue with God. If the priest is a "man of God", one who belongs to God and helps others to know and love him, he cannot fail to cultivate a deep intimacy with God, abiding in his love and making space to hear his Word. Prayer is the first form of witness which awakens vocations. Like the Apostle Andrew, who tells his brother that he has come to know the Master, so too anyone who wants to be a disciple and witness of Christ must have "seen" him personally, come to know him, and learned to love him and to abide with him.

Another aspect of the consecration belonging to the priesthood and the religious life is the complete gift of oneself to God. The Apostle John writes: "By this we know love, that he laid down his life for us; and therefore we ought to lay down our lives for the brethren" (1 Jn 3:16). With these words, he invites the disciples to enter into the very mind of Jesus who in his entire life did the will of the Father, even to the ultimate gift of himself on the Cross. Here, the mercy of God is shown in all its fullness; a merciful love that has overcome the darkness of evil, sin and death. The figure of Jesus who at the Last Supper, rises from the table, lays aside his garments, takes a towel, girds himself with it and stoops to wash the feet of the Apostles, expresses the sense of service and gift manifested in his entire existence, in obedience to the will of the Father (cf. Jn 13:3-15). In following Jesus, everyone called to a life of special consecration must do his utmost to testify that he has given himself completely to God. This is the source of his ability to give himself in turn to those whom Providence entrusts to him in his pastoral ministry with complete, constant and faithful devotion, and with the joy of becoming a companion on the journey to so many brothers and sisters, enabling them too to become open to meeting Christ, so that his Word may become a light to their footsteps. The story of every vocation is almost always intertwined with the testimony of a priest who joyfully lives the gift of himself to his brothers and sisters for the sake of the Kingdom of God. This is because the presence and words of a priest have the ability to raise questions and to lead even to definitive decisions (cf. John Paul II, Post-Synodal Apostolic Exhortation *Pastores Dabo Vobis*, 39).

A third aspect which necessarily characterizes the priest and the consecrated person is a life of communion. Jesus showed that the mark of those who wish to be his disciples is profound communion in love: "By this all men will know that you are my disciples, if you have love for one another" (Jn 13:35). In a particular way the priest must be a man of communion, open to all, capable of gathering into one the pilgrim flock which the goodness of the Lord has entrusted to him, helping to overcome divisions, to heal rifts, to settle conflicts and misunderstandings, and to forgive offences. In July 2005, speaking to the clergy of Aosta, I noted that if young people see priests who appear distant and sad, they will hardly feel encouraged to follow their example. They will remain hesitant if they are led to think that this is the life of a priest. Instead, they need to see the example of a communion of life which can reveal to them the beauty of being a priest. Only then will a young man say, "Yes, this could be my future; I can live like this" (*Insegnamenti* I, [2005], 354). The Second Vatican Council, in speaking of the witness that awakens vocations, emphasizes the example of charity and of fraternal cooperation which priests must offer (cf. Decree *Optatam Totius*, 2).

Here I would like to recall the words of my venerable Predecessor John Paul II: "The very life of priests, their unconditional dedication to God's flock, their witness of loving service to the Lord and to his Church – a witness marked by free acceptance of the Cross in the spirit of hope and Easter joy – their fraternal unity and zeal for the evangelization of the world are the first and most convincing factor in the growth of vocations" (*Pastores Dabo Vobis*, 41). It can be said that priestly vocations are born of contact with priests, as a sort of precious legacy handed down by word, example and a whole way of life.

The same can be said with regard to the consecrated life. The very life of men and women religious proclaims the love of Christ whenever they follow him in complete fidelity to the Gospel and joyfully make their own its criteria for judgement and conduct. They become "signs of contradiction" for the world, whose thinking is often inspired by materialism, self-centredness and individualism. By letting themselves be won over by God through self-renunciation, their fidelity and the power of their witness constantly awaken in the hearts of many young people the desire to follow Christ in their turn, in a way that is generous and complete. To imitate Christ, chaste, poor and obedient, and to identify with him: this is the ideal of the consecrated life, a witness to the absolute primacy of God in human life and history.

Every priest, every consecrated person, faithful to his or her vocation, radiates the joy of serving Christ and draws all Christians to respond to the universal call to holiness. Consequently, in order to foster vocations to the ministerial priesthood and the consecrated life, and to be more effective in promoting the discernment of vocations, we cannot do without the example of those who have already said "yes" to God and to his plan for the life of each individual. Personal witness, in the form of concrete existential choices, will encourage young people for their part to make demanding decisions affecting their future. Those who would assist them need to have the skills for encounter and dialogue which are capable of enlightening and accompanying them, above all through the example of life lived as a vocation. This was what the holy Curé of Ars did: always in close contact with his parishioners, he taught them "primarily by the witness of his life. It was from his example that the faithful learned to pray" (*Letter Proclaiming the Year for Priests*, 16 June 2009).

May this World Day once again offer many young people a precious opportunity to reflect on their own vocation and to be faithful to it in simplicity, trust and complete openness. May the Virgin Mary, Mother of the Church, watch over each tiny seed of a vocation in the hearts of those whom the Lord calls to follow him more closely, may she help it to grow into a mature tree, bearing much good fruit for the Church and for all humanity. With this prayer, to all of you I impart my Apostolic Blessing.

From the Vatican, 13 November 2009

MESSAGE
FOR THE 44th WORLD DAY
OF SOCIAL COMMUNICATIONS

23 January 2010

The Priest and Pastoral Ministry in a Digital World:
New Media at the Service of the Word.

The theme of this year's World Communications Day – *The Priest and Pastoral Ministry in a Digital World: New Media at the Service of the Word* – is meant to coincide with the Church's celebration of the Year for Priests. It focuses attention on the important and sensitive pastoral area of digital communications, in which priests can discover new possibilities for carrying out their ministry *to* and *for* the Word of God. Church communities have always used the modern media for fostering communication, engagement with society, and, increasingly, for encouraging dialogue at a wider level. Yet the recent, explosive growth and greater social impact of these media make them all the more important for a fruitful priestly ministry.

All priests have as their primary duty the proclamation of Jesus Christ, the incarnate Word of God, and the communication of his saving grace in the sacraments. Gathered and called by the Word, the Church is the sign and instrument of the communion that God creates with all people, and every priest is called to build up this communion, in Christ and with Christ. Such is the lofty dignity and beauty of the mission of the priest, which responds in a special way to the challenge raised by the Apostle Paul: "The Scripture says, *'No one who believes in him will be put to shame ... everyone who calls on the name of the Lord will be saved.'* But how can they call on him in whom they have not believed? And how can they believe in him of whom they have not heard? And how can they hear without someone to preach? And how can people preach unless they are sent?"(Rom 10:11, 13-15).

Responding adequately to this challenge amid today's cultural shifts, to which young people are especially sensitive, necessarily involves using new communications technologies. The world of digital communication, with its almost limitless expressive capacity, makes us appreciate all the more St Paul's exclamation: "Woe to me if I do not preach the Gospel" (1 Cor 9:16) The increased availability of the new technologies demands greater responsibility on the part of those called to proclaim the Word, but it also requires them to become more focused, efficient and compelling in their efforts. Priests stand at the threshold of a new era: as new technologies create deeper forms of relationship across greater distances, they are called to respond pastorally by putting the media ever more effectively at the service of the Word.

The spread of multimedia communications and its rich "menu of options" might make us think it sufficient simply to be present on the Web, or to see it only as a space to be filled. Yet priests can rightly be expected to be present in the world of digital communications as faithful witnesses to the Gospel, exercising their proper role as leaders of communities which increasingly express themselves with the different "voices" pro-vided by the digital marketplace. Priests are thus challenged to proclaim the Gospel by employing the latest generation of audiovisual resources (images, videos, animated features, blogs, websites) which, alongside traditional means, can open up broad new vistas for dialogue, evangelization and catechesis.

Using new communication technologies, priests can intro-duce people to the life of the Church and help our contem-poraries to discover the face of Christ. They will best achieve this aim if they learn, from the time of their formation, how to use these technologies in a competent and appropriate way, shaped by sound theological insights and reflecting a strong priestly spirituality grounded in constant dialogue with the Lord. Yet priests present in the world of digital communications should be less notable for their media savvy than for their priestly heart, their closeness to Christ. This will not only enliven their pastoral outreach, but also will give a "soul" to the fabric of communications that makes up the "Web".

God's loving care for all people in Christ must be expressed in the digital world not simply as an artifact from the past, or a learned theory, but as something concrete, present and engaging. Our pastoral presence in that world must thus serve to show our contemporaries, especially the many people in our day who experience uncertainty and confusion, "that God is near; that in Christ we all belong to one another" (Benedict XVI, *Address to the Roman Curia*, 21 December 2009).

Who better than a priest, as a man of God, can develop and put into practice, by his competence in current digital technology, a pastoral outreach capable of making God concretely present in today's world and presenting the religious wisdom of the past as a treasure which can inspire our efforts to live in the present with dignity while building a better future? Consecrated men and women working in the media have a special responsibility for opening the door to new forms of encounter, maintaining the quality of human interaction, and showing concern for individuals and their genuine spiritual needs. They can thus help the men and women of our digital age to sense the Lord's presence, to grow in expectation and hope, and to draw near to the Word of God which offers salvation and fosters an integral human development. In this way the Word can traverse the many crossroads created by the intersection of all the different "highways" that form "cyberspace", and show that God has his rightful place in every age, including our own. Thanks to the new communications media, the Lord can walk the streets of our cities and, stopping before the threshold of our homes and our hearts, say once more: "Behold, I stand at the door and knock. If anyone hears my voice and opens the door, I will enter his house and dine with him, and he with me" (Rev 3:20).

In my Message last year, I encouraged leaders in the world of communications to promote a culture of respect for the dignity and value of the human person. This is one of the ways in which the Church is called to exercise a "diaconia of culture" on today's "digital continent". With the Gospels in our hands and in our hearts, we must reaffirm the need to continue preparing ways that lead to the Word of God, while being at the same time constantly attentive to those who continue to seek; indeed, we should encourage their seeking as a first step of evangelization. A pastoral presence in the world of digital communications, precisely because it brings us into contact with the followers of other religions, non-believers and people of every culture, requires sensitivity to those who do not believe, the disheartened and those who have a deep, unarticulated desire for enduring truth and the absolute. Just as the prophet Isaiah envisioned a house of prayer for all peoples (cf. Isa 56:7), can we not see the web as also offering a space – like the "Court of the Gentiles" of the Temple of Jerusalem – for those who have not yet come to know God?

The development of the new technologies and the larger digital world represents a great resource for humanity as a whole and for every individual, and it can act as a stimulus to encounter and dialogue. But this development likewise represents a great opportunity for believers. No door can or should be closed to those who, in the name of the risen Christ, are committed to drawing near to others. To priests in particular the new media offer ever new and far-reaching pastoral possibilities, encouraging them to embody the universality of the Church's mission, to build a vast and real fellowship, and to testify in today's world to the new life which comes from hearing the Gospel of Jesus, the eternal Son who came among us for our salvation. At the same time, priests must always bear in mind that the ultimate fruitfulness of their ministry comes from Christ himself, encountered and listened to in prayer; proclaimed in preaching and lived witness; and known, loved and celebrated in the sacraments, especially the Holy Eucharist and Reconciliation.

To my dear brother priests, then, I renew the invitation to make astute use of the unique possibilities offered by modern communications. May the Lord make all of you enthusiastic heralds of the Gospel in the new "agorà" [places of assembly] which the current media are opening up.

With this confidence, I invoke upon you the protection of the Mother of God and of the Holy Curè of Ars and, with affection, I impart to each of you my Apostolic Blessing.

From the Vatican,
24 January 2010, Feast of Saint Francis de Sales.

VI.

MEETINGS
WITH THE CLERGY

MEETING
WITH THE PARISH PRIESTS
AND THE CLERGY
OF THE DIOCESE OF ROME

Hall of Blessings
Thursday, 26 February 2009

Fr Gianpiero Palmieri: *Holy Father, I am the parish priest of San Frumenzio ai Prati Fiscali. I would like to ask you a question about the Christian community's mission to evangelize today, and in particular, the role and formation priests have in this regard. In the face of the task of evangelization, we sometimes feel unprepared and inadequate. From both the cultural and the human perspectives, at times we fail to grasp the fundamental currents, positive or wanting, of contemporary thought. We risk being too narrow minded, incapable of a wise understanding of the hearts of people today. Is not the proclamation of salvation in Jesus also the proclamation of the new man Jesus, the Son of God, in whom our poor humanity is redeemed, authenticated, and transformed by God? So, my question is this: Do you share these thoughts? In our Christian communities so many people are wounded. Where and how can we help others to come to know Jesus? And also, how can we priests build within us a beautiful and fruitful humanity? Thank you, Your Holiness!*

The Holy Father: Thank you! Dear brothers, first of all I would like to express my great joy at being with you, the parish priests of Rome: my parish priests, we are a family. The Cardinal Vicar has rightly mentioned that this is a moment of spiritual rest. I too am grateful that I can begin Lent with a moment of spiritual rest, a spiritual breathing space, in contact with you. He also said that we have come together so that you can tell me of your experiences, your struggles and also your successes and joys. It is not an oracle who stands before you to whom you ask questions. We are having a family conversation. And for me, it is very important to become acquainted here, through you, with parish life, with your experiences of the word of God in the context of today's world. I too wish to learn, drawing close to the realities from which anyone in the Apostolic Palace is a little too removed. This also limits my answers. You live in direct contact, day after day, with today's world. I have contact with the world in different, but also very helpful, ways. For example, I have just had the ad limina visit of the Bishops of Nigeria. Through the Bishops I could visualize – feel the joys and suffering – the life of the Church in this important country of Africa the largest, with 140 million inhabitants, and a large number of Catholics. And this obviously gives me spiritual calmness, because it is a Church like we see in the Acts of the Apostles. A Church in which there is the fresh joy of having found Christ, of having found the Messiah of God. A Church which lives and grows every day. The people are joyful at finding Christ; they have vocations and thus have *fidei donum* priests in various of the world's countries. To see not just a weary Church, as is often found in Europe, but also a youthful Church, full of the joy of the Holy Spirit, is certainly spiritually refreshing. However alongside all these universal experiences, it is also important for me to see my own Diocese, the difficulties and all the other realities that are experienced in this Diocese.

In this sense, essentially, I agree with you: it is not enough to preach or to carry out pastoral work with the precious knowledge acquired in the study of theology. This is important and fundamental but it must be assimilated: from academic knowledge, which we have learned and upon which we have reflected, within a personal vision of life, in order then to reach out to other people. In this regard I would say that while on the one hand it is important to make the great word of faith concrete, by our personal experience of faith, in time spent with parishioners, it is also important not to lose its simplicity. Obviously, great words of our tradition such as "expiatory sacrifice", "redemption of the sacrifice of Christ", "original sin" are today almost incomprehensible. We cannot simply work with lofty formulas, though true, without placing them within the context of today's world. Through study, and what our theology teachers and our personal experience with God tell us, we must concretize and express these great words in such a way that they form part of the proclamation of God to the people of today.

On the other hand, we must not shroud the simplicity of the word of God with commentaries so dense that they distance us. I remember a friend who, after hearing sermons that included long anthropological reflections intended to lead us to the Gospel, used to say: "I am not interested in these approaches, I want to understand what the Gospel says!". I often think that instead of longwinded preambles, it would be better to say, as I used to: "We do not like this Gospel, we are opposed to what the Lord says! But what exactly is it trying to say?". If I say with sincerity that at first glance I do not agree, we have already awakened attention. It is obvious that, as a man of today, I would like to understand what the Lord is saying. Thus without taking a long circuitous route we can reach the heart of the word. And we must also bear in mind, free of oversimplifications, that the Twelve Apostles were fishermen, tradesmen, from the province of Galilee. They had no special training, no knowledge of the great Greek and Latin world. Yet they went to every part of the Empire and even beyond the Empire, as far as India, and proclaimed Christ with simplicity and with the power of the clarity of what is true. It is important, in my view, not to lose the simplicity of the truth. God exists. God is not a distant, hypothetical being. Rather, God is close; he has spoken to us, he has spoken to me. And thus we simply say what he is and how our understanding of him can and must be naturally explained and developed. Let us not lose sight of the fact that we are not proposing reflections; we do not propose a philosophy, rather we propose the simple proclamation of God who has acted. And he works within me, too.

PRIESTS OF JESUS CHRIST

Now to the question of the cultural contextualization which is absolutely necessary in our case, that of Rome, I would say that the first thing that can help is our personal experience. We are not living on the moon! I am a man of this time if I live my faith sincerely in the culture of today with the mass media of today, with dialogue, with the realities of the economy, etc if I myself take my own experience seriously, and seek to adapt to this reality. In this way we are on the way to making ourselves understood by others. St Bernard of Clairvaux said in his book *De Consideratione*, for his student, Pope Eugene: contemplate drinking from your own well, that is, from your own humanity. If you are sincere with yourself and begin to realize what faith is for yourself, from your human experience now, drinking from your own well as St Bernard put it, then you will also be able to say to others what needs to be said. And in this regard I think it is important to be truly attentive to today's world but also to the Lord within: to be a man of this time and at the same time a believer of Christ, who in himself transforms the eternal message into a current message for today.

Who knows the men and women of today better than the parish priest? The rectory is not in the world; rather it is in the parish. And people often come here to the parish priest, usually openly, with no pretext other than suffering, sickness, death or family matters. And they come to the confessional stripped of any veneer, with their very being. No other "profession", it seems to me, gives this possibility of knowing the person as he is, in his humanity, rather than in the role he plays in society. In this sense, we can truly study the person in his core, beyond roles, and learn ourselves what it is to be human, what it is to be in the school of Christ. To this end, it is absolutely important to come to understand the human being, the human being of today, in ourselves and with others, but also always listening attentively to the Lord and accepting in myself the seed of the word, so that it may become leaven within me and become communicable to others.

Fr Fabio Rosini: *I am the parish priest of Santa Francesca Romana all'Ardeatino. Faced with the current process of secularization and its obvious social and existential impact, we have opportunely received through your Magisterium an exhortation concerning the urgent need for the first evangelization, for pastoral zeal in evangelization or re-evangelization, and for the adoption of a missionary outlook. We have realized how important the transformation of ordinary pastoral activity is, no longer content with caring only for that portion of believers who persevere in Christian life but, more decisively and more systematically, caring also for the many sheep who are lost or bewildered. Many priests of Rome have tried different approaches to respond to this urgent objective, the need to "refound" or even "found" the faith. Experiences of first evangelization are increasing and the results are very encouraging. But what ought to be the indispensable criteria for this urgent evangelizing action? What, in your view, are the elements that guarantee that one does not rush in vain into the pastoral demands of proclaiming Christ to our generation? I humbly ask you to point out to us, with your prudent discernment, the parameters to respect and to observe in order to carry out an evangelizing mission that is genuinely Catholic and bears fruit in the Church.*

The Holy Father: I am glad to hear that this first evangelization is happening and that it goes beyond the confines of the faithful community, beyond the parish, in search of the so-called 'lost sheep'; and that an effort is being made today to reach out to those who live without Christ, or who have forgotten Christ, in order to proclaim the Gospel to them. And I am glad to hear not only that this is being done but also that satisfying and numerically significant results are being achieved. Clearly, you are able to speak to those people whose faith has withered or in whom it was never present.

I can give no recipes for this practical work because the paths to follow differ according to the people, their professions, and the particular situation. The catechism points out what is essential to proclaim. However, it is those who are familiar with the particular situations who must read the signs, who must find a method for opening hearts and inviting people to set out with the Lord and with the Church.

You speak of criteria of discernment to avoid rushing in vain. I would like to say first of all that both parts are important. The community of the faithful is a precious thing and we must not underestimate even noticing the many who are distant the positive and beautiful reality constituted by these faithful, who say "yes" to the Lord in the Church, who seek to live the faith, who try to walk in the Lord's footsteps. We must help these members of the faithful, as we have already noted, to see the presence of faith, to understand that it is not something just of the past but shows the way today, teaches us how to live as human beings. It is very important that they truly find in their parish priest a pastor who loves them and helps them to hear the word of God today; to understand that it is a word for them, and not only for people of the past or of the future. It is important that he help them progress in their sacramental life, in the experience of prayer, in listening to the word of God and in the life of justice and charity, because Christians must be leaven in our society with its many problems, dangers and much corruption.

In this way, I believe that communities of the faithful can also play a missionary role "without words", if they truly live a righteous life. In this way they witness how it is possible to live worthily, following the paths pointed out by the Lord. Our society needs precisely such communities, capable of living justice today, not only for themselves but also for others: people who know how to live, as we heard today in the First Reading. This reading opens saying: "Choose life". It is easy to say "yes". But then it continues: "Your life is God". Thus, choosing life is choosing the option for life, which is the option for God. If there are individuals or communities who make this choice of life completely and who show others that the life they have chosen is truly life, they are bearing a very valuable witness.

And so I come to a second reflection. For proclamation we need two elements: the word and witness. As we know from the Lord himself, we need the word that says what he has told us, that makes the truth of God appear, the presence of God in Christ, the path that unfolds before us. Therefore it is a question of evangelization in the present, as you said, which expresses the words of the past in the world of our experience today. It is absolutely indispensable, fundamental, to give credibility to this word through witness so that it does not only appear as a lofty philosophy or a fine utopia, but as reality, a reality with which it is possible to live, but this is not all: a reality that is life-giving. In this regard I consider that the witness of the community of the faithful, as a background to the word, to the proclamation, is of the utmost importance. With the word we must open up avenues to experience faith for those who are seeking God. This is what the ancient Church did with the catechumenate; it was not only catechesis, something doctrinal; it was also a place for a gradual experience of the life of faith in which the word is opened up, and understood when interpreted through life experiences, made concrete by life.

So, I think that together with the word, the presence of a hospitable place of faith, a place in which one has a progressive experience of faith, is also important. And here I see one of the tasks of the parish: offering hospitality to those who have no experience of normal parish life. We must not be a circle closed in on ourselves. We have our customs but still we must be open and endeavour to create "vestibules", that is, places which will draw others closer. Someone who comes from afar cannot immediately enter parish life, which already has its own practices. For such a person everything is novel, far removed from his own life. Therefore, with the help of the word, we must seek to create what the early Church created with the catechumenates: spaces in which one begins to live the word, to follow the word, to make it understandable and realistic, corresponding to forms of actual experience. In this sense I think that what you noted is very important, that is, the need to associate the word with the witness of a just life, being for others, opening oneself to the poor, to the needy, and also to the rich who need to have their hearts opened, to feel someone knocking at their hearts. So, it is a question of different avenues, according to the situation.

I would say, little can be said in theory but practical experience will show us the paths to follow. And naturally, we must be within the great communion of the Church an ever important criterion to follow even if perhaps still a little distant. In other words, one needs to be in communion with the Bishop, with the Pope, and hence in communion with the great past and the great future of the Church. In fact, being in the Catholic Church does not imply only being part of a great journey that precedes us. It also means looking with great openness to the future, a future that only unfolds in this manner. We could continue speaking about its components, but on another occasion.

Fr Giuseppe Forlai: *Holy Father, I am parochial vicar at St John Chrysostom parish, in the northern sector of our diocese. Difficulties in education, of which you have authoritatively spoken, Your Holiness, include, as we all know, difficulties with the educators, specifically, I believe, in two aspects. Firstly, I feel it is necessary that the length of stay of the educator-priest be given more consideration. The second aspect: I believe that the fundamental "game-plan" of pastoral care of youth is played on the cultural front; culture understood as emotive-relational ability and the mastery of the words that concepts contain. Young people without this culture can become the poor of the future, at risk of emotional breakdown or crisis in the workplace. That young people come to our after school catechesis and recreation centres to spend some of their free time does not suffice. I would like these oratories or centres to become communities of people who come up with the right questions to guide young people to a religious sense. And this should give rise to a serious reflection on the collaboration between these centres and religion teachers. Your Holiness, please give us an authoritative*

word on these two aspects of the challenges facing educators: the
necessary length of appointment and the urgent need for priest-
teachers who are adequately prepared culturally. Thank you.

The Holy Father: Let us commence with the second point: it is
broader and in a certain sense easier. Of course, an after-school
centre where only games were played and refreshments provided
would be absolutely superfluous. The point of an after-school
catechetical and recreation centre must be cultural, human and
Christian formation for a mature personality. About this we are
entirely in agreement. It seems to me, that currently we are
experiencing a cultural impoverishment. So many things are
known, but without a heart, without an interior connection,
because a communal vision of the world is lacking. For this
reason a cultural solution inspired by the faith of the Church,
and by knowledge of God, is absolutely essential. I would say
that this is precisely the role of such a centre, that one not only
finds possibilities there for one's leisure time but above all for an
integral human formation that completes the personality.

Therefore, of course, the priest as an educator must himself
have received a good training and must fit into today's culture,
and be deeply cultured if he is to help young people to enter a
culture inspired by faith. I would naturally add that in the end,
the central point of orientation in every culture is God, God
present in Christ. We see today that there are people with very
great knowledge but lacking an inner orientation. Thus
knowledge can also be dangerous because without a profound
ethical orientation it leaves the individual to his own devices,
and hence without the necessary indicators to become truly
human. In this regard, the core of all cultural training, which is
so necessary, must undoubtedly be faith: to know the face of
God, revealed in Christ, and thus to have the fundamental
point of reference for the rest of culture, which would otherwise
become disoriented and disorienting. A culture without a
personal knowledge of God and without a knowledge of the
face of God in Christ is a culture that could be destructive,

because it would have no knowledge of the necessary ethical bearings. In this regard, I think, we really have a profound cultural and human mission, which opens people to all the wealth of the culture of our time but also provides the criterion, the discernment to test what is true culture and what might become anti-culture.

The first question is far more difficult for me, the question is also addressed to His Eminence that is, the length of appointment of young priests so as to ensure that young people receive direction. There is no doubt that a personal relationship with the educator is important and demands a certain amount of time so that he and the young people may get used to each other. In this sense I agree that the priest, a reference point for youth, cannot change every day or else this focus would be lost.

Yet the young priest must also have different experiences in different cultural settings, so that he ends up with the necessary cultural background to be, as a parish priest, a long-term reference point in the parish. I would also say that the measure of time in a young person's life is different than in an adult's. The three years from the age of 16 to 19 are at least as long and important as the years between 40 and 50. It is exactly in this period, in fact, that the personality is formed: it is an inner journey of great importance, of great existential growth. Thus I would say that three years for an assistant priest is a good time for training a generation of young people; and in this way he can also become acquainted with other contexts, learn about other situations in other parishes and thus enrich his human skills. And, this is not too short a time to have a certain continuity, an educational process of experience in common, of learning to be a human person. Moreover, as I said, three years when one is young is a crucial and very long period, because within this time the future personality is really formed. I therefore think that both needs can be reconciled: on the one hand, the young priest can have different experiences to enrich his own human experience; and on the other, the need to be with young people for a certain length of time, to be able to introduce them into life, to teach them to be human people, is recognized. Here I am thinking of the compatibility of the two aspects: different experiences for a young priest, and continuity in the guidance of young people to direct them in life. But I do not know what the Cardinal Vicar will tell us about this.

The Cardinal Vicar Agostino Vallini: *Holy Father, of course I agree with these two needs, the balance between the two needs. It seems to me, with the little that I have been able to learn, that in Rome a certain stability of young priests in parishes for at least a few years has been preserved, with a few exceptions. There can always be exceptions. However, a difficulty sometimes stems from serious needs or particular situations, especially in the relations between the parish priest and the parochial vicar, and here I am touching a raw nerve, and also from the scarcity of young priests. As I was also able to tell you when you received me in Audience, one of the serious problems in our Diocese is precisely the number of vocations to the priesthood. I am personally convinced that the Lord calls and continues to call. Perhaps we must also do more. Rome can and will produce vocations, I am sure. But many facets impinge on this complex matter. I believe of course that a certain stability has been guaranteed, and I too will act along the lines that the Holy Father has pointed out to us to the best of my ability.*

Fr Giampiero Ialongo: *Your Holiness, I am one of the many parish priests who exercises his ministry on the outskirts of Rome. I work at Torre Angela, bordering on Torbellamonaca, Borghesiana, Borgata Finocchio, Colle Prenestino. These suburbs, like so many others, are often forgotten and neglected. And perhaps, more than the other districts of our city, our suburbs feel the hardship that the international financial crisis is having on the life of many families. We carry out many initiatives that primarily aim to listen, but then also to provide material, aid to those who turn to us without distinction of race, culture or religion. Nevertheless, we are realizing increasingly that we are facing a real crisis. The food parcels we prepare, articles of clothing, and occasional financial aid to pay bills or the rent can indeed be a help but not, I believe, a solution. I am convinced that as Church we should question ourselves more on what we can do, and even more on the causes that have led to this widespread crisis. We must have the courage to denounce a radically unjust economic and financial system. And I do not think, in the face of these inequalities introduced by this system, that merely a little optimism will suffice. What is needed is an authoritative word, an unbiased word, that will help Christians as you have already said in some way, Holy Father, to manage with evangelical wisdom and responsibility the goods that God has given, and has given for everyone and not only for a few. I should like to hear you speak on this subject again. Thank you, Your Holiness!*

The Holy Father: First of all I would like to thank the Cardinal Vicar for his words of trust: Rome can provide more candidates for the Lord's harvest. Above all else we must pray to the Lord of the harvest, and also do our part to encourage young men to say "yes" to the Lord. And of course, young priests themselves are called to set an example to the young people of today showing that it is good to work for the Lord. In this way we are full of hope. Let us pray to the Lord and do our part.

Now, for this question which touches the raw nerve of the problems we are facing. I would distinguish between two levels. The first is the level of the macroeconomy which through its functioning reaches every citizen, all of whom feel the effects of a faulty structure. Naturally, it is the Church's duty to denounce this. As you know, for quite some while we have been preparing an Encyclical on these matters. I see now how difficult it is to speak with competence on this subject. If we do not deal competently with the matter, it will not be credible. On the other hand, it is also necessary to speak with great ethical awareness, created and awakened, so to speak, by a conscience formed by the Gospel. Hence it is necessary to expose the fundamental errors, the basic mistakes, now being shown up by the collapse of important American banks. In the end, it is a question of human avarice in the form of sin or as the Letter to the Colossians says, avarice as idolatry. We must condemn this idolatry which stands against the true God, as well as the falsification of the image of God with another God, "*mammona*". We must do so courageously and concretely, for lofty moralizing does not help if it is not substantiated by knowledge of the facts, which also helps one understand what it is possible to do in practice to gradually change the situation. And, of course, to do this will require the understanding of this truth and the good will of all.

Here we come to the crux: does original sin really exist? If it did not exist we could simply appeal to lucid reason, with arguments accessible and indisputable by all, and to the good will that exists in everyone. In this way we could make good headway and reform humanity. But it is not like this: reason including our own is obscured, we notice this every day. For selfishness, the root of avarice, lies in wanting above everything only for myself, in being concerned for the world only as far as it serves me. It exists in all of us. It clouds reason which can be very learned, the finest scientific arguments, yet still obscured by false premises. In this way we can move along with great intelligence, bounding ahead, but on the wrong road. The will too, as the Fathers say, is distorted, it is not simply inclined to do good, but can seek above all else itself or its own interests. To find the way of reason, of true reason, is therefore already something far from easy, and is developed only with difficulty in dialogue. Without the light of faith that penetrates the shadows of original sin, reason cannot progress. But faith itself then comes up against the resistance of our will. The latter does not want to take the path of self-denial and a correction of the individual will in favour of the other rather than for ourselves.

I would say, therefore, that these errors should be addressed with reasonable and reasoned arguments, not with high moralizing but with concrete reasons that are understandable by economics today. The condemnation of these errors is important; it has always been a part of the Church's mandate.

We know that in response to the new situation created by industrialization, the social doctrine of the Church, starting with Leo XIII, has sought to address these matters not just by denouncing them, because that does not suffice but also by showing the difficult paths along which, step by step, the assent of reason and the assent of the will are called for, together with the correction of one's conscience, and a readiness to deny oneself, in order then to collaborate with what is the true aim of human life, of the human family.

That said, the Church always has the task of being watchful, of seeking with the best resources she has to understand the logic of the economy, to enter into its reasoning and to illuminate this line of reasoning with the faith which sets us free from the selfishness of original sin. It is the duty of the Church to enter into this discernment process, this reasoning, and to make herself heard, at the various national and international levels, in order to help and to correct. This is not an easy task because so many individual interests and national groups oppose any radical rectification. Perhaps this sounds pessimistic, but to me it seems realistic: as long as there is original sin we will never attain radical and total correction. Nevertheless, we must do all we can at least for provisional solutions, sufficient to allow humanity to live and to block the domination of selfishness, when presented under pretexts of science, and national and international economics.

This is the first level. The other is to be realists, to ensure that the great aims of macroscience are not achieved in microscience: macroeconomics in microeconomics without the conversion of hearts. Without just individuals there will be no justice. We must recognize this. Therefore, education in justice is a priority goal, we might even say, "the" priority. St Paul says that justification is the effect of Christ's work. This is not an abstract concept, regarding sins that no longer concern us, but refers precisely to integral justice. God alone can give us this, but he gives it to us only with our cooperation at various levels, at all levels possible.

Justice cannot be created in the world solely through good economic models, necessary though they are. Justice is achieved only if there are upright people. And there cannot be just people without the humble, daily work of conversion of hearts, of creating justice in hearts. This is the only way to extend corrective justice. For this reason the work of the parish priest is so fundamental, not only for the parish but also for humanity, for if there are no upright people, as I said, justice will remain theoretical. Good structures cannot be established if they are opposed by people's selfishness, technically competent though they may well be.

This work of ours, humble and conducted day in day out, is fundamental if we are to achieve the great goals of humanity. We must work together at all levels. The universal Church must denounce, but also suggest what might be done and how it can be done. Bishops' Conferences and individual Bishops must act. And everyone must teach justice. I think that still today Abraham's dialogue with God is true and realistic (Gn 18:22-33), when Abraham says will you indeed destroy the city? Perhaps there are fifty righteous people, perhaps ten? And ten of the righteous are enough to ensure the city's survival. Now, if ten righteous people are lacking, notwithstanding all the economic teaching, society will not survive. Therefore we must do what is necessary to educate and to provide at least ten just people, but if possible far more. And it is precisely through our evangelization that we ensure that there are numerous righteous people and that justice may be present in the world.

In effect, the two levels are inseparable. If, on the one hand, we do not proclaim macrojustice, microjustice fails to grow. On the other hand, if we do not do the very humble work of microjustice, macrojustice will not grow either. And as I said in my first Encyclical, despite all the systems that can spread in the world, in addition to the justice that we seek, charity always remains necessary. Opening hearts to justice and charity is educating in faith, it is guiding people to God.

Fr Marco Valentini: *Holy Father, I am the vicar at the parish of Sant'Ambrogio. When I was in formation I did not understand, as I do today, the importance of the liturgy. I now ask myself what would charity be without the liturgy and whether, without it, our faith would be reduced to a moral code, an idea, a doctrine or an event of the past, and if we priests might not seem to be teachers or counsellors rather than mystagogues who introduce people into the mystery. Thus I come to the question. Without taking anything from the human, philosophical or psychological formation in universities and seminaries, I would like to understand whether our specificity requires a better liturgical formation or whether the present procedure and structure of studies already sufficiently satisfy the Constitution* Sacrosanctum Concilium *n. 16, where it says that the liturgy should be counted as one of the necessary and most important, principal subjects whose theological, historical, spiritual, pastoral and legal aspects should be taught and that the teachers of other subjects should take care that the connections between these and the liturgy are clear.*

The Holy Father: If I have understood correctly, the question is: within our many-faceted, multi-dimensional pastoral work, what is the space and place for liturgical training and the reality of celebrating the mystery? This is also a question about the unity of our proclamation and our pastoral work, which has so many dimensions. We must seek the unifying point to ensure that our numerous activities may together constitute the work of a pastor. If I have properly understood, you are of the opinion that the unifying point which creates the synthesis of all the dimensions of our work and our faith could be, precisely, the celebration of the mysteries and therefore the mystagogy which teaches us to celebrate.

To me, it is important that the sacraments, the Eucharistic celebration of the sacraments, not be something, as it were, out of place alongside more contemporary studies such as education in morals or economics things that we have already mentioned. It can easily happen that the sacraments remain somewhat isolated in a more pragmatic context and become a reality not fully integrated into the totality of our humanity. Thank you for the question, because really what we must teach is how to be human. We must teach this great art: how to be a human being. As we have seen, this requires many things: from the important denouncement of original sin found among the roots of our economy and branching into numerous aspects of our lives, to practical guides to justice and the evangelization of non-believers. The mysteries, however, are not something exotic in the cosmos of more practical realities. Mystery is the heart from which our power comes and to which we return to find this centre. For this reason I believe that catechesis that we might call mystagogical is very important. Mystagogical also means realistic, referring to our life as people of today. If it is true that the human being's "measuring stick" for what is just and what is not lies not within but without, in God, it is important that this God is not distant but recognizable, concrete, and that he enter our life and truly be a friend with whom we can speak and who can speak with us. We must learn to celebrate the Eucharist, to learn to know intimately Jesus Christ the God with the human face and really come into contact with him. We must learn to listen to him and learn to let him enter into us. Sacramental Communion is precisely this interpenetration between two persons. I do not take a piece of bread or meat, I take or open my heart so that the Risen One may enter the context of my being, so that he may be within me and not only outside me. In this way he speaks within me and transforms my being, giving me the meaning of justice, the dynamism of justice and zeal for the Gospel.

This celebration, at which God not only comes close to us but also enters the very fabric of our existence, is fundamental to being able truly to live with God and for God and to carry the light of God in this world. Let us not go into too many details here. However, it is always important that sacramental catechesis be an existential catechesis. Naturally, while accepting and learning more and more about the aspect of mystery where words and reasoning leave off it is also completely realistic, because it brings me to God and God to me. And it brings me to the other because the other receives the same Christ. Therefore if the same Christ is in him and in me, the two of us are no longer separate individuals. Here emerges the doctrine of the Body of Christ, because we are all incorporated if we receive worthily the Eucharist in the same Christ. Therefore our neighbour is truly near: no longer are we two separate "selves" but we are united in the same "self" of Christ. In other words, Eucharistic and sacramental catechesis must really reach the heart of our existence. It must be an education that opens us to God's voice, that lets us be opened so that the original sin of selfishness may be broken, that in the depths of our existence we may become open, in order to also become truly just. In this regard I think we must always learn the liturgy better not as something exotic but as the heart of our Christian being which while not easily accessible to one who is distant is, in fact, exactly that openness to the other, to the world. We must all work together to celebrate the Eucharist ever more profoundly: not only as a rite, but as an existential process that touches me in the very depths of my being, more than any other thing, and changes me, transforms me. And in transforming me, it also begins the transformation of the world that the Lord desires and for which he wants to make us his instruments.

Fr Lucio Maria Zappatore: *Holy Father, I am a Carmelite, a parish priest of Santa Maria Regina Mundi at Torrespaccata. Last Sunday, during the Angelus concerning the Petrine ministry, you spoke of the singular and specific ministry of the Bishop of Rome who presides over the whole assembly of charity. I ask you to continue this reflection, extending it to the universal Church: what is the particular charism of the Church of Rome, and what are the characteristics that make her, through a mysterious gift of Providence, unique in the world? What does having as her Bishop the Pastor of the universal Church imply for her mission, especially today? Not that we want to know our privileges as it was once said:*

Parochus in urbe, episcopus in orbe (Pastor in the city, bishop in the world) rather, we would like to know how to live this charism, this gift of living as priests in Rome, and what is expected of us Roman parish priests. In a few days you will be visiting the Campidoglio [Capitol] to meet the civil authorities of Rome and will speak of the material problems of our city: today we ask you to speak to us of the spiritual problems of Rome and of her Church. And, as regards your visit to the Campidoglio, allow me to dedicate to you the following sonnet in the Roman dialect, hoping that you might enjoy listening to it. (Proceeds to recite sonnet).

The Holy Father: Thank you. We have heard the Roman heart speak, a poetic heart. It is very beautiful to hear something in the Roman dialect and to learn that poetry is deeply rooted in the Roman heart. Perhaps this is a natural privilege that the Lord has granted Romans. It is a natural charism that precedes the charisms of the Church.

Your question, if I have understood it correctly, consists of two parts. First of all, what, in practice, is the responsibility of the Bishop of Rome today? But then you justly extend the Petrine privilege to the entire Church of Rome this is also how it was considered in the ancient Church and ask what the obligations of the Church of Rome are in response to this vocation of hers.

It is not necessary to develop here the doctrine of primacy, which you all know very well. What is important is that we reflect on the fact that the Successor of Peter, the ministry of Peter, truly guarantees the universality of the Church: this transcendence over forms of nationalism and other barriers that exist in humanity today, in order to be truly one Church in the diversity and richness of a multitude of cultures.

We see that other ecclesial communities too, other Churches, feel the need for a unifying point in order not to lapse into nationalism, into identification with a specific culture in order to be really open, all things to all people, and to be almost constrained to open up towards everyone else. I think this is the fundamental ministry of the Successor of Peter: to guarantee this catholicity that implies multiplicity, diversity, richness of cultures and respect for diversity. At the same time, it excludes absolutization and unites everyone obliging all to open themselves, to let go of the absolutizing of their own experiences in order to find themselves in the unity of God's family which the Lord desired, and which the Successor of Peter guarantees, as unity within diversity.

Naturally the Church of the Successor of Peter together with her Bishop must carry this weight, this joy of the gift of her responsibility. Indeed, in the Book of Revelation the Bishop appears as an angel of his Church, that is, a little like the embodiment of his Church, to which the Church herself must answer. Therefore the Church of Rome, together with the Successor of Peter and as his particular Church, must guarantee this universality, this openness, this responsibility for the transcendence of love, this presiding in love which excludes any form of particularism. The Successor of Peter must also guarantee fidelity to the Word of the Lord, to the gift of faith, which we have not invented but which is truly a gift that could only come from God himself. This is and always will be the duty, but also the privilege, of the Church of Rome: against trends, against particularism, against the absolutization of only some aspects, against heresies which are always the absolutization of a single aspect. It is also her duty to guarantee universality and fidelity to the whole, to the richness of her faith, of her path through history that is always open to the future. Together with this witness and faith and universality, naturally she must give an example of charity.

This is what St Ignatius tells us when, in somewhat enigmatic words, he identifies the sacrament of the Eucharist with the action of loving others. And this, to return to the previous point, is very important: that is, this identification with the Eucharist which is *agape,* charity, the presence of charity that is given in Christ. There must always be charity, the sign and cause of charity in being open to others, giving of the self to others, this responsibility towards the needy, the poor, the forgotten. This is a great responsibility.

Presiding at the Eucharist is followed by presiding in charity, to which only the community itself can bear witness. I think this is the great task, the great question for the Church of Rome: truly to be an example and a starting point of charity. In this sense it is a bulwark of charity.

In the presbyterate of Rome we come from all the continents, we are of all races, all philosophies and all cultures. I am glad that the presbyterate of Rome itself expresses universality: in the unity of this little local Church, the universal Church is present. It is more difficult and more demanding to be true models of witness, of charity, of being among others with our Lord. We can only pray the Lord to help us in individual parishes, in individual communities, so that together we may be truly faithful to this gift, to this mandate to preside in charity.

Fr Guillermo M. Cassone: *Holy Father I come from the community of the Schnöstatt Fathers in Rome, parochial vicar at Santi Patroni d'Italia, San Francesco e Santa Caterina, in Trastevere. After the Synod on the Word of God, reflecting on* Propositio n. 55, *"Maria Mater Dei et Mater fidei", I wondered how to improve the relationship between the Word of God and Marian piety, both in priestly spiritual life and in pastoral action. Two images help me: the Annunciation for listening, and the Visitation for preaching. I would like to ask you, Your Holiness, to enlighten us on this topic with your teaching. I thank you for this gift.*

The Holy Father: It seems to me that you have also provided the answer to your question. Mary really is the woman of listening: we see it in her encounter with the Angel and we see it again in every episode of her life, from the Wedding at Cana, to the Cross and to the day of Pentecost, when she was in the midst of the Apostles precisely to receive the Spirit. She is the symbol of openness, of the Church that awaits the coming of the Holy Spirit.

In the moment of the Annunciation, we can already detect an attitude of listening true listening, a listening that becomes interiorized, which does not simply say "yes" but assimilates the word, grasps the word and follows it with true obedience, as if it were an interiorized word, that is, as if it had become a word in me and for me, almost a form of my life. I find this very beautiful: to see this active listening, that is, a listening that attracts the word in such a way that it enters and becomes a word within me, reflecting on it and accepting it in the depths of my heart. Thus the word becomes an incarnation.

We see it in the *Magnificat*. We know that it is a fabric woven from Old Testament words. We see that Mary is truly a woman of listening, that she knew Scripture in her heart. She did not only know a few texts, but she identified with the word to the extent that the Old Testament words were summed up in a hymn forming within her heart and on her lips. We see that her life was really penetrated by the word. She had entered into the word, assimilating it, and it became life within her, and it was thus transformed into words of praise and a proclamation of God's greatness.

I believe St Luke, referring to Mary, says at least three times, perhaps four, that she assimilated and conserved the words of Scripture in her heart. For the Fathers she was the model of the Church, the model of the believer who cherishes the word, who carries the word within and not only reads it but interprets it with the intellect, to discern what it meant at that time and what the philological questions are. All this is interesting and important, but it is more important to hear the word that should be conserved and that becomes a word within me, becomes life and the presence of the Lord within me. So, the connection between Mariology and the theology of the word is important. The Synod Fathers also spoke of this and we shall speak of it in the Post-Synodal Document.

It is obvious: The Madonna is a word of listening a silent word, but also a word of praise and of proclamation because in listening to the word, it becomes flesh again and thus a presence of God's greatness.

Fr Pietro Riggi: *Holy Father, I am a Salesian working in the Don Bosco Boys Town. I wanted to ask you the following: the Second Vatican Council brought many important renewals to the Church, but it did not abolish what already existed. It seems to me that some priests and theologians would like to pass off as the spirit of the Council some ideas which have nothing to do with it. One example is indulgences; there is a Manual of Indulgences published by the Apostolic Penitentiary. Through indulgences one can draw on the treasures of the Church and relieve the sufferings of souls in Purgatory, but many priests no longer mention this. Similarly, a manual of the blessings exists that provides for the blessing of persons, households and offices, objects and meals. But some priests consider them pre-conciliar and send away the faithful who are asking for what they are entitled to. The first Fridays of the month were not abolished by the Second Vatican Council, but many priests no longer speak of them. Today there is a general aversion to all these practices because they are seen as antiquated and harmful, whereas I consider that these Christian prayers and practices are up to date and important and feel they should be properly explained to the People of God in a balanced way and in the light of the truth that shines from the Second Vatican Council. I also wanted to ask you this: speaking of Fatima, you once said there is a link between Fatima and Akita, Japan's weeping Virgin. Both Paul VI and John Paul II celebrated a solemn Mass in Fatima and used the same passage from Sacred Scripture: Revelation 12, about a woman adorned with the sun, fighting a decisive battle with the ancient serpent, the devil, Satan. Is there an affinity between Fatima and Revelation 12?*

The Holy Father: These are matters about which the Council did not speak but which it presumed as realities in the Church. They live in the Church and are developing. This is not the moment to bring up the vast subject of indulgences. Paul VI reordered the topic and gave us guidelines for understanding it. I would say that it is simply an exchange of gifts, that is, all the good that exists in the Church is there for everyone. With the "key" of indulgences we can enter into this communion of the Church's goods. Protestants are opposed to this, claiming that the only treasure is Christ. But for me the marvellous thing is that Christ who is really more than sufficient in his infinite love, in his divinity and humanity wished to add our poverty to all that he had done. He does not consider us solely as objects of his mercy, but also makes us subjects of mercy and love together with him, almost as though even if not quantitatively, at least in the sense of mystery he wished to add to the great treasure of the Body of Christ. He wanted to be the Head with the Body. And he wanted the mystery of his Redemption to be completed with the Body. Jesus wanted to have the Church as his Body, in which all the richness of what he did is realized. It is precisely from this mystery that a *tesaurus ecclesiae* came into existence and that the Body, like the Head, gives so much and that we can receive so much from each other and give so much to each other.

And this is also true for other things you mention. For instance, the Fridays of the Sacred Heart: this is a very beautiful devotion in the Church. These are not necessary practices, but they have developed through the richness of meditation on the mystery. Thus, the Lord offers us these possibilities in the Church. I do not think this is the moment to go into all the details. Everyone can basically understand what is more or less important; but no one should scorn these riches, developed down the centuries as an offering, a kind of multiplication of the lights of the Church. Christ's light is unique. It appears in all its hues and offers knowledge of the wealth of his gift, the interaction between Head and Body, the interaction among the members, so that we may truly be together a living organism in which each one gives to all and all give to the Lord, who gave us his entire self.

CONCLUSION OF
THE YEAR FOR PRIESTS

VIGIL ON THE OCCASION
OF THE INTERNATIONAL MEETING
OF PRIESTS

DIALOGUE OF THE
HOLY FATHER BENEDICT XVI
WITH PRIESTS

St Peter's Square
Thursday, 10 June 2010

AMERICA

Holy Father, I am Don José Eduardo Oliveira y Silva and I come from America, namely Brazil. Most of us here are committed to the parish apostolate, and not to just one community. Sometimes we pastors are in charge of several parishes or else of particularly large communities. We try our best to meet the needs of a society that has changed much, it is no longer entirely Christian, and we come to realize that our "doing" is not enough. How should we proceed, your Holiness? What direction should we take?

Dear friends,
First of all I would like to express my great joy because gathered here are priests from all parts of the world, in the joy of our vocation and in our willingness to serve with all our strength the Lord in our time. As regards to the question, I am well aware that today it is very difficult to be a parish priest, also and above all in the countries of ancient Christianity. Parishes have become more extensive pastoral units... and it is impossible to

know everyone, it is impossible to do all the work we would expect of a parish priest. So really, we are wondering how to proceed, as you said. But I would first like to say: I know there are many parish priests in the world who really give all their strength for evangelization, for the Lord's presence and for his sacraments. And to these faithful parish priests who work with all the strength of their lives, with our being passionate for Christ, I want to say a big "thank you" at this moment. I said that it is not possible to do all we would like to do, that perhaps we should do, because our strength is limited and there are difficult situations in an increasingly diversified, more complicated society. I think that, above all, it is important that the faithful can see that the priest does not just perform a "job" with working hours, and then is free and lives only for himself, but that he is a passionate man of Christ who carries in himself the fire of Christ's love. If the faithful see that he is full of the joy of the Lord and understand also that he cannot do everything, they can accept limits and help the parish priest. This seems to me the most important point: that we can see and feel that the parish priest really feels his call from the Lord, that he is full of love for the Lord and for his faithful. If there is this, you understand and you can also see the impossibility of doing everything. So, being full of the joy of the Gospel with our whole being is the first condition. Then they must make choices, have priorities, to see what is possible and what is impossible. I would say that we know the three fundamental priorities: they are the three pillars of our being priests. First, the Eucharist, the Sacraments. The Eucharist: to make possible and present the Eucharist, above all on Sundays, for as many as possible, for everyone, and to celebrate it so that it becomes really the visible act of the Lord's love for us. Then, the Proclamation of the Word in all its dimensions: from the personal dialogue to the homily. The third point is *caritas*, the love of Christ: to be present for the suffering, for the little ones, for the children, for people in difficulty, for the marginalized; to make really present the love of the Good Shepherd. And then, a very high priority is also the personal relationship with Christ. In the Breviary, on 4 November, we read a beautiful text by St Charles Borromeo, a great shepherd, who truly gave all of himself, and says to us, to all priests, "Do not neglect your own soul. If your soul is neglected, even to others you can not give what you should give. Thus, even for yourself, for your soul, you must have time". Or, in other words, the personal colloquy with Christ, the personal dialogue with Christ is a fundamental pastoral priority in our work for the others! And prayer is not a marginal thing: it is the "occupation" of the priest to pray, as representative of the people who do not know how to pray or do not find time to pray. The personal prayer, especially the *Prayer of the Hours*, is fundamental nourishment for our soul, for all our actions. Finally, to recognize our limitations, to open ourselves up even to this humility. Recall a scene from Mark, chapter 6, where the disciples are "stressed out", they want to do everything, and the Lord says: "Come away by yourselves to a lonely place, and rest a while" (Mk 6:31). Even this is work I would say pastoral work: to find and to have the humility, the courage to rest. So, I think, that passion for the Lord, love for the Lord shows us the priorities, the choices, helps us to find the road. The Lord will help us. Thank you all!

AFRICA

Your Holiness, I am Mathias Agnero and I come from Africa, from Côte d'Ivoire. You are a Pope-theologian, while we, when we can, just read some books on theology for formation. However, it seems to us that a rift has been created between theology and doctrine, and even more between theology and spirituality. One feels the need that studies should not all be academic but nourish our spirituality. We feel the need in the same pastoral ministry. At times theology does not seem to have God and Jesus Christ at the centre as the first "theological place", but it instead has diffused tastes and trends. The consequence is the proliferation of subjective opinions permitting the introduction, even in the Church, of non-Catholic thought.

How can we stay focused in our lives and in our ministry, when it is the world judging faith and not vice versa? We feel "off-centre"!

Thank you. You touched upon a very difficult and painful problem. There is actually a theology that wants above all to be academic, to appear scientific and forgets the vital reality, the presence of God, his presence among us, his talking today not just in the past. Even St Bonaventure distinguished two forms of theology in his time and said: "There is a theology that comes from the arrogance of reason, that wants to dominate everything, God passes from being the subject to the object of our study, while he should be the subject who speaks and guides us". There is really this abuse of theology, which is the arrogance of reason and does not nurture faith but overshadows God's presence in the world. Then, there is a theology that wants to know more out of love for the beloved, it is stirred by love and guided by love. It wants to know the beloved more. And this is the true theology that comes from love of God, of Christ, and it wants to enter more deeply into communion with Christ. In reality, temptations today are great. Above all, it imposes the so-called "modern vision of the world" (Bultmann, *modernes Weltbild*), which becomes the criterion of what would be possible or impossible. And so, because of this very criterion that everything is as usual, that all historical events are of the same type, the newness of the Gospel is excluded, the irruption of God is excluded, the real news that is the joy of our faith. What should we do? I would say first to all theologians: have courage. And I would like to say a big "thank you" to the many theologians who do a good job. There are abuses, we know, but in all parts of the world there are many theologians who truly live the Word of God. They are nourished by meditation, are living the faith of the Church and want to help so that faith is present in our today. To these theologians I would like to say a big "thank you". And I would say to theologians in general: "Do not be afraid of this ghost of science!" I have been following theology since 1946. I began to study theology in January '46 and, therefore, I have seen about three generations of theologians, and I can say that the hypotheses that in that time, and then in the 1960s and 1980s, were the newest, absolutely scientific, absolutely *almost* dogmatic, have since aged and are no longer valid! Many of them seem almost ridiculous. So, have the courage to resist the apparently scientific approach, do not submit to all the hypotheses of the moment, but really start thinking from the great faith of the Church, which is present in all times and opens for us access to the truth. Above all, do not think that positivistic thinking, which excludes the transcendent that is inaccessible is true reason! This weak reasoning, which only considers things that can be experienced, is really an insufficient reasoning. We theologians must use a broader reason which is open to the greatness of God. We must have the courage to go beyond positivism to the question about the roots of being. This seems to me of great importance. Therefore, we must have the courage to use the great, broader reason and we must have the humility not to submit to all the hypotheses of the moment and to live by the great faith of the Church of all times. There is no majority against the majority of the Saints. Saints are the true majority in the Church and we must orient ourselves by the Saints! Then, to the seminarians and priests I say the same. Do not think that Sacred Scripture is an isolated Book; it is living in the living community of the Church, which is the same subject in all ages and guarantees the presence of the Word of God. The Lord has given us the Church as a live subject with the structure of the Bishops in communion with the Pope. This great reality of the Bishops of the world in communion with the Pope guarantees to us the testimony of permanent truth. We trust this permanent Magisterium of the communion of the Bishops with the Pope, which represents to us the presence of the Word. Besides, we also trust in the life of the Church while, above all, exercising critical thought. Certainly theological formation – I would like to tell seminarians – is very important. In our time, we must know Sacred Scripture well, in order to combat the attacks of the sects. We must really be friends of the Word. We must also know the currents of our time to respond reasonably in order to give – as St Peter says – "reason for our faith". Formation is very important. But we must also be critical. The criterion of faith is the criterion with which to see also theologians and theologies. Pope John Paul II gave us an absolutely sure criterion in the *Catechism of the Catholic Church*. Here we see the synthesis of our faith, and this Catechism is truly the criterion by which we can judge whether a given theology is acceptable or not. So, I recommend the reading, the study, of this text, so we can go forward with a critical theology in the positive sense. That is critical of the trends of fashion and openness to the true news, the inexhaustible depths of the Word of God, which reveals itself anew in all times, even in our time.

EUROPE

Holy Father, my name is Fr Karol Miklosko and I come from Europe, from Slovakia, and I am a missionary in Russia. When I am celebrating Mass, I find myself and I understand that there I meet my identity as well as the root and energy of my ministry. The Sacrifice of the Cross reveals to me the Good Shepherd who gives all of himself for the flock, for each sheep. And when I say: "This is my body … this is my blood" given and poured out as a sacrifice for you, then I understand the beauty of celibacy and obedience, which I promised freely at the moment of my ordination. Despite the natural difficulties, celibacy seems obvious to me, looking at Christ. But I am stunned to read so much worldly criticism of this gift. I ask humbly, Holy Father, to enlighten us about the depth and the true meaning of ecclesiastical celibacy.

Thank you for the two parts of your question. The first, which shows the permanent and vital foundation of our celibacy. The second, which shows all the difficulties in which we find ourselves in our times. The first part is important, i.e. the centre of our life must really be the daily celebration of the Holy Eucharist. Central here are the words of consecration: "This is my Body, this is my Blood", which means that we speak "*in persona Christi*". Christ allows us to use his "I", we speak in the "I" of Christ. Christ is "drawing us into himself" and allows us to be united. He unites us to his "I". So, through this action, the fact that he "draws" us to himself so that our "I" becomes united to his, he realizes the permanence, the uniqueness of his Priesthood. Therefore, he is at all times the unique Priest. Yet, he is very present to the world because he "draws" us to himself and so renders present his priestly mission. This means that we are "drawn" to the God of Christ. It is this union with his "I" which is realized in the words of the consecration. Also in the "I absolve you" because none of us could absolve from sins it is the "I" of Christ, of God, who alone can absolve. This unification of his "I" with ours implies that we are "drawn" also into the reality of his Resurrection; we are going forth towards the full life of resurrection. Jesus speaks of it to the Sadducees in Matthew, chapter 22. It is a "new" life in which we are already beyond marriage (cf. Mt 22:23-32). It is important that we always allow this identification of the "I" of Christ with us, this being "drawn" towards the world of resurrection. In this sense, celibacy is anticipation. We transcend this time and move on. By doing so, we "draw" ourselves and our time towards the world of the resurrection, towards the newness of Christ, towards a new and true life. Therefore, celibacy is an anticipation, a foretaste, made possible by the grace of the Lord, who draws us to himself, towards the world of the resurrection. It invites us always anew to transcend ourselves and the present time, to the true presence of the future that becomes present today. And here we come to a very important point. One great problem of Christianity in today's world is that it does not think anymore of the future of God. The present of this world alone seems sufficient. We want to have only this world, to live only in this world. So we close the doors to the true greatness of our existence. The meaning of celibacy as an anticipation of the future is to open these doors, to make the world greater, to show the reality of the future that should be lived by us already as present. Living, then, as a testimony of faith: we truly believe that God exists, that God enters into my life, and that I can found my life on Christ, on the future life. And now we know the worldly criticism of which you spoke. It is true that for the agnostic world, the world in which God does not enter, celibacy is a great scandal, because it shows exactly that God is considered and experienced as reality. With the eschatological dimension of celibacy, the future world of God enters into the reality of our time. And should this disappear!? In a certain sense, this continuous criticism against celibacy may surprise in a time when it is becoming increasingly fashionable not to get married. But this not-getting married is something totally, fundamentally different from celibacy. The avoidance of marriage is based on a will to live only for oneself, of not accepting any definitive tie, to have the life of every moment in full autonomy, to decide at any time what to do, what to take from life; and therefore a "no" to the bond, a "no" to definitiveness, to have life for oneself alone. While celibacy is just the opposite: it is a definitive "yes". It is to let oneself be taken in the hand of God, to give oneself into the hands of the Lord, into his "I". And therefore, it is an act of loyalty and trust, an act that also implies the fidelity of marriage. It is the opposite of this "no", of this autonomy that accepts no obligations, which will not enter into a bond. It is the definitive "yes" that supposes, confirms the definitive "yes" of marriage. And this marriage is the biblical form, a natural way of being man and woman, the foundation of the great Christian culture, of great cultures around the world. And if that disappears, the root of our culture will be destroyed. So celibacy confirms the "yes" of marriage with its "yes" to the future world. So, we want to go ahead and make present this scandal of a faith that bases all existence on God. We know that besides this great scandal that the world does not want to recognize, there are also the secondary scandals of our shortcomings, our sins, which obscure the true and great scandal and make people think: "They are not really living on the foundation of God". But there is also so much loyalty! Celibacy

– as its adverse criticism shows – is a great sign of faith, of the presence of God in the world. We pray to the Lord to help us, to set us free from the secondary scandals in order to make relevant the great scandal of our faith: the confidence, the strength of our life, which is founded in God and in Jesus Christ!

ASIA

Holy Father, I am Fr Atsushi Yamashita and I come from Asia, from Japan. The priestly model that Your Holiness has given us this Year, the Curé of Ars, sees at the centre of our life and ministry, the Eucharist, the Sacrament of Penance and personal repentance; and love for worship, worthily celebrated. I see before me signs of the rigorous poverty of St John Vianney and his passion for everything connected to worship. How can we live these fundamental aspects of our priestly life, without falling into clericalism or an estrangement from reality that the world today does not permit us?

Thank you. So the question is how to live the centrality of the Eucharist without conducting a purely cultic life, as a stranger to the everyday life of other people. We know that clericalism is a temptation for priests in all ages, today as well. And it is even more important to find the true way to live the Eucharist, which is not closure to the world, but openness to the world's needs. We must keep in mind that in the Eucharist is realized this great drama of God who goes out of himself, leaves as said in the Letter to the Philippians his own glory, goes out and lowers himself to be one of us, even unto death on the Cross (cf. Phil 2). This is the adventure of God's love, which leaves, abandons himself to be with us – and this becomes present in the Eucharist. The great act, the great adventure of God's love is the humility of God who gives himself to us. In this sense, the Eucharist is to be considered as entering into this path of God. St Augustine says in *De Civitate Dei*, Book X: "*Hoc est sacrificium Christianorum: multi unum corpus in Christ*", i.e. the sacrifice of Christians is being united by love of Christ in the unity of the one body of Christ. The sacrifice consists precisely in going out of ourselves, in allowing entrance into the communion of the one bread, of the one Body and, therefore, to enter into the great adventure of God's love. So, we must celebrate, live and meditate always on the Eucharist, as the school of liberation from my "I": to enter into the one bread, which is the Bread of all that unites us in the one Body of Christ. Therefore, the Eucharist is, in itself, an act of love and it obliges us to this reality of love for others: that the sacrifice of Christ is the communion of all in his Body. So, this is how we must learn the Eucharist, which then is the opposite of clericalism, of closure in oneself. We think also of Mother Teresa, truly the great example in this century, at this time. A love that leaves itself, which leaves every type of clericalism, of estrangement from the world, and goes to the most marginalized, to the poorest, to those nearing death and totally gives herself up to love of the poor, the marginalized. But Mother Teresa who gave us this example and the community that follows in her steps, supposed always as the first condition of one foundation, the presence of a tabernacle. Without the presence of the love of God who gives himself, it would not have been possible to realize that apostolate. It would not have been possible to live in that abandonment to self. Only by inserting their self-abandonment in God, in this adventure of God, this humility of God, they could and can perform today this great act of love, this openness to all. In this sense, I would say that living the Eucharist in its original sense, in its true depth, is a school of life. It is the surest protection against the temptation of clericalism.

OCEANIA

Most Holy Father, I am Fr Anthony Denton and I come from Oceania, from Australia. Here tonight are many priests. But we know that our seminaries are not full and that in the future, in various parts of the world, we expect a decline, even sharp. What can we do to encourage new vocations? How can we propose our way of living, all that is great and beautiful in it, to a young man of our time?

Thank you. You too have touched upon a great and painful problem of our time: the lack of vocations, because of which local Churches are in danger of perishing, for lack of the Word of life, missing the presence of the Eucharist and other Sacraments. What's to be done? The temptation to take things into our own hands is great, the temptation to transform the priesthood – the Sacrament of Christ, to be chosen by him – into a normal profession, a "job" with specific working hours, and for the rest one belongs only to oneself. If we do so, we make it just like any other vocation; we make it accessible and easy. But this is a temptation that does not solve the problem. It reminds me of the story of Saul, the King of Israel, who before the battle against the Philistines waits for Samuel for the necessary sacrifice to God. When Samuel does not arrive at the expected time, Saul himself makes the sacrifice, although not a priest (cf. 1 Sam 13). He thought to resolve the problem, which of course he does not, because if one tries to take in hand what he cannot do, he makes himself God, or nearly so, then one cannot expect that things really go in the way of God. If we too only perform a profession like any other, giving up the sacred, the novelty, the diversity of the sacrament which only God can give, that can only come from his calling and not from our "doing", we would not solve anything. The more we should – as the Lord invites us – pray to God, knock on his door, at the heart of God, to give us vocations, to pray with great insistence, with great determination, even with great conviction. For God does not close himself to a persistent, permanent, confident prayer, even when he makes us wait, like Saul, beyond the time we expected. This seems to me the first point: to encourage the faithful to have this humility, this confidence, this courage to pray insistently for vocations, to knock at the heart of God to give us priests. In addition to this I would like to make some three points. The first: each of us should strive to live his priesthood in such a way as to be convincing. In such a manner that young people might say this is a true calling, one can live in this way, in this way one can do essential things for the world. I think that none of us would have become a priest if we had not met convincing priests who were on fire with the love of Christ. So this is the first point: Let us strive to be convincing priests. The second point is that we must invite, as I said before, people to join in prayer, to have this humility, this trust to speak to God forcefully, decisively. The third point: have the courage to talk with young people about whether God is calling them, because often a human word is required to open one to hear to the divine call. Talk with young people and especially help them find a vital context in which they can live. Today's world is such that the maturation of a priestly vocation seems to be ruled out. Young people need environments in which to live their faith, in which to experience the beauty of faith, in which to feel that this is a way of life, "the" way of life. And help them find movements, or the parish the community in the parish or elsewhere, where they really are surrounded by faith, by God's love, and can therefore become open so that the call of God may arrive and help them. Moreover, we thank the Lord for all the seminarians of our time, for the young priests, and we pray. The Lord will help us! Thank you all!

PRAYER FOR
THE YEAR FOR PRIESTS

Lord Jesus, in St John Mary Vianney you gave your Church an impressive model of your own pastoral charity. Sustained by his example and his spiritual closeness, may we live to the full this Year for Priests.

Grant that, kneeling before the Blessed Sacrament like St John Mary, we may learn the directness and simplicity of your word which instructs us, the tenderness of your love which welcomes repentant sinners, and the consolation born of trusting abandonment to the embrace of your Immaculate Mother.

Lord Jesus, through the intercession of the Holy Curé of Ars, may Christian families become "little churches" where every vocation and charism bestowed by your Holy Spirit is accepted and cherished. May we echo with similar fervour the prayers which he often raised to you:

"I love you, my God, and my sole desire is to love you to my dying breath.

I love you, my God, who are infinitely worthy of love, and I would prefer to die for love of you, rather than live for a moment without your love.

I love you Lord, and the only favour I ask of you is this: to love you for all eternity.

My God, though my tongue cannot tell you at every moment that I love you, I would have my heart repeat it to you with every breath I take.

I love you, my divine Saviour, because you were crucified for my sake, and here below you keep me ever united to your Cross. My God, grant me the grace to die in your love, concious to the end of my love for you."
Amen.

APOSTOLIC JOURNEY OF
POPE BENEDICT XVI TO PORTUGAL
ON THE OCCASION OF THE TENTH
ANNIVERSARY OF THE BEATIFICATION
OF JACINTA AND FRANCISCO, YOUNG
SHEPHERDS OF FÁTIMA

ACT OF ENTRUSTMENT
AND CONSECRATION
OF PRIESTS TO THE
IMMACULATE HEART OF MARY

PRAYER

Church of the Most Holy Trinity – Fátima
Wednesday, 12 May 2010

Immaculate Mother,
in this place of grace,
called together by the love of your Son Jesus
the Eternal High Priest, we,
sons in the Son and his priests,
consecrate ourselves to your maternal Heart,
in order to carry out faithfully the Father's Will.

We are mindful that, without Jesus,
we can do nothing good (cf. Jn 15:5)
and that only through him, with him and in him,
will we be instruments of salvation for the world.

Bride of the Holy Spirit,
obtain for us the inestimable gift
of transformation in Christ.

Through the same power of the Spirit that
overshadowed you,
making you the Mother of the Saviour,
help us to bring Christ your Son
to birth in ourselves too.
May the Church
be thus renewed by priests who are holy,
priests transfigured by the grace of him
who makes all things new.

Mother of Mercy,
it was your Son Jesus who called us
to become like him:
light of the world and salt of the earth
(cf. Mt 5:13-14).

Help us,
through your powerful intercession,
never to fall short of this sublime vocation,
nor to give way to our selfishness,
to the allurements of the world
and to the wiles of the Evil One.

Preserve us with your purity,
guard us with your humility
and enfold us with your maternal love
that is reflected in so many souls
consecrated to you,
who have become for us
true spiritual mothers.

Mother of the Church,
we priests want to be pastors
who do not feed themselves
but rather give themselves to God for their brethren,
finding their happiness in this.
Not only with words, but with our lives,
we want to repeat humbly,
day after day,
our "here I am".

Guided by you,
we want to be Apostles
of Divine Mercy,
glad to celebrate every day
the Holy Sacrifice of the Altar
and to offer to those who request it
the sacrament of Reconciliation.

Advocate and Mediatrix of grace,
you who are fully immersed
in the one universal mediation of Christ,
invoke upon us, from God,
a heart completely renewed
that loves God with all its strength
and serves mankind as you did.

Repeat to the Lord
your efficacious word:
"They have no wine" (Jn 2:3),
so that the Father and the Son will send upon us
a new outpouring of
the Holy Spirit.
Full of wonder and gratitude
at your continuing presence in our midst,
in the name of all priests
I too want to cry out:
"Why is this granted me,
that the mother of my Lord should come to me?" (Lk 1:43).

Our Mother for all time,
do not tire of "visiting us",
consoling us, sustaining us.
Come to our aid
and deliver us from every danger that threatens us.
With this act of entrustment and consecration,
we wish to welcome you
more deeply, more radically,
for ever and totally
into our human and priestly lives.

Let your presence cause new blooms to burst forth
in the desert of our loneliness,
let it cause the sun to shine on our darkness,
let it restore calm after the tempest,
so that all mankind shall see the salvation
of the Lord,
who has the name and the face of Jesus,
who is reflected in our hearts,
for ever united to yours!

Amen!